CHANGING
THE SCRIPT

CHANGING
THE SCRIPT

AN AUTHENTICALLY FAITHFUL
AND AUTHENTICALLY
PROGRESSIVE POLITICAL
THEOLOGY FOR THE 21ST CENTURY

DANIEL SCHULTZ

PUBLISHING

BROOKLYN, NEW YORK

Printed in the United States of America
10 9 8 7 6 5 4 3 2 1

Portions of this book originally appeared in *Religious Dispatches*
magazine and *Dispatches from the Religious Left*, Ig Publishing, 2008.

Ig Publishing
392 Clinton Avenue
Brooklyn, NY 11238
www.igpub.com

Library of Congress Cataloging-in-Publication Data

Schultz, Daniel.
 Changing the script : an authentically faithful and authentically progressive political theology for the 21st century / Daniel Schultz.
    p. cm.
 ISBN 978-1-935439-14-1
 1. Liberalism--Religious aspects--Christianity. 2. Christianity and
politics--United States. 3. Political theology--United States. 4. Brueggemann, Walter. I. Title.
 BR526.S37 2010
 261.7--dc22
                              2010023044

For my wife Jennifer and our children Abigail and William. I hope the world will be a better place for you.

CONTENTS

INTRODUCTION

In 2008, I was asked to contribute to an anthology called *Dispatches From The Religious Left*. I immediately set about detailing the demographic, organizational, philosophical and theological differences between the Religious Right and the Religious Left—and between the lower case elements of the religious left. I plotted out a detailed examination of these qualities, using public opinion surveys, voting data, organizational charts and religious history.

Two and a quarter pages and nine footnotes into the project, I was hopelessly bogged down.

For the record, I still believe there's value in a thorough sociological examination of the Religious Left and what makes it unique. Mercifully, however, what needs to be said for our present purposes is simple.

What the Religious Left is doing is not working.

The Religious Left—both upper and lower case—is bedeviled by a number of problems, if you'll excuse the phrase. What follows are several points of bedevilment—and some thoughts about a way the way out. Many if not most of these points boil down to two persistent issues. First, there is an inability or an unwillingness to speak a word of judgment in the political realm, as progressive religious folks have been schooled too well in reconciliation and engagement with leaders. Second, there is an equal inability or unwillingness to think imaginatively about faith and the public square, with too great a willingness to accept current realities as immutable.

To a certain extent, these problems are the logical result of certain characteristics of the religious left, which is far too varied and complex a movement to speak with one voice. The religious left is made up of congregations, denominational offices from local to national levels, other religious representatives, ecumenical and interfaith organizations, social-justice and peace activists, single-issue groups, Washington insiders, Democratic Party outreach initiatives, seminaries, institutes and bloggers. None of these groups work the same way, or on precisely the same concerns. And where secular progressives have to deal with political and strategic differences, religious liberals also have to factor in theological and ecclesiastical gaps. In many ways, this diversity is also a core strength, but such diversity also requires a common, coherent, strategic vision. Currently, the religious left does not have one.

Things have improved since Faith in Public Life, an outgrowth of the Center for American Progress, arrived on the scene in 2006. But a persistent lack of organization and funding for infrastructure across the movement leads to messaging that is diffused and ineffective. More seriously, it leads to the perception that the Religious Left doesn't believe in much of anything. It doesn't help that for a movement based on religious *values*, the Religious Left has an odd tendency to lose itself in the fog of *issues*.

One classic example of this tendency was a press release issued by the National Council of Churches the day before the 2004 election that called on the Bush administration to repatriate Uighur prisoners held at Guantanamo Bay. Amy Sullivan's reaction to this release in an article for the *Washington Monthly* the following March was caustic, but on-target: "I have no doubt that advocacy on behalf of Chinese Muslim prisoners is a worthy cause," she wrote. "I also have no doubt that it confirms the irrelevance of the once-powerful religious left."[1]

Much of the malfeasance of the Bush administration was known before the 2004 election. A relevant religious voice would have asked about the rush to war, Abu Ghraib, or the inexcusable immorality of the Guantanamo prison itself. The NCC chose instead to target a single, narrowly-defined issue. By not "breaking the frame" of the debate, the Religious Left has often conceded morally unacceptable situations before the fight has even begun.

The Religious Left is also split between spiritual development and political action. Progressive religion has long been uncomfortable with conflating the two, unlike its conservative counterparts. This tension, coupled with long-term membership declines, has led some Protestant denominations to withdraw from the public square. Religious front groups for right-wing political and financial interests such as the Institute for Religion and Democracy have happily encouraged this tendency with well-funded campaigns to paint the leadership of progressive churches as radical leftists, and by stoking internal denominational disputes. Despite this meddling, some denominations have embraced a liberal political or public policy identity, and of course, progressive elements are active within more conservative denominations as well. But the reality is that for many reasons—cultural, numerical and theological—the Protestant mainline and the "social Catholics" are no longer as visible as they once were.

Then there is the personal element. For many faithful progressives, ambivalence is the emotion of first resort when considering politics. Because they tend to define faith over and against the dirty, judgmental business of winning elections, such people are, unsurprisingly, reluctant to jump into the partisan shark tank. Instead, they pursue "spiritual activism," or understand "progressive" to modify theology more than politics. Others who share the same tendency have become embittered commentators on the state of a game they refuse to play. And many maintain an uneasy line between religious and political commitments without ever being able to give their hearts undivided to either side of the equation. This conflict is particularly acute for Christians raised on sermons about loving one's enemy or being "in the world, but not of it."

In many ways, this is a healthy, even fruitful tension. As we shall see, one of the unique strengths the Religious Left can leverage is its moral authority, an authority that is only increased by the ability to stay out of petty political bickering. But it is equally true that the Religious Left's claim to influence on public affairs has been withered by its general failure to address the aggression of movement conservatism. As Jeff Sharlet points out, some right-wing evangelicals don't even consider progressive believers to be Christians. No doubt this is largely influenced by the perception that religious liberals won't stand to testify for their beliefs. What's more, many progressive activists without deep ties to religious communities are confused by the Religious Left's apparent powerlessness and silence before the reactionary elements of Christianity, and harshly critical of its refusal to articulate a simple, clear and effective moral critique of conservative ideas and policies. However Christ-like it may be in its ethical approaches, as a political movement, the Religious Left is in danger of being declared neither hot nor warm—and being spit out accordingly.

A PRESCRIPTION FOR THE RELIGIOUS LEFT: POLITICAL THEOLOGY

Ignoring the political dimension of faith in favor of spirituality without context has lost mainline churches a generation of believers. For belief to be relevant, it must demonstrate that it makes a difference in this world *and* the next. Whining that progressives have values, too, accomplishes nothing. It keeps alive conservative frames about amoral liberals without offering a meaningful alternative. Finally, trying to make the Democratic Party more "friendly to faith" in order to draw "persuadable" social conservatives is a waste of resources. This is likely to be a controversial assertion, as many progressives want to establish as broad a coalition as possible, and see nothing wrong with being "faith friendly." But this strategy does not provide a positive vision, only a defensive reaction to conservative criticism.

One unworkable solution deserves a bit more scrutiny: The idea that the Religious Left can show the nation a kinder, gentler way to do politics without partisanship. On a practical level, voters have demonstrated again and again that they want Democrats to provide a meaningful alternative to Republicans' reactionary ideology. The progressive agenda is a popular one, while conservatism represents an ever-smaller slice of the electorate. Thus, there is no political need to compromise with a radical movement that is declining in popularity. Ethically, this seemingly principled desire to accomplish something "beyond politics" while remaining engaged with the political system rests on dubious assertions, namely that there is some divine method to "take the politics out of politics."[2] There is no such transcendent way. Until the Kingdom come, those who want to create and sustain social change are stuck with morally ambiguous involvement in the world of partisan politics. Those who want to keep their hands clean should find another hobby or withdraw from the political realm altogether.

The eagerness to heal politics also involves the perverse notion that one party should be able to drag the nation through an almost infinite variety of dirty tricks, at the end of which the other party should be reconciled to them, letting bygones be bygones. However satisfactory that might be to those raised on an ethos of turning the other cheek, it does little to establish justice. Wrongs have been done in the conservative ascendancy of the past forty years. They will need to be set right. This is not a time to cry "peace, peace" when there is no peace. This is a time to articulate a *political theology*. By this I mean a normative politics rooted in "a view of God and his purposes, and their relation to human action in history, even though our normative thought doesn't derive directly from any theological premises, revealed or rationally arrived at," to borrow a quick-and-dirty definition from the philosopher and social critic Charles Taylor.[3] The Religious Left needs to put forward a simple, clear and effective moral critique not just of conservatism, but of all American life. This critique must lay out clear ethical distinctions and suggest political (but not necessarily partisan) choices to be made as a result.

A workable progressive political theology should be consistent with broadly progressive values, yet incisive enough that it is able to establish clear responsibility for living up to those values. It must offer insight into social, cultural, economic and political problems. It is not enough to say, for example, that "fighting poverty is a moral value." Voters must understand not only what the value is, but why it is important and who they should hold accountable if it is not upheld. In short, it must lend a standard for judging the contemporary political scene, and suggest meaningful alternatives to it.

THE POLITICAL THEOLOGY OF WALTER BRUEGGEMANN

In a 2005 *Christian Century* article, the Old Testament scholar and theologian Walter Brueggemann laid out a series of nineteen theses about the Bible's countercultural witness to our society. He discerned the presence of "scripts" in our lives: dynamic, normative stories that actualize our values in patterns of behavior, often below the threshold of consciousness. The Biblical narrative of relationship with what Brueggemann termed the "elusive, irascible God" calls these scripts into question. The God of Abraham, Isaac and Ishmael is a jealous God, and will brook no divided loyalties.[4]

The primary script in control of our lives, according to Brueggemann, is "the script of therapeutic, technological, consumerist militarism that permeates every dimension of our common life." By this, he means certain acculturated assumptions about the way life should work. Brueggemann writes:

> I use the term therapeutic to refer to the assumption that there is a product or a treatment or a process to counteract every ache and pain and discomfort and trouble, so that life may be lived without inconvenience.

> I use the term technological, following Jacques Ellul, to refer to the assumption that everything can be fixed and made right through human ingenuity; there is no issue so complex or so remote that it cannot be solved.

I say consumerist, because we live in a culture that believes that the whole world and all its resources are available to us without regard to the neighbor, that assumes more is better and that "if you want it, you need it." Thus there is now an advertisement that says: "It is not something you don't need; it is just that you haven't thought of it."

The militarism that pervades our society exists to protect and maintain the system and to deliver and guarantee all that is needed for therapeutic technological consumerism. This militarism occupies much of the church, much of the national budget and much of the research program of universities.

This script, says Brueggemann, promises to make us "safe and happy," and yet has failed to do either. For our health and the health of the world, we must let it go and grasp a new one. Though his aim is to strengthen the theology of the church, not assist partisan ideology, Brueggemann describes this in straightforwardly political terms:

It is clear to all but the right-wing radio talk people and the sponsoring neoconservatives that the reach of the American military in global ambition has served only to destabilize and to produce new and deep threats to our society. The charade of a national security state has left us completely vulnerable to the whim of the very enemies that our security posture has itself evoked. A by-product of such attempts at security, moreover, has served in astonishing ways to evoke acrimony in the body politic that makes our democratic decisionmaking processes nearly unworkable.

We are not safe, and we are not happy. The script is guaranteed to produce new depths of insecurity and new waves of unhappiness. And in response to new depths of insecurity and new waves of unhappiness, a greater resolve arises to close the deal according to the script, which produces ever new waves and new depths.

This is a more insightful analysis of the current state of the union than anything I've ever read in corporate journalism. Brueggemann has sussed out the framework that underlies much of our contemporary politics, and the utter faithlessness of its premises. His critique couldn't be simpler or more clear. Though it is not shy about evaluating moral or political stances, its targets go well beyond a single ideology to attack shared, flawed assumptions. Attempting to live life without contingency or responsibility to others is wrong and unsustainable. That, it seems to me, is the central critique progressive faith can offer.

PUTTING COUNTERSCRIPTS INTO PLAY

In a 2008 article for *The Nation*, Democratic New York State Senator Eric Schneiderman described the differences between what he called *transactional* and *transformational* politics. The former is the simple and pragmatic art of securing the best possible deal given today's circumstances, while the latter is "the work we do today to ensure that the deal we can get on gun control or immigration reform in a year—or five years, or 20 years—will be better than the deal we can get today." Schneiderman's description of this project seems tailor-made for the Religious Left:

> Transformational politics requires us to challenge the way people think about issues, opening their minds to better possibilities. It requires us to root out the assumptions about politics or economics or human nature that prevent us from embracing policies that will make our lives better.[5]

Questioning assumptions, imagining new possibilities, keeping an eye on the human bottom line of public policy: this is the natural work of faithful people engaged in an ongoing ethical encounter with a dynamic God. God is still speaking indeed, and still working to recreate our world. Religious progressives should be fearless in proclaiming the social and political implications of that reality. If they can do that, they will take control of the so-called Overton Window, the spectrum of "commonly held ideas, attitudes and presumptions [that] frame what is politically possible."[6] By using the moral authority traditionally accorded to religious leaders in America, the Religious Left can influence which ideas are or are not considered acceptable in political discourse.

Perhaps the finest recent example of this was Barack Obama's response in 2008 to fierce criticism launched against the Reverend Jeremiah Wright's analysis of the state of contemporary race relations. Even as he rejected his pastor's ideas, Obama accepted the legitimacy of the questions Wright raised. That single-handedly restored the issue of racial justice to public discourse for the first time in forty years. To put it in Brueggemann's frame, Obama established a counter to the conformist script that had been running more or less unchallenged in our society since the time of Martin Luther King.

Using the idea of counterscripts to foster critical discourse in this way will allow religious progressives to work across both partisan and confessional lines, an area of major concern for this renascent movement. It also enables critiques of both Democrats and Republicans, and perhaps will even allow one day for the establishment of new coalitions based on shared values. And because it relies on shared observation rather than revelation or a single theological framework, it can hold together both secular and religious progressives.

However, make no mistake about it: Brueggemann's biblical theses are faithful—and progressive. They do not sell out or tone down for political convenience the kind of values articulated by George Lakoff's Rockridge Institute: strength, safety and protection, fulfillment, fairness, freedom, opportunity, prosperity, community, cooperation, trust, honesty and openness. But they do ask in a distinctly religious voice to what end these values are upheld and whether they are ultimate or partial goals.

Establishing accountability through counterscripts is also fairly simple. No politician will ever be able to usher in the Kingdom of God, of course, even if they were able to move the nation as a whole away from destructive scripts to healthier ways of being. But as a relative matter, evaluating the extent of their cooperation with the technological, therapeutic, consumerist, conformist and militarist scripts is almost as simple as opening the *Congressional Record*. In order to do this, however, we will have to lose our scruple about calling things what they truly are. Prophets who are unwilling to judge present realities against a vision of God's possibilities are by definition unnecessary. Unfortunately, standing in judgment goes against the grain of many religious progressives. Developing a righteous anger therefore may well be the most difficult change to make, but also the most necessary.

COUNTERSCRIPTS: JUDGMENT, AMBIGUITY AND NEW GROUND

We are not safe, and we are not happy. This frank evaluation is the starting point for any meaningful conversation about the current state of our nation. If the Religious Left wants to find relevance beyond easy slogans and "me-too-ism," it will have to find a way to help our fellow citizens understand how to reorder their commitments in light of the scripts' failure to perform as advertised. Otherwise, the Religious Left will be remaindered as a not-particularly-effective electoral adjunct to the centrist wing of the Democratic Party.

How might we start this conversation in a way that advances the progressive cause yet honors "a view of God and his purposes"? That, of course, is the question of questions. We will hear many answers to it in the years to come. Brueggemann for his part is explicit that his statements are not utilitarian politics but theology:

Liberals tend to get so engaged in the issues of the day, urgent and important as those issues are, that we forget that behind such issues is a meta-narrative that is not about our particular social passion but about the world beyond our control. The claim of that alternative script is that there is at work among us a Truth that makes us safe, that makes us free, that makes us joyous in a way that the comfort and ease of the consumer economy cannot even imagine.

It will not be easy for religious progressives to work toward the counterscripting of our present society, for a number of reasons. Scripture guides them to build an alternative society in the countercultural world of the church, not to attempt the redemption of the public square. Moreover, the God Brueggemann has in sight is not an easy boss, nor is the textual container for his good news always user-friendly. Though the tensions between secular and religious liberals are often overstated, they do exist, and they will continue for the simple reason that their experiences and overarching goals overlap but are not identical.

Perhaps most vexing of all, the judgment of the God Walter Brueggemann knows often seems to take the form of dragging us before our ambivalence and making us face it. This is a feature, not a bug. Brueggemann writes that:

One of the crucial tasks of ministry is to name the deep ambiguity that besets us, and to create a venue for waiting for God's newness among us. This work is not to put people in crisis. The work is to name the crisis that people are already in, the crisis that evokes resistance and hostility when it is brought to the surface and named.

God may yet lead us anew where liberals and conservatives can disrupt the shrillness long enough to admit that variously we are frightened by alternative patterns of sexuality.

We do not want to kill all gays as the book of Leviticus teaches, but we are in fact uneasy about changes that seem so large.

God may yet lead us anew when conservatives and liberals can interrupt our passion for consumer goods and lower taxes long enough to admit that we believe neighbors should be cared for, even with taxes. We have a passion for social programs but are nonetheless aware of being taxed excessively, and it causes us alarm.

God may yet lead us so that liberals and conservatives can stop the loudness to know that the divestment that costs us nothing is too easy, whether directed at Israel or the Palestinians; the core divestment to which we are first called comes closer to our own entitlements. The Spirit has always been, for the church and beyond the church, 'a way out of no way.'

These statements will no doubt make many progressives squirm. There are good reasons for that. Brueggemann addresses here the work of the church, not the state or the society, and the work of the church is to stay together above all else. In that it is no less political than any other venue of human activity, but it is a politics directed at a certain aim—unity—that does not always map well onto larger spheres.

Then there is the less than full-throated support for a progressive agenda, particularly on questions of sexual identity, a difficulty Brueggemann himself points out. But the essential insight seems correct: there are any number of issues where honesty compels religious progressives to admit conflicted feelings. More important, there are any number of issues where honesty compels religious progressives to challenge their self-perception as morally pure agents. It is precisely at such junctures that the search for fertile new ground, spiritually and politically, must be launced.

Take one of Brueggemann's examples. We might say that 9/11 has left our society ambivalent about what it means to be safe in an age of terror. However, such a statement does not require us to surrender to the belief that we must undermine our democratic liberty and the rule of law in order to erect an American security state, as the Bush administration did in the years following the September 11 attacks. At the same time, we should also confess that many of us enabled the Bush administration's lunacy by "supporting the troops" if not actually voting for Bush and Cheney. Certainly, most Americans paid their war taxes, and all of us benefitted from the militarism it funds. Once we have admitted our moral compromises before and after September 11, 2001, we can recognize an opportunity for transformation.

The attacks on New York City, Pennsylvania and Washington D.C. should have sparked a reconsideration of an already dangerously unbalanced American security policy. That rethinking is now long overdue. Until we are able to surface and address our ambiguous desires to be kept safe and free, the reconsideration will remain undone, and we will be subject to "the charade of a national security state" in one form or another because we will not have changed the crucial assumption that the force of arms alone can keep us safe. That keeps us wedded to the morality of violence and the politics of militarism and all those things entail.

Working with such deeply embedded scripts may blunt the transactional effectiveness of the Religious Left in the short run. The movement can seldom offer a promised land, as it were, only an ongoing journey with a cranky, temperamental God and a destination that is perpetually just around the corner. There's a reason Brueggemann speaks of where "God may yet lead us." An honest faith demands that we admit that we have no idea where exactly God is directing us. After all, we've never been there before.

Again, this will be distressing for those who look to progressive faith to provide an electoral counterweight to the right-wing—and centrist—idolatry of power. They no doubt will want to know what religious believers can contribute today toward securing the immediate electoral or governmental fortunes of the progressive movement. There's no reason they shouldn't. Politics as it is currently worked is a short-range, bottom-line oriented business. If you can't deliver money or votes, then you have no power. The Religious Right is able to bring both to the table; therefore they still have considerable power. But I hope that what I have been able to demonstrate is that transactional politics is not the calling of progressive religious. Instead, the main function of the Religious Left is to ask the questions, not line up behind the answers. Where the Religious Right has been the cash machine and ground troops for the conservative movement, the Religious Left can and should be the engine for *transformational* progressive politics. And where religious conservatives have been the stout defenders of everything that is clear and solid and unchanging, religious liberals are the "astronauts of inner space," relentlessly pushing through uncertainty toward newer, higher ground. Thus, it ought to be taken as a good sign when that drive "evokes resistance and hostility" and charges of judgmentalism. It means progress is being made.

It may be helpful here to recall the old joke that says the purpose of good preaching ought to be to comfort the afflicted and afflict the comfortable. I think that goes in spades for the Religious Left. The movement is, and always have been, a ragged, disputatious lot following a ragged, disputatious narrative toward an irascible, hidden God. What has worked for it hasn't been a comfortable groove but affliction and an inborn, restless stubbornness that forever keeps it on the move. Progressive faith has been generative not in its support for established powers or settled narratives but in its eternal, persistent, damnably disruptive questioning of the seemingly self-evident way things must be. Religious liberals are meant to be gadflies in the service of the Lord, asking through political theologies difficult questions about what truly makes us safe, what truly makes us happy, and where it is that the mystery and promise of God is leading us.

So I offer the following chapters not as an agenda, but as illustrations of how counterscripts can be used to ask the necessary questions. I have borrowed the scripts Dr. Brueggemann names to scaffold my book, but really they are points of departure, not rigid definitions. As Brueggemann himself says, there are many other scripts that could and perhaps should be named. And while I have tried to understand and reflect Brueggemann's take on each one, I cannot guarantee that our analyses are exactly in sync.

Another qualification is in order. Though I consider political and policy options, finding the optimal outcomes for each is not the ultimate goal of this book. Rather, following Brueggemann's work in *The Prophetic Imagination* (discussed in more detail with the Consumerist script), I have tried to point the way toward a critical but imaginative discourse. Readers looking for the keys to more effective, short-term transactional politics will find themselves frustrated. I cannot tell Democrats how to win midterm congressional election cycles, nor am I particularly interested in doing so.

One last thing before we summarize the chapters: in my experience, political theology tends to provoke a lot of anxiety from secular readers. They often wonder what role religious belief should play in the public square. They ask: Why should public policy require God's blessing? How can you argue facts against dogma? Shouldn't we do the right thing whether or not God commands it? These are all vital questions, and I share many of the concerns secular people have about the way religious authority is used to drive political ends in our society. However, they are not questions germane to the present subject. I intend this book to sharpen the ways religious people— particularly Christians, for I speak out of my own tradition—think about what their faith has to say about the common life of the nation. It is meant as an invitation to reflect upon politics and to imagine new ways of doing and being. If I seem to speak *ex cathedra* at some times, I beg my readers' forgiveness, particularly the secular ones. Nothing here is meant to announce God's commandment. I'm not qualified for that!

The normative aspects of this political theology are only so if you agree with my "view of God and his purposes." If you do not, then I invite you to listen in and see if you might overhear something of the gospel, to paraphrase Fred Craddock. Perhaps we might imagine together a better future for our nation, even if we don't agree on how it is we will get there.

The book breaks down into three uneven sections, each of which contains a current topic in politics and pairs it with one of Brueggemann's scripts. The first part of the book looks at abortion and how it has developed as a political cause in recent years. I have tried to provide substantial background on abortion opinion in the United States., as well as how the conversation about abortion has been used—and often misused—to advance a certain vision of the Religious Left as it evolved after 2004. In particular, I look at the "common ground" strategy on abortion, the "culture war" that surrounds it, and the violence that has been used against reproductive service providers. I suggest that the abortion controversy is a proxy war for the place of women in American society, and conclude that a proper understanding of the therapeutic script challenges us to consider how our use of medical technology reflects the distribution of power in our society.

The next section concerns the collapse of the world economy that began in 2007 and has only recently begun to ease. It traces the roots of the "rigged game" that has left so many average workers feeling helpless before an oppressive economic machine, the systemic corruption in the financial sector that made the economic crisis almost inevitable and the continuing aftermath. This section considers two of Brueggemann's scripts—the Consumerist and the Technological—to bring into view the temptations that led us into the crisis, and the temptations that will have to be avoided in order for us to be led out of it. I propose engaging a process of criticizing the economy, delegitimizing its current structures, drawing contrasts, confronting the ambivalence provoked by the economy and lamenting the real sorrows it causes, seeking new energy and new beginnings and finally finding amazement and cause for praise in God's new possibilities.

The final part of the book takes up American use of torture during the Global War on Terror, both against "enemy combatants" and against battlefield prisoners captured in Iraq and Afghanistan. The torture regime points to flaws in the project of American military might and its goal of establishing security through the use of force. I argue that torture ought to elicit a response from religious progressives that goes beyond human-rights sloganeering to proclaiming an alternative witness to the military machine itself, with the aim of removing the social approval of militarism. This is a daunting task that will require religious people to rework their own communities before they can hope to affect the larger society.

In the end, it is all daunting. Meaningful change will come to our nation slowly and fitfully, if it comes at all. But as I argue, religious progressives are not called to provide the answers to America's problems. They—we—are called, rather, to ask the questions and to move into the newness we have been promised. To journey with trust in God and reciprocity for our fellow citizens is not an easy calling. But it is the faith we know, and most days, with God's help, it will do. I would suggest that any group that purports to call itself the Religious Left start there and work its way forward, slowly, tentatively, and with one eye always set firmly on where God may yet lead us.

1. The Therapeutic Script: Abortion

"I want to underwrite what I call the Tonto Principle of Christian Ethics. The Tonto Principle is based on the Lone Ranger and Tonto finding themselves surrounded by 20,000 Sioux. The Lone Ranger turns to Tonto and says, "What do you think we ought to do, Tonto. Tonto replies, "What do you mean we, white man?" We Christians have thought that when we address the issue of abortion and when we say "we," we are talking about anybody who is a good, decent American. But that is not who "we" Christians are. If any issue is going to help us discover that, it is going to be the issue of abortion."—Stanley Hauerwas[1]

Christians find themselves in an impossible situation in a liberal democracy. On one hand, they must be the church, faithful to their own standards and beliefs. But they also must be more than the church: they must be citizens, mindful of the beliefs and practices of the many, whose moral standards may be aligned outside of or even in opposition to those of the church.

Even the assumption that "the church" speaks with one voice is problematic. About three-quarters of all Americans claim some degree of Christian faith, which means there are at least 225 million possible definitions of what it means to be a follower of Christ in the United States. However, reconciling the beliefs of the ultra-conservative Church of Christ with my own mostly liberal United Church of Christ is enough to make Jesus' prayer "that they may all be one" (John 17:21) seem less like operating instructions than a lament over its perpetual division.

The tension between religious commitment and public responsibility is not unique to Christianity, of course. Any thoughtful, honest participant in the public square will struggle to distinguish between their core beliefs and what is right for a nation of millions. This is as true of Judaism or neo-Paganism as it is of Christianity or atheism. More difficult is to see that our ideologies—the definitional ideas of our social networks—are equally conditional. Still, when pressed, most adults can grasp that a liberal or conservative political perspective is not identical to what the nation needs.

This differentiation between belief and policy is a particular problem for American Christians, though, precisely because their religion is socially dominant. In many parts of the nation, Christian moral reasoning is assumed to be normative, much as the Lone Ranger assumes his perspective is the norm until he is disabused of this notion by Tonto. Because Christianity is so dominant, the moral discourse is often understood in terms of Christians speaking to fellow believers. That is a problem in itself. America is not now, nor has it ever been, a Christian nation, as some ideologues hold. It was not founded to advance the religion or its specific moral principles, and it has never been the sole province of a single faith. It has always been, and continues to be, a contested land.

But the imposition of a monolithic moral conversation introduces other perversions as well. As noted, it is often assumed that Christians speak with a single voice on particular social issues. Another popular assumption is that the principle of Christian unity requires believers to paper over differences at all costs, such that any divisions that do exist are suppressed "for the good of the body." Both of these assumptions are ideological expressions designed to bolster the power of certain parties. Neither of them should seen as morally or politically neutral.

I want to take up the subject of abortion, then, as a way of understanding how unacknowledged scripts dominate American political life. Other issues might be chosen to bring the therapeutic script into view, but the subject of abortion is definitional for both society and the Religious Left. I hope to show that despite ambiguity in who can speak for American Christians, there is far less controversy over the practice of abortion than its opponents would like it to seem, and that such controversy as exists is perpetuated by conservatives bent on rolling back reproductive rights. Likewise, to the extent that there is a "Culture War" in America today, it is a one-sided affair, with hostility and violence originating exclusively from the right wing. Thus, calls to find "middle ground" in ideas like "abortion reduction" give disproportionate strength to conservative positions. They also betray faithful values, properly understood. A truly *progressive* Religious Left will need to stand its ground on abortion. A truly *faithful* movement will need to seek hope and freedom for women beyond medicalized regulation of their bodies. Only when we understand that women must be empowered as a principled matter of justice will we be able to break new ground on this social, political *and* religious dead zone.

THE ABORTION CONVERSATION

It is important to explore public opinion on abortion in some detail in order to develop a true picture of the political dimensions of the issue. In the past thirty years, Americans' views on the subject have been remarkably stable: A thin majority supports relatively unhindered abortion rights, a super-majority endorses it in the case of rape, incest or to preserve the mother's life, and a small but vocal minority opposes it altogether.

The National Election Survey has tracked attitudes toward abortion since 1980. In that time, the number of Americans who believe abortion should be "a matter of personal choice" has hovered around 40%, while those who believe it "should never be permitted" has shown a modest increase, from 10% of respondents in 1980 to 15% in 2008. A "mushy middle ground" approves of legalized abortion in more or less restrictive circumstances: around 30% say "yes" in the case of rape or incest, and about 20% agree to a needs-tested standard. Other surveys return similar results. According to the General Social Survey, 90% of Americans approve of abortion if the mother's health is in danger, while about 80% agree that abortion is justified in the case of rape or birth defects. Lower numbers—in the mid-40's—say the same thing if the woman is single, does not want or cannot afford more children, or for other, unspecified reasons. In 2008, only 10% of respondents thought that abortion should be illegal under any circumstances.[2]

The Pew Charitable Trust tracked opinion on abortion from July 1995 to August 2008, asking respondents if abortion should be always legal, mostly legal, mostly *illegal*, or always illegal. Their results, despite swings in either direction, ended up almost the same as when they began. In 1995, 59% believed abortion should be legal, and 40% believed it should be illegal. In 2008, the proportions were 54% to 41%.

These myriad survey results illustrate the ambiguous nature of the abortion divide. While most Americans express a desire for a "middle ground" on abortion, when push comes to shove, the majority goes with a "pro-choice" position: abortion should available with few, if any, restrictions. A super-majority endorses some exceptions. Only a tiny but persistent minority believes that abortion should be illegal altogether. That group reverses the general trend in society. According to a Pew Forum survey, 66% of Americans believe there is room for middle ground in abortion policy. However, those who want to ban the practice believe the opposite: 66% of them say there is *no room* for compromise.[3]

Despite the best, and often successful, efforts of the Religious Right to depict Christians as uniformly anti-abortion, in reality there is a considerable range of opinion on the subject even within religious traditions. White Evangelical Protestants are typically the most opposed to legalized abortion, but according to Pew, 9% of them believe it should be always legal, and 24% think it should be mostly legal. Catholics are split right down the middle: 49% say it should be always or mostly legal, 48% not. The religiously unaf-filiated are the most accepting of abortion: almost three-quarters of them approve. Mainline Protestants are not far behind at 69%. Again, the numbers seeking an outright ban are relatively small: only 15% of white Evangelicals and Catholics, and 6% of white mainline Protestants.[4]

So when someone says that "we Christians" believe this or that on the subject of abortion, it is important to respond: who is we? There is simply no single, authoritative voice for Christians in the United States. Nor, on most issues, is there a single position uniting the body of Christ. In the case of abortion, however, there is a rough consensus that it should be available in one form or another.

And those who disagree with that consensus are increasingly congregating in the Republican Party. A 2007 self-study of the party, confirmed by later research, found that the GOP was becoming old-er, more conservative, more Protestant, and increasingly concerned with social issues. Importantly, the GOP's so-called "moralists" were the most likely to vote on a candidate's position on issues, rather than his or her leadership qualities. They were also far more likely—by a margin of fifty points—to disagree with the following statement:

> The Republican Party has spent too much time focusing on moral issues such as abortion and gay marriage and should instead be spending time focusing on economic issues such as taxes and government spending.

And by thirty points, moralists declared themselves less likely to vote for a candidate who disagreed with them on abortion, even if that candidate agreed with their position on other issues. Little wonder the survey declared that the moralists had a "laser-like focus on moral issues."[5]

Two surveys released in mid-2009 might lead one to believe that the moralists' anti-abortion focus had spread into the general population. A Gallup poll headlined "More Americans 'Pro-Life'

Than 'Pro-Choice' for First Time" claimed that opinion had shift-ed from a 50-44 pro-choice split in 2008 to a 51-42 *pro-life* gap in 2009.[6] A Pew survey titled "Public Takes Conservative Turn on Gun Control, Abortion" returned similar results.[7] A closer look at the numbers, however, reveals that the movement was almost en-tirely among Republicans, particularly self-described "moderates" and "conservatives." This is not surprising, considering the pro-life invective thrown at President Obama.[8]

It is worth emphasizing here that despite predictions of large swings, by and large, socially conservative voters have stuck with the Republican Party. While Obama improved on John Kerry's perfor-mance with religious voters, he only equaled Al Gore's 2000 numbers among generic Protestants, and actually lost ground among white evangelicals relative to Gore. This backs up the common political observation that George W. Bush had a special relationship with evangelical voters. Obama did make inroads among younger evan-gelicals, even though they remain both overwhelmingly Republican and overwhelmingly opposed to abortion.[9]

The clear picture that should emerge from recent polling on abor-tion is a static difference of opinion, with only those firmly opposed becoming more polarized in their views. In addition, there is not a general outcry for the question to be resolved, despite survey results showing support for middle or common ground. Abortion and other "moral values" questions routinely rank near the bottom of voters' pri-orities. In recent years, open-ended questionnaires about priorities of-ten don't even return significant results for "abortion" or "homosexual rights." In general, then, there is no true culture war around the issue of abortion. The vast majority of Americans want it to be available, even if they disagree on the extent to which it should be restricted.

ABORTION AND THE "CULTURE WAR"

To the extent that there is a culture war, it is one largely fomented by a radicalized Religious Right. Frederick Clarkson points out that it was the ultra-nationalist Pat Buchanan who introduced the term "culture war" itself to American politics in an inflammatory speech at the 1992 Republican National Convention:

> Buchanan's speech epitomizes the Religious Right's general view of the "culture war"—as a "religious war" that manifests itself on many "cultural" fronts, most urgently abortion, homosexuality (especially, now, marriage equality), education privatization, and curriculum content of the public schools. So the culture war is not simply conflict over abortion or gay marriage. It is a one sided war of aggression against the civil rights advances of women and minorities and the rights of individual conscience that we generally discuss under the rubric of religious pluralism and of separation of church and state. For these political aggressors, war is not merely a metaphor or the equivalent of a sports analogy. It is far more profound and stems from the conflict of "world view," usually described as a "Biblical World view" against everything else. It is explicitly understood by its proponents as a religious war and waged accordingly on multiple fronts, mostly in terms we have come to define as "cultural." How the conflict plays out takes on political dimensions and sometimes physical conflict. This war is theocratic in nature, and seeks to roll back decades, and depending on the faction, centuries of democratic advances.

The "culture war" speech wasn't Buchanan's introduction to the politics of division. As early as 1971, he was writing memos for Richard Nixon calling on the president to "use abortion and parochial-school aid to deepen the split between Catholics and social liberals."[10] Buchanan's advice eventually bore fruit—if not with Nixon, then with the Republican Party, and with evangelicals as well as Catholics. In *Thy Kingdom Come*, Randall Balmer names what he calls "the abortion myth" that the organized Religious Right began in reaction to *Roe v. Wade*. He cites Religious Right architect Paul Weyrich to the effect that the movement began as a response to a 1980 decision removing the tax-exempt status of Bob Jones University. This is apparently confirmed by the attitude of conservative strategist and evangelical elder statesman Chuck Colson, who believed that overturning Roe would not accomplish much, but that the abortion issue itself would provide a useful "wedge" for introducing conservative Christian values into the political mainstream. Like Buchanan, Colson proved prescient.[11]

Clarkson calls the culture war a "one sided war of aggression." Unfortunately, that is all too often not hyperbole. According to the National Abortion Federation, between 1977 and the murder of Dr. George Tiller in May 2009, there had been seven murders of abortion service providers in the United States and Canada. There had also been 17 attempted murders, 41 bombings, 175 arsons, 96 attempted bombings or arsons, 1400 instances of vandalism, 100 "Butyric acid attacks," 659 Anthrax threats, 179 assaults, 406 death threats, 4 kidnappings, 151 burglaries, and 525 episodes of stalking. This tally disregards trespassing incidents, clinic invasions, bomb threats and hoaxes, pickets, and other attempts to disrupt clinic services.[12]

Let us be very clear here: not all anti-abortion activists are violent. Only a tiny fraction of the pro-life movement even engages in direct action, much less violence. However, it is important to recognize that the national conversation about abortion takes place against a backdrop of violence and intimidation. This terror campaign has been abetted by the violent rhetoric of hard right, but mainstream, leaders seeking to achieve certain cultural and political goals. Again, there is not so much a "culture war" as a small group of hardline activists on the right dedicated to upsetting the status quo.

COMMON GROUND ON ABORTION

In recent years, a movement to break new ground on the subject of abortion has sprung up within the Democratic Party. Initially a reaction to the perception that John Kerry lost the 2004 election because of Republican appeals to "moral values voters," the "common ground" argument quickly shifted to a critique of the Democratic approach to social conservatives. Since Barack Obama's arrival at the White House, this movement has become more focused on sustaining a broad middle coalition for the party by offering an ostensibly less partisan approach to politics. The urge for common ground has resulted in an impetus to break the stalemate by building a consensus around "abortion reduction." It has also sparked a great deal of rhetoric suggesting that both pro-life and pro-choice advocates are equally responsible for the cultural division over abortion.

The tensions of this approach are apparent in "Come, Let Us Reason Together," a foundational 2007 paper sponsored by the centrist think tank Third Way and signed by a variety of self-described moderate evangelical leaders. The paper lauds the "Reducing the Need for Abortion and Supporting Parents Act," commonly known as Ryan-DeLauro after its principal co-sponsors:

> This legislation is the first bill to join together the most effective strategies, regardless of their identification with the pro-choice or pro-life side, to minimize the need for abortions. The legislation finds common ground on reducing the number of abortions in America by both preventing unintended pregnancies and supporting pregnant women who wish to carry their pregnancies to term.

> Among its central provisions, Ryan-DeLauro calls for sex education with an abstinence emphasis and medically accurate contraceptive information, better access to contraception for low-income women, after-school programs for kids, and help for parents on communicating their values to their teens. It also expands Medicaid coverage of pregnant women and S-CHIP coverage of children, addresses domestic violence against pregnant women, helps pregnant women and young mothers stay in school, and expands adoption assistance.[13]

At first glance, this seems quite reasonable, even commonsensical. But as Debra Haffner of the Religious Institute on Sexual Morality, Justice and Healing points out, it presents as new ground points that were agreed upon as commonly held by both progressive and conservative believers in 1999:

- Promoting sexual responsibility
- Fostering equality and respect for women
- Strengthening parent-child communication about sexuality
- Working to reduce teenage pregnancies
- Improving prenatal and maternal care
- Supporting the choice of adoption
- [Reducing] the conditions that lead to unplanned pregnancies.[14]

"Come, Let Us Reason Together" praises its evangelical supporters for being eight years behind the curve, in other words. And though Ryan-DeLauro is presented as attractive to centrist believers, some of the bill's supporters cited a subtle but key difference with the paper's approach:

> [This legislation] finds a common ground approach to protecting life and supporting families. Its strategy for reducing abortions...is effective and serious. These are very worthy goals and deserve the full support of the Christian community and pro-life organizations across the country.—Randy Brinson, M.D., Founder and Chairman, Redeem the Vote

> [This legislation] is an important step toward preventing abortion and supporting pregnant women. For too long, too many people have been satisfied with only a contentious debate over simplified positions of "life" and "choice." A better approach is to foster more energy for and commitment to

advancing a dialogue that aims for solutions.—Reverend Jim Wallis, *Sojourners/Call to Renewal*

We are told that this reflects a compromise on the part of abortion opponents. Rather than seeking an outright ban or the overturn of *Roe v. Wade*, these activists will settle for the common ground of reducing the number of abortions performed each year. But closer inspection reveals that this compromise is something less than advertised. "Preventing abortions" (or "reducing abortions") is not the same as "reducing the *need* for abortion," nor is it identical to "the reduction of unwanted pregnancies." The first is a formulation used almost exclusively by abortion opponents, while the latter two phrases are used by pro-choice advocates, with pregnancy prevention usually being the choice of activists. Despite attempts to conflate the last with the first, reduction of unwanted pregnancies is currently the official stance in the Democratic Party platform and the policy of the Obama administration.

As Frederick Clarkson has documented, the abortion reduction strategy has its roots in the pro-life movement, which indeed settled upon it as a compromise to legal bans on abortion, a goal the movement had decided was unattainable. Examining a 1996 paper published in the conservative Catholic journal *First Things*, Clarkson noted that the idea has more to do with erecting barriers to abortion than changing the circumstances of women seeking abortions:

> While the signers agreed that the regulations upheld in the Casey decision "do not afford any direct legal protection to the unborn child," they emphasized that "experience has shown that such regulations—genuine informed consent, waiting periods, parental notification—reduce abortions in a locality, especially when coupled with positive efforts to promote alternatives to abortion and service to women in crisis.

Furthermore, abortion reduction was conceived "in the context of the wider goal of criminalization":

> Having declared abortion to be among other things, child killing, an act of "lethal violence," and a usurpation of the rule of law, the signatories added: "Any criminal sanctions considered in such legislation [then being considered by Congress] should fall upon abortionists, not upon women in crisis." They further urged Congress to "recognize the unborn child as a human person entitled to the protection of the Constitution.[15]

The signers Clarkson writes about include some of the very same people who endorsed "Come, Let Us Reason Together," most notably Jim Wallis, David Gushee, and Ron Sider. Wallis later affirmed that it reflected his current thinking, and Gushee refused to reject it.

THE TROUBLE WITH COMMON GROUND

With abortion reduction at the center of the so-called common ground on abortion, the conversation becomes decidedly tilted toward the frames of abortion opponents. When this has been pointed out by critics of the common ground approach (including myself), the response has been accusations of spiritual and political divisiveness, as though the critics were undermining a widely-held consensus position, rather than stating the obvious: that abortion reduction unnecessarily favors a minority position.

Take, for example, a blog post written by Susan Brooks Thistlethwaite, in response to comments I and others had made on the common-ground strategy:

> Also, in a more spiritual sense, increasing tolerance and building pluralistic community is the right thing to do. There is true joy in finding the unexpected ally, the bet-

ter position that benefits more people. Sure there are road-blocks, and temptations to confuse common ground with lowest common denominator. But true change is possible. And religious faith is all about possibility, unexpected joy and the movement of grace...Among people who self-iden-tify as liberal or progressive, there should be room for diver-sity of opinion on how to best effect the change we need. And really, if we can't honor diversity, aren't we betraying that fundamental principle of historic liberalism?[16]

Thistlethwaite conflates leeriness of the consequences of a particular political strategy with a rejection of grace and a betrayal of liberal values. An Op-Ed published by two Catholic activists in the *Cleveland Plain Dealer* and later reprinted by *Sojourners* takes a similar, albeit more aggressive tack, equating activists on either side of the issue as disruptive ideologues:

When both the left and right begin sharpening their knives, it means you are on to something. This new threat raising the hackles of liberals and conservatives still hunkered down in culture-war bunkers? It's a movement focused on comprehensive strategies to reduce abortions by providing economic supports for vulnerable women and preventing unintended pregnancies. A chorus of critics across the ide-ological spectrum has lined up to malign these common-ground efforts with all the righteous zeal of those who make "the perfect" the enemy of "the good."

Liberal bloggers slam Catholics and evangelicals work-ing on this approach as radical "anti-choice" hard-liners cozying up to the religious right. Religious conservatives denounce the effort as a betrayal of faith and question re-search that finds that abortions decline when women have quality health care and access to robust social services...

While these reactions run the gambit from the predictable to the absurd, they share a scorched-earth rhetorical style and an absolutist devotion to hardened agendas. If politics is the art of the possible, these common-ground naysayers seem more comfortable defending turf and demonizing opponents than seizing a unique political moment when pro-choice and pro-life public officials are finally doing more than exploiting abortion as a "wedge issue" to divide voters and win elections.[17]

This sets up abortion reduction as a sensible (not to mention faithful) middle ground, when in truth, the strategy is far closer to the anti-abortion pole than the true center point of the issue.

This no doubt seems like so much inside baseball to many readers. To some extent it is. But these debates also reflect real differences on political process. More importantly, they reveal significant differences on an issue involving the rights of millions—and as Michelle Goldberg has documented, perhaps billions—of women.[18] Those differences are more deeply rooted than simple politics. They involve profound philosophical, even theological, commitments that have the power to shape the course of our common life for decades to come.

THE TROUBLE WITH ABORTION REDUCTION

One of the enduring critiques of the strategy of reducing abortion has been that it does not respect women's moral agency. The critics have not been reassured by the words of abortion reduction's supposedly liberal proponents. Jim Wallis, for example, took to his blog to respond to readers' questions about the strategy:

> Support for women caught up in difficult situations and tragic choices is a better path than coercion for really reducing the abortion rate. Yes, I agree there is never a "need" for abortion except in the case where the health of the mother

is threatened. But until we can reach out to women who "feel" the need for abortion and support them in alternative choices, we will never change the shameful abortion rate that both sides seem content to live with while they just attack each other. It is time to move from symbols to solutions.[19]

Wallis' response reveals a characteristic myopia. Support is better than coercion. Gentler, anyway. But it is no less authoritarian. Rather than trust women to make the painful decision to terminate a pregnancy, even with the assistance of their physicians or loved ones, Wallis breezily dismisses the need for abortion in all but a few cases. He then compounds the error by presuming to know what women ought to feel about abortion, and the legitimacy of men such as himself correcting their mistaken feelings. This comes wrapped in the twin assumptions that the abortion rate is "shameful," raising the question of who ought to be ashamed, and that abortion is a problem in search of a "solution."

All in all, this is quite a display of entitlement masquerading as moral concern. It's certainly a far cry from the "fundamental principle of historic liberalism" known as self-determination. It's also a far cry from the radical egalitarianism of the early church, where the apostle Paul could boldly decry patriarchal attitudes by proclaiming "there is no longer male and female" in Christ. It is worth pausing here to consider the full context of that quote:

Now before faith came, we were imprisoned and guarded under the law until faith would be revealed. Therefore the law was our disciplinarian until Christ came, so that we might be justified by faith. But now that faith has come, we are no longer subject to a disciplinarian, for in Christ Jesus you are all children of God through faith. As many of you as were baptized into Christ have clothed yourselves with Christ. There is no longer Jew or Greek, there is no longer slave or free, there is no longer male and female; for all of you are one in Christ Jesus. And if you belong to Christ, then you are Abraham's offspring, heirs according to the promise.

My point is this: heirs, as long as they are minors, are no better than slaves, though they are the owners of all the property; but they remain under guardians and trustees until the date set by the father. So with us; while we were minors, we were enslaved to the elemental spirits of the world. But when the fullness of time had come, God sent his Son, born of a woman, born under the law, in order to redeem those who were under the law, so that we might receive adoption as children. And because you are children, God has sent the Spirit of his Son into our hearts, crying, 'Abba! Father!' So you are no longer a slave but a child, and if a child then also an heir, through God.[20]

Christians, according to Paul, stand in a new relationship to one another and to Jewish law. They have been freed by faith from the law. This may be their own faith, or by Jesus' faithfulness to God's purposes, suggesting that the grace offered by Christ overcomes any human sin. In that freedom, Christians are joint heirs of God's promise, adults radically and equally capable of making their own decisions, with no room for domination of one party over another.

In sharp contrast to this perspective, abortion foes have been emboldened by recent legal and political developments to infantilize women through "informed consent" and other tactics to steer women to what these opponents consider appropriate choices.[21] Jill Filipovic, among many others, rightly derided this strategy in a blog post sarcastically titled, "Because respecting women means making all their decisions for them."[22]

This perception is only furthered by the logical difficulty of attempts to outlaw abortion that attach criminal penalties to the doctors who perform the procedures, but not to the women who seek them. As opponents of such laws point out, persons who solicit contract killings are themselves charged with murder. If abortion is to be considered murder, why should women not be given corresponding charges?[23] A particularly repellent variation on the theme of infantilizing women involves saving them from the regrets of abortion:

> "While we find no reliable data to measure the phenomenon, it seems unexceptionable to conclude some women come to regret their choice to abort the infant life they once created and sustained," Justice Kennedy wrote, alluding to the brief. "Severe depression and loss of esteem can follow."[24]

This is a complete denial of a woman's ability to make her own moral choices—even choices that she will later come to regret—by depending upon discredited medical research that reinforces discriminatory cultural stereotypes about the inability of pregnant women to understand the consequences of their decisions. In other words, it makes the law a disciplinarian to children, claiming it's for their own good. For example, abortion opponents in South Dakota attempted to ban abortion outright in that state in part by perverting the value of women's moral decision-making to suggest that they would never choose to end a pregnancy of their own free will. Therefore, according to this logic, a ban on the practice would protect women's choices, health, and welfare.[25] A bill outlawing abortion except in the case of a threat to the mother's health—identical to Jim Wallis' stated position and conceived as a challenge to Roe—was signed into law in early 2006[26], but voters soundly rejected it in consecutive referendums, even after exceptions for incest and rape were added.[27]

Another South Dakota law that was unaffected by the referendums requires doctors to describe the medical and mental health risks of abortion, as well as the gestational stage of the fetus. Doctors are required to

tell any woman seeking an abortion that she is terminating
the life of "a whole, separate, unique, living human being"
with whom she has an "existing relationship," that her relationship "enjoys protection under the United States Constitution and under the laws of South Dakota," and that abortion terminates that relationship along with "her existing
constitutional rights with regards to that relationship."[28]

However, laws aimed at reducing abortion do not need to be as restrictive as South Dakota's to undermine self-determination. Measures such as mandatory counseling, waiting periods, and spousal
notification do little to nothing to prevent abortion. Rather, they
burden the women who seek to end their pregnancies, and treat
them as unable to make informed decisions without the intercession
of doctors, husbands, and their own second-guessing. Restrictions
such as these also have the perverse effect of specially taxing poor
women with few resources to cope with an unintended pregnancy,
while not much affecting wealthier individuals with more alternatives. As Scott Lemieux says, this is theoretically consistent with a
thoroughgoing pro-life position, but how it can be squared with a
nominally pro-choice stance is something of a mystery.[29]

While many of the examples cited here stem from the debate
over the Partial Birth Abortion Act of 2006, the problem is hardly one of the past. After the murder of Kansas abortion provider
George Tiller, *New York Times* columnist Ross Douthat took it upon
himself to question the necessity of Tiller's perfectly legal work, not
trusting that the women Tiller served could (or would) make a good
decision in consultation with their physician. While conceding that
late-term abortions often arise from the most difficult of circumstances, Douthat postulated that

the argument that some abortions take place in particularly
awful, particularly understandable circumstances is not a
case against regulating abortion. It's the beginning of pre-

cisely the kind of reasonable distinction-making that would produce a saner, stricter legal regime.[30]

In other words, understanding the tragic choices women must make when having a regulated third-trimester abortion indicates that there should be less freedom when it comes to the 90 percent of unregulated abortions performed in the first weeks of pregnancy. This dizzying logic leads Douthat to the rather remarkable conclusion that the state has underperformed its paternal duties by not stepping in to make "reasonable distinctions" in medical decisions made by women.

Douthat's column points to a common problem in the arguments for reducing abortion: the lack of a plausible explanation for why the government has an interest in making a *safe* and *legal* medical procedure *rare*. (Ironically, antichoice activists recognize this contradiction immediately.)

WHY SHOULD ABORTION BE DISCOURAGED?

Proponents of the abortion-reduction strategy often speak of it as though it were a self-evident good. I have already noted Jim Wallis' comments on America's "shameful abortion rate." Likewise, the website RealAbortionSolutions.org (a project of Faith in Public Life) challenges its readers to "Be inspired by religious leaders who are calling for Democrats and Republicans to come together around common ground solutions based on results, not rhetoric." Those religious leaders turn out to be many of the same people who signed the "Come, Let Us Reason Together" statement.[31] Another example comes from a press release challenging what it called Republicans' "failed abortion policies":

> "The Republican strategy regarding abortion is more about rhetoric than results," said Chris Korzen, executive director of Catholics United. "People of faith and pro-life activists are tired of empty promises. It's time to move beyond the

abortion stalemate and support public policies that help women and families choose life." [32]

While it may seem obvious from a pro-life perspective that the abortion rate needs to be reduced, there is in fact no solid policy reason that government ought to "help women and families choose life." The abortion rate is already declining, according to the Guttmacher Institute, going from "roughly 29 per 1,000 in 1979 to between 18 and 19 per 1,000 in 2005." Likewise, the teen abortion rate went from "about 43 per 1,000 between 1979 and 1989 to 20 per thousand in 2003." [33] This raises the question of why the government should encourage "better choices" when women are increasingly making those very same choices on their own.

More to the point, however ethically preferential it might be, there is simply no government interest in abortion reduction. Abortion, after all, is in the vast majority of cases a safe and relatively minor medical procedure. The scientific studies claiming to demonstrate psychological harm to women who have had abortions have been debunked, as have ideas about long-lasting health problems. There may be a government interest in helping women avoid invasive and unnecessary procedures, but that is a weak argument, as millions of elective medical procedures are carried out every year in the United States. Why should this particular one be discouraged? Why in this one particular case should it be assumed that a woman's capacity to make medical decisions in consultation with her family and doctors is insufficient?

This might easily be mistaken for an argument against the regulation of abortion itself. It is not. As with any other medical procedure, there is a legitimate government interest in making sure that abortions are carried out safely and effectively. Given the unique circumstances of a developing human life, there is even legitimate interest in a presumption against late-term abortions. But abortion has already met those tests. There is no reason other than deference to particular moral precepts to burden the practice further with policies designed to steer women away from it.

Abortion reduction proponents argue that their proposals benefit women as a whole. According to Third Way, for example, the Ryan-DeLauro bill would fund a variety of programs, including sex education, family planning services, adoption assistance, children's health care, and prevention programs directed at teen pregnancy, domestic violence, and sexual assault.[34]

These proposals are meant to "reduce the need for abortion" by providing alternatives rather than punitive measures. But while they may or may not be worthy goals in their own right, here they are offered as instruments to reaching an overarching goal whose worthiness is never addressed. Instead, we are left to infer that the means justify the end, as it were.

As it happens, those means appear to have much more to do with politics than policy. The Third Way white paper creating the abortion reduction frame says that it "maintains the progressive principle of supporting abortion rights, while reflecting people's desire for common ground, as well as their concerns about the morality of abortion." That sounds good enough, until one realizes the absence of a tangible policy goal. According to Third Way, the core purpose of Ryan-DeLauro isn't to advance any of the programs listed above, *but to solve the political problem of abortion.* That assessment may sound overly cynical at first, but the paper itself states its goals: "This memo offers new guidance on how to approach the abortion issue in a way that addresses the concerns of the vast and conflicted middle and maintains supports for abortion rights." In other words, the message comes first, and the policy follows. A later section in the paper on common ground confirms this perception:

> Americans recognize that the abortion debate is bitter, polarized, and destructive. By a 69-28% margin, they say that "the abortion debate is too angry." And by a margin of 74-20%, Americans wish elected leaders would look for common ground on the issue of abortion.

...

Does common ground exist? Yes, Americans find that common ground through the goal of reducing the prevalence of abortion while still protecting the right. Specifically, the following statement was supported by a 69-28% margin:

I support abortion rights, but I believe we can find common ground to reduce the need for abortions in America while still protecting a woman's right to have one.

Setting aside the dubious proposition that approval of a general statement translates into support for a specific proposal, the memo says nothing about policy, and contradicts itself morally. It very well may be an effective means to overcome the political stalemate around abortion. It may be the ticket to attracting socially conservative evangelicals and Catholics to the Democratic Party. But while it claims to recognize the moral complexity of abortion, the Third Way memo avoids taking a firm stand on the issue one way or another. In fact, it studiously avoids the question of why the need for abortion ought to be reduced. The only answer it provides is that such a policy would soothe American's frayed nerves on a "culture war" issue. That, it should be said, is less-than-satisfying. The business of government is not to assuage moral qualms, but to provide sensible policies for its citizens. As the blogger Digby writes on another subject,

These are not issues on which compromise is possible and being pragmatic in this regard results in incoherence and a diminishment of moral authority.[35]

No amount of dancing around the subject can close the gap. If abortion is to be legal, there should be no need to reduce its occurrence or the need for it. A far more supportive frame would to be to seek to prevent unintended pregnancies. Unlike abortion reduction, preventing unplanned pregnancies has measurable policy outcomes, such as better health for women, increased education, and savings on Medicaid costs. It is also consistent with the progressive value of self-determination. Unfortunately, it also involves increasing the availability of contraception and other reproductive services to poor women, which would require moderate compromisers to confront social conservatives. This could be a truly prophetic moment, but somehow I doubt that it will come to pass.

THE PARTISANSHIP OF ABORTION REDUCTION

Abortion reduction rests on weak ethical ground. It diminishes women's self-determination, it relies on contradictory moral premises, and it offers political messaging in response to policy questions. As if all that weren't bad enough, it might also be bad politics. The strategy of compromise ignores the evidence of polling on the subject, as we have seen. It also neglects, perhaps intentionally, the history of partisanship on the abortion issue.

By that, I mean both the political contention between Democrats and Republicans and the wrangling that takes place within the parties. Republicans have famously used abortion as a wedge issue to pry away evangelical and Catholic voters from the Democratic Party. There is some evidence to suggest that the issue has lost salience among Catholics in recent elections,[36] but it appears to continue its hold on evangelicals, even among younger voters.[41] Less well known are Republican attempts to woo black and Hispanic voters,[38] who tend to be more socially conservative than white Democrats.[39] Moreover, abortion remains an important part of conservative identity politics and a central rallying point for the religious right.[40]

The potency of abortion amongst Republicans was evident in the 2008 presidential race, when religious conservatives fretted about the possibility of a Rudolph Giuliani candidacy[41], threatened to stay home rather than vote for the insufficiently pro-life John McCain[42], pledged to "revolt" if McCain did not choose a pro-life running mate,[43] and finally exulted in Sarah Palin's nomination for Vice-President.[44]

Abortion's use as a litmus test is not limited to presidential politics among Republicans. It—or related life issues—has been used against state-level candidates and U.S. Representatives, including from the pulpit of a Catholic church.[45] Nor is abortion as an issue limited to Republican intramurals: it has long been a favorite weapon of social conservatives to criticize Democratic politicians. President Obama has been criticized as "the most committed pro-abortion president in our history" by James Dobson[46], to no one's surprise. More interesting, Obama's friend Rick Warren attempted to trap him at a candidate forum with a surprise question on when life begins.[47] Before the forum, Eric McFadden, a former Hillary Clinton campaign aide, pleaded for Warren to move the conversation "beyond the question of the legality of abortion and move towards actually reducing the need for abortion."[48] Meanwhile, despite attempts by Democratic-leaning evangelicals to spin the Democratic Party platform on reproductive rights as a victory for the cause of abortion reduction, the new plank may have actually strengthened party support for the principle of choice and the policy of pregnancy prevention.[49]

Catholic Democrats have been special targets of abortion politics. In 2008, Robert Novak attempted to steer Democrats away from nominating Kathleen Sebellius as a "A Pro-Choicer's Dream Veep,"[50] and Denver Archbishop Charles Chaput called on Vice President Joe Biden to refrain from taking communion in the Catholic church.[51] More generally, as Amy Sullivan has extensively documented in her book *The Party Faithful*, there has been a long tradition of Catholic bishops challenging pro-choice Catholic politicians,[52] often walking right up to the line separating church and state. Sullivan argues convincingly that this history caused the Democratic Party to shy away unnecessarily from religious outreach altogether for many years, assuming that they would get the same reception from other religious groups.

On the other hand, Sullivan herself gives no help to Catholic Democrats, repeating the oft-told canard that Pennsylvania Governor William Casey Sr. was prevented from speaking at the 1992 Democratic Convention because of his opposition to abortion. The truth is more complex—and antagonistic. As the watchdog group Media Matters points out, eight other pro-life speakers took the platform at the convention. Unlike those speakers, Casey had refused to endorse Bill Clinton, even going so far as to call on the convention to find another nominee.[53] Media Matters says that Casey's planned speech was "for a single purpose: attacking the Democratic party," which is not quite accurate. It is true that Casey's text, later released as an op-ed essay with the combative title "The Speech The Democratic Party Didn't Want You To Hear," was a stern rebuke to his own party. Casey never mentions Clinton or running mate Al Gore in the speech, preferring to open with the following declaration:

> The national Democratic Party has embraced abortion on demand. I believe this position is wrong in principle and out of the mainstream of our party's historic commitment to protecting the powerless. I also believe this position is politically self-defeating because it excludes not only pro-life voters, but also those who are ambivalent but believe the number of abortions should be reduced and the practice made subject to reasonable regulation.[54]

Casey seemed determined to tear down the Democratic Party unless it was rebuilt around the value of life, understood in explicitly Catholic terms. "By rejecting abortion on demand, we can move our party back to the mainstream," Casey promised in an oddly partisan conclusion to an intensely ideological speech, asserting that a pro-life position would draw Reagan Democrats back to the party.

But electoral politics was not the only thing on Casey's mind. He also called on Democrats to "do all that we can to make life worth living for both mother and child," using a combination of social welfare initiatives and "reasonable regulations" including a ban on third-trimester abortions or those performed for sex selection, parental notification, informed consent, and waiting periods. The planned speech seems to have formed the kernel for an essay laying out a "A New American Compact" on abortion that was published during the convention as a full-page ad in the *New York Times* and later reprinted in *First Things*. Comparing the documents is fascinating work. Casey's original highlighted women as the recipient of social concern:

> Our respect for the wonders of pregnancy must be matched by a sensitivity to the traumas of pregnancy. When a woman is faced with a crisis pregnancy, we must reach out to her with compassion and understanding. We must give her the support she needs to get through her pregnancy with dignity and security.[55]

The version that ran in *First Things* drops mentions of a new regulatory scheme and plays up the idea of supporting pregnant women, using language that anticipates that of abortion-reduction proponents in years to come:

> At the same time, a public policy that more adequately expresses the traditions and convictions of the American people will do more than restore legal protection to the unborn.

> It will take seriously the needs of women whose social or economic circumstances might tempt them to seek the abortion "solution." It will recognize our shared responsibility, in public and private settings, to make realistic alternatives to abortion available to such women. It will support women in caring for the children they choose to raise themselves, and it will help them find homes for those they

cannot raise. It will work to provide a decent life for mother and child before and after birth.

In sum, we can and we must adopt solutions that reflect the dignity and worth of every human being and that embody understanding of the community's shared responsibility for creating policies that are truly prowoman and prochild. What we seek are communities and policies that help women to deal with crisis pregnancies by eliminating the crisis, not the child.[56]

Whether or not Casey was denied a speaking slot because of his pro-life views, the narrative of his refusal has survived in large part because it has been useful to pro-life Democrats. However, the abortion issue is not a simple matter of pro-life Republicans and pro-choice Democrats. There are movements within both parties pushing the anti-abortion agenda. There are also movements working across party lines, leading Digby to declare a "two-front" war on reproductive rights. She, like me, had harsh words for Jim Wallis' attempts to negotiate a compromise on the issue of abortion that dismissed women's self-determination. Digby went further, though, to attack the compromise itself:

> These two assaults on women's reproductive rights—the "gentle" persuasion of our new friends who say "we just want to make women realize they don't need to have abortions" combined with the harsh assault by the religious right to limit women's access to birth control makes it obvious that this battle is now being fought on twin fronts.

> And one day soon, I'm sure we'll see a brilliant compromise brokered between the Democrats and Republicans—the Republicans will reluctantly allow the government to "force" people to dispense birth control against their consciences

and the Democrats will reluctantly agree that it's necessary to force women to have children against their will. A lovely bipartisan outcome.[57]

This is the partisanship of abortion reduction: the fight for a cause, rather than a party. Those who have sought compromise around the supposed middle ground of abortion reduction have learned the hard way that not all sides are interested. In the summer of 2009, as the Obama administration prepared to release its abortion policies, Third Way staffer Rachel Laser floated a trial balloon, touting the Ryan-DeLauro bill as a way to "dial down the culture wars."[58] But because the bill included money for contraception and comprehensive sex education, as well as abortion reduction measures, it was opposed by the U.S. Council of Catholic Bishops and the Southern Baptist Convention, who wanted the two sides of the proposal severed. Reminded that the White House called for a reduction in the *need* for abortion, rather than abortion reduction itself, the Catholic Bishops reiterated through a spokeswoman that

> The phrase "reducing the need for abortion" is not a common-ground phrase. We would say that there is no need for abortion, that abortions are signs that we have not met the needs of women. There is no authentic need for abortion.[59]

So much for compromise.

THE CASE OF GEORGE TILLER
On Sunday, May 31, 2009, Dr. George Tiller was shot to death in the lobby of his church in Wichita, Kansas.[60] Tiller, an OB/GYN, had long been a target of anti-abortion activists because he performed late-term abortions. His murder shocked the nation, outraging pro-choice activists and worrying pro-life groups concerned that his murder would set back their cause. Many abortion opponents—including James Dobson and Albert Mohler—quickly denounced

the killing.[61] Though the gunman, Scott Roeder, had few formal ties to extremist groups like Operation Rescue, let alone mainstream abortion opponents, he was found with the phone number of Cheryl Suellenger, Operation Rescue's political director, in his car. Suellenger later admitted that she had been feeding Roeder information about Tiller's court appearances.[62]

Tiller's murder took place against a backdrop of what can only be described as hate speech and the suborning of violence. Unfortunately, ugly rhetoric has been a staple of the anti-abortion movement for decades. Randall Terry, founder of Operation Rescue, has long used the dictum "If you think abortion is murder, act like it."[63] Terry's successor at Operation Rescue agreed, calling Tiller a "murderer" and "killer."[64] Terry himself remained unrepentant after Tiller's death, saying

> George Tiller was a mass-murderer. We grieve for him that he did not have time to properly prepare his soul to face God. I am more concerned that the Obama administration will use Tiller's killing to intimidate pro-lifers into surrendering our most effective rhetoric and actions. Abortion is still murder. And we still must call abortion by its proper name: murder. Those men and women who slaughter the unborn are murderers according to the law of God. We must continue to expose them in our communities and peacefully protest them at their offices and homes, and yes, even their churches.[65]

This kind of rhetoric is not limited to the fringes of the anti-abortion movement. Frank Pavone, director of Priests for Life, in discussing Tiller's murder, compared abortion to a "holocaust." Bishop Robert Finn of the Catholic Diocese of Kansas City and St. Joseph declared "We are at war!" at an anti-abortion conference just five weeks before Tiller's death.[66] Even Rick Warren, normally held up as a model of a centrist evangelical, echoed the language of "holocaust," telling reporter Dan Gilgoff after the Saddleback Forum,

For many evangelicals, of course, if they believe that life begins at conception, that's a deal breaker for a lot of people. If they think that life begins at conception, then that means that there are 40 million Americans who are not here [because they were aborted] that could have voted. They would call that a holocaust, and for them it would like if I'm Jewish and a Holocaust denier is running for office. I don't care how right he is on everything else, it's a deal breaker for me. I'm not going to vote for a Holocaust denier...[67]

Media figures have also taken part in the egregious rhetoric. The ever-ghoulish Ann Coulter has referred to the murder of abortion providers as a "procedure by rifle." She also told Fox News host Bill O'Reilly, "I don't really like to think of it as a murder. It was terminating Tiller in the 203rd trimester." When O'Reilly pressed her on this statement, Coulter replied, "I am personally opposed to shooting abortionists, but I don't want to impose my moral values on others."[68]

O'Reilly himself has much to answer for as attacks on Tiller as a "baby killer" and "murderer" were a regular staple of his show for years. In 2007, he made the chilling declaration to then-Governor Kathleen Sebellius that "if the state of Kansas doesn't stop this man, then anybody who prevents that from happening has blood on their hands."[69] Tucker Carlson defended O'Reilly's comments comparing Tiller to Hitler, al-Qaeda, and NAMBLA, saying, "Every one of those descriptions of Tiller is objectively true. I sincerely think it's appalling that he was murdered. But Tiller was a monster, no doubt."[70]

Many on the right are careful to disavow the use of violence in opposing abortion. Bishop Finn, for example, told his audience that their battle was spiritual, "We cannot hate these human enemies, and we must find a way to love them."[71] And as Thomas Frank explained shortly after Tiller's death, culture war rhetoric is conceived as entertainment and a vehicle for fundraising, not a call to physical violence. Frank wrote that

> According to the unwritten rules of the culture wars, the "base" isn't supposed to act on it when the performers describe a world gone crazy. They're an audience; they're supposed to hiss, applaud, donate, vote and go home.[72]

Thus it comes as a shock to many conservative leaders when violence actually does erupt. They are apparently unaware that "what we know from experience about volatile, unstable actors like [Scott Roeder] is that they can be readily induced into violent action by hateful rhetoric that demonizes and dehumanizes other people." Religious figures like Rick Warren who compare legalized abortion to the Holocaust and media figures like Bill O'Reilly who call abortion providers "killers" may not intend for their words to result in violence, but the inevitable result of their irresponsible rhetoric is to push extremists over the edge.

VIOLENCE AND COMMON GROUND

Common ground proponents often cite just such examples as evidence for the need for tempered speech on abortion. For example, John Buchanan, editor and publisher of *The Christian Century* wondered if Tiller's murder could "possibly lead people of good will on both sides to show more civility and respect as we continue to talk about the issue?"[73] Faith in Public Life released a statement from religious leaders—once again, many of the same people who signed the "Come, Let Us Reason Together" statement—deploring the killing and reiterating their position:

> As people of faith working to create civility and common ground on abortion, this reprehensible attack reminds us of our moral obligation to respect the humanity of those on both sides of this issue. Wherever we stand, this act offends us all.[74]

Statements such as these create a false equivalence between "both sides of this issue." As Timothy Rutten of the *Los Angeles Times* noted, "Over the years, no abortion-rights advocate has physically harmed an antiabortion partisan. Since 1973, antiabortion extremists have killed eight times."[75] Pro-choice activists can be strident in their rhetoric, even dismissive of their opponents. Yet they have not strayed into calls for the elimination of their foes, nor suggested that violence against them might be justified. As Fred Clarkson says, so far the culture war has been "a one-sided war of aggression."

Nor are calls on both sides to turn down the rhetoric effective in marginalizing extremists like Randall Terry. As journalist Bill Berkowitz wrote in response to the Faith in Public Life statement, "What good is a condemnation of Tiller's murder if the hate speech that often inspires—perhaps even drives—one to commit such murders is not also condemned?"[76] Indeed, even before Tiller was buried, abortion opponents turned their attention to his colleague LeRoy Carhart, publishing photos of his Nebraska clinic, home, and work addresses. Operation Rescue started a "research project" on Carhart, soliciting information from women who had sought abortions from him in the past five years. "If experience is any guide," says Kansas City journalist Barb Shelly,

> this "research project" will result in unverifiable and downright bogus allegations, which the group will make public. It's the sort of information that just might inflame an unbalanced person like Scott Roeder, the man accused of shooting Tiller in his church—where, by the way, Operation Rescue had protested and disrupted services numerous times.[77]

Shelly's concerns are not ill-founded. Scott Roeder was a member of an anti-government militia, and the scene of the murder he committed recalled Jim Adkisson's 2008 attack on a Unitarian Universalist congregation in Tennessee. The Tillers' participation at their church was detailed at dr-tiller.com, a site aggregating the research done on him. Moreover, while Roeder may not have had formal ties with anti-abortion activists, he was friendly with a number of extremists, many with ties to the militia and white supremacist worlds, leading Daily Kos contributing editor Hunter to declare, "if he weren't white, we'd be calling this a 'terror cell.'"[78] That is more than a joke: a Department of Homeland Security report released in spring 2009 warned against just such violence. Perpetrators like Roeder are seldom the "lone gunmen" they are made out to be, often traveling in loose associations such as the Army of God and following patterns of violence and intimidation that are refined by their networks over time.[79] Easy calls for common ground do little to address the sources of this violence, nor do they do anything to address the legitimate security concerns it raises. Reconciliation requires a just and accurate understanding of the situation. As it stands now, the murder of physicians like Dr. Tiller means that women in desperate situations have even fewer places to turn for treatment, while advocates for their care are chided for divisive language and the people whose words created the climate for violence are ignored. It was little wonder, then, that the support for common ground seemed to collapse after Tiller's death:

> Tiller's death is a "massive setback" in the search for common ground, said Cristina Page, a New York City author and abortion rights advocate. "It's sort of like having a family member murdered and then being asked to make nice with the assassin's family. It's unnatural."[80]

That by itself would not make it impossible, or even undesirable. But it is not something that can be compelled, or even asked, and certainly not for partisan gain. It can only be volunteered. Otherwise, it's just one more violation.

BRUEGGEMANN AND THE THERAPEUTIC SCRIPT

At first glance, Walter Brueggemann's vision of the therapeutic script doesn't seem to offer a way out of this morass. In fact, it might be taken as a broadside against "abortion on demand":

> I use the term therapeutic to refer to the assumption that there is a product or a treatment or a process to counteract every ache and pain and discomfort and trouble, so that life may be lived without inconvenience.[81]

Only the coarsest of analysts would suggest that women terminate their pregnancies as lightly as they would seek treatment for foot pain. More often, it is a wrenching and difficult decision brought on by dire necessity. What Brueggemann seems to have in mind is less chiding women for their choices than the medicalization of health care and the kind of "moralistic therapeutic deism" described by the sociologist Christian Smith. This "de facto dominant religion" understands God as a kindly but distant deity who wants us "to be good, nice, and fair to each other," and the good life as being happy and feeling good about oneself.[82]

Against this deity, Brueggemann posits a God who is a tenacious (if not always sympathetic) presence in the midst of suffering, but who calls his people to leave comfort and security behind. Brueggemann's God "refuses domestication," and "will not let our lives be domesticated either." This God consistently offers an alternative to the unkept promises of the world to keep us safe and happy without cost to ourselves. The plain fact is that we cannot live without pain and discomfort and trouble. The vision of God that Brueggemann offers is one who will walk beside us in the midst of these things and challenge us to find a new vision of what it means to be whole outside the easy understandings of doctors and pharmaceutical companies and psychotherapists.

Applying Brueggemann's vision of the therapeutic script to the specific case of abortion does provide some useful insight. Abortion for the sake of gender selection is hard to square with the "ragged, disjunctive" narrative of life God calls us to. Less clear is abortion performed when genetic tests indicate a high probability of mental retardation or significant but not life-threatening disease. In such situations, and in the absence of other considerations, the needs of the mother must be weighed carefully against the quality of the potential new life.

I hasten to add that these are ethical calculations, not policy considerations. They ought to be carried out by women, their partners, physicians, and those they trust to give advice. No two cases will be alike, and there is no warrant for second-guessing by intrusive scolds. Nor, given the relative rarity of such cases, is there grounds for government intervention that will undoubtedly burden others seeking abortions for their own reasons. The value in considering the therapeutic script in this light is to affirm that abortion, like any aspect of humanity, is not beyond the reach of ethics. Some choices will be better or worse given the situation, the values and commitments of those involved. The decision to have an abortion is often an imperfect one. For believers at least, it should be made with a careful consideration of the ways in which the promise of medical treatment has often failed in its promise to keep us safe and happy.

ABORTION AND THE PROXY WAR

While the decision to terminate a pregnancy is often imperfect, it is also often the least bad option available. More to the point, it is also often one made by individuals who do not share the values of any one particular religious tradition. Christians in particular must be careful not to legislate their morality, first because they may discover that not many of the "we" will turn out to be pale-faces, but also because to do so offers the easy illusion that steering women away from abortion is everything needed to "choose life."

In a sense, this is to invert Brueggemann's formula. We cannot, by withholding a product or a treatment or a process, ensure the safety and happiness of women and their children. We cannot do this in the name of a God "who keeps life ragged and open," and we certainly cannot do this to our fellow citizens in the service of a dominant ideology. It is not faithful either to the counterscripting God or to the pluralistic values of a liberal democracy. It might be fairly objected that pluralistic values *are* a dominant ideology. Indeed, this is the very argument that social conservatives use against an American culture they see as depraved and full of death. That is their right, but it should not be mistaken for anything other than what it is: an attempt to exert power within the social and political spheres.

Power is very much a part of the equation here. In considering abortion, Stanley Hauerwas asks a trenchant question: who is holding men accountable for their choices?

The legalization of abortion can be seen as the further abandonment of women by men. One of the cruelest things that has happened over the last few years is convincing women that Yes is as good as No. That gives great power to men, especially in societies (like ours) where men continue domination. Women's greatest power is the power of the No. This simply has to be understood. The church has to make it clear that we understand that sexual relations are relations of power. Unfortunately, one of the worst things that Christians have done is to underwrite romantic presuppositions about marriage. Even Christians now think that we ought to marry people simply because they are "in love." Wrong, wrong, wrong! What could being in love possibly mean? The romantic view underwrites the presumption that, because people are in love, it is therefore legitimate for them to have sexual intercourse, whether they are married or not. Contrary to this is the church's view of marriage. To the church, marriage is the public declaration that two people have pledged to live together faithfully for a lifetime.[83]

However regressive the vision of sexuality is here, there is an underlying and fundamentally sound point: *sexual relations are relations of power*. Until this is understood, the consequences of those relationships cannot be adequately understood. Specifically, the nature of the debate around abortion cannot be adequately understood. Abortion, as a political issue, is a proxy war for who will determine the place of women in American society. For example, the "Statement of Principle and Concern" published in *First Things* declared that

> The abortion license is inextricably bound up with the mores of the sexual revolution. Promotion of the pro-life cause also requires us to support and work with those who are seeking to reestablish the moral linkage between sexual expression and marriage, and between marriage and procreation. We believe that a renewal of American democracy as a virtuous society requires us to honor and promote an ethic of self-command and mutual responsibility, and to resist the siren song of the false ethic of unbridled self-expression.[84]

Southern Baptist theologian Albert Mohler echoed this line of thinking in denouncing contraception:

> "I cannot imagine any development in human history, after the Fall, that has had a greater impact on human beings than the pill," Mohler continued. "It became almost an assured form of contraception, something humans had never encountered before in history. Prior to it, every time a couple had sex, there was a good chance of pregnancy. Once that is removed, the entire horizon of the sexual act changes. I think there could be no question that the pill gave incredible license to everything from adultery and affairs to premarital sex and within marriage to a separation of the sex act and procreation."

These are transparent efforts to place women back in the roles determined for them in the so-called traditional family by regulating their sexuality. In this line of thought, women's individual desires (and reproductive rights advocates argue their needs) take second place to the creation of a virtuous society.[85]

It is one thing to argue that sexuality ought to be an expression of faithful relationship, as Hauerwas does. That is a theological precept applied to the teachings of the church without reference to public policy. Believers ought to be—and in fact are—free to hold such values and pass them on within their families and private communities. But it is quite another thing to say any sexual expression outside of marriage for the purpose of procreation reflects a selfish license destructive of community. While this is still a theologically based moral precept, it casts its net wider to make claims on society at large. There is nothing wrong with that by itself: the members of a democratic society determine its shape and future largely through moral arguments, and there is no reason to disavow specifically religious thought because it produces an unwelcome result. But while this reasoning makes claims on society as a whole, it founds those claims on the behavior of individual women.

Because women literally bear the consequences of sexual activity—that is, pregnancy—attempts to regulate sexuality by establishing its consequences force women to be responsible not just for the potential life growing within them but for the character of their community, imposing upon them an enormous burden. This is the definition of legislating religious morality. It requires the state to prefer a particular vision of social and sexual norms over and against any others. Moreover, it requires the state to make normative judgments about individual behavior without any clear benefit beyond the preservation of particular ways of organizing the family.

When translated into the realm of policy, this line of thought can become absurd and vicious. This is made clear in the lengths some conservatives will go to establish consequences for sexual activity, even when one of its participants was not a willing partner.

During the 2008 presidential campaign, bloggers and journalists revealed that as Mayor of Wasilla, Alaska, Sarah Palin transferred the costs of "rape kits" from city funds to the victims themselves. When pressed on the issue, Palin's office responded with a carefully-worded statement that she "does not believe, nor has she ever believed, that rape victims should have to pay for an evidence-gathering test."[86] Why then would she oppose state funding for such kits? The obvious conclusion was that they contained emergency contraceptives, frequently derided as a form of abortion by social conservatives.[87]

This is an admittedly extreme example, but it reflects some widely-held ideas. The Bush administration, for example, fought to keep emergency contraceptives from being sold over the counter, and stressed abstinence in pregnancy prevention initiatives both domestically and abroad. In 2008, President Bush was given an "International Medal of Peace" by Rick Warren in recognition of his AIDS prevention program, which heavily promoted abstinence and fidelity, with poor results. The same day, then President-elect Barack Obama issued a statement echoing Warren's praise, saying "This epidemic can't be stopped by government alone, and money alone is not the answer either."[88]

Likewise, in one of its final policy initiatives, the Bush administration broadened a "conscience clause" exempting medical professionals, including pharmacists, doctors, and nurses from providing emergency contraceptives if doing so violated their beliefs. The previous standard had been to require health care workers to make alternate arrangements for their patients, but the Bush regulations would have allowed them to refuse to refer or even discuss contraceptives or abortion.[89] The Obama administration quickly rescinded the Bush policy, but reiterated its support for a "carefully crafted conscience clause legislation," citing the need to balance "the rights of providers and the health of women and their families."[90] Obama later promised a "robust" conscience clause[91] while noting that his Faith Advisory Council—charged in part with looking at supporting women and children, addressing teenage pregnancy, and reducing the need for abortion and filled with religious moderates—could not bridge divides on sex education and contraceptives.[92]

It seems commonplace, even trite, to say so, but the proxy war around abortion refights the battles of the 1960s and 70s. James Dobson is explicit on this point:

> Illegitimate births, heartbreak, shattered personalities, abortions, disease, even death—this is the true vomitus of the sexual revolution, and I am tired of hearing it romanticized and glorified. God has clearly forbidden irresponsible sexual behavior, not to deprive us of fun and pleasure, but to spare us the disastrous consequences of this festering way of life. Those individuals and those nations choosing to defy His commandments on this issue will pay a dear price for their folly.

Dobson is equally clear that he understands the "new morality" as a rejection of Christianity:

> There has been a general understanding for thousands of years that premarital and extramarital sexual behavior is dangerous. Those who broke the rules put themselves at risk for syphilis, gonorrhea, unwanted pregnancy, and social rejection. Women, even more than men, understood the dangers of promiscuity and tried to protect themselves from it. There were exceptions, of course, but the culture generally recognized and supported Christian standards of morality.

> This commitment to premarital chastity and marital fidelity was widely supported in our society from 1620 to 1967. Then, suddenly, adherence to the biblical standard disintegrated.[93]

This is not the first time that such battles have been fought in American society. In the mid 1800s, evangelical activists answered changing family and social patterns by helping to forge a new regime for sexual regulation in opposition to "abortion, contraception, and the public expression of sexuality in art and literature."[94]

CHANGING THE SCRIPT ON ABORTION: SCRIPTURE

Given all this history, as well as the stultified debate of the past forty years and beyond, how can faithfully engaged progressives offer a new word on the subject of abortion? How can they liberate their neighbors from the "assumption that there is a product or a treatment or a process to counteract every ache and pain and discomfort and trouble" without trampling their rights?

For Christians at least, the search begins with scripture. This is done not to find some kind of spiritual trump card in political debate, nor to find easy answers to difficult questions. For Christians, scripture is normative in the shaping of arguments. It is also *dialectical:* as Brueggemann is acutely aware, scripture provides a conversation partner that brings to light and challenges the moral suppositions that Christians bring to the public square. Moreover, scripture sharpens the decisions Christians make in the public realm, and calls them to authenticity and accountability, if not to God, then to the larger community. This is often no simple matter, and abortion is no exception.

The word itself is nowhere to be found in scripture. The closest reference is in Exodus 21:22:

> When people who are fighting injure a pregnant woman so that there is a miscarriage, and yet no further harm follows, the one responsible shall be fined what the woman's husband demands, paying as much as the judges determine.

This seems to treat the fetus (literally "offspring") as not a full life, for the very next verse states:

> If any harm follows, then you shall give life for life, eye for eye, tooth for tooth, hand for hand, foot for foot, burn for burn, wound for wound, stripe for stripe.

The New Testament does not contain even this much on the subject. There are several warnings against drugs that may or may not refer to abortifacients, but that is the sum total.[95]

Arguments for and against abortion on the basis of scripture must therefore be made by inference. Here, anti-abortion advocates find themselves on very weak ground. For example, it is true that the Old Testament treats children as a blessing, and there is the commandment against killing in both Exodus and Deuteronomy. But there are many examples of killing in both testaments, including that of children. Another ambiguity: Amos decries Ammonites who "ripped open pregnant women in Gilead" (1:13) but this judgment takes place in the context of aggression against the Israelites, not personal decisions to terminate a pregnancy. And Leviticus 27:6 and Numbers 3:15 suggest that full status as a person is not accorded to newborns until after the first month.

It is not necessary to go into an exhaustive consideration of all the arguments and counter-arguments to be made from scripture, but two more citations deserve mention. Psalm 139 and similar passages are sometimes used to show that the unborn are full persons:

> For it was you who formed my inward parts;
> you knit me together in my mother's womb.

But this is poetic language describing God's omnipresent care and concern. Indeed, the rest of the psalm describes the divine providence as almost oppressive:

> Where can I go from your spirit?
> Or where can I flee from your presence?

Again, Deuteronomy 30:19 exhorts: "Choose life so that you and your descendants may live." Taking this as a specific prohibition against abortion mangles the context beyond repair. Reading the original setting of the verse reveals that it is an exhortation to live in renewed covenant with the God of the Israelites, according to the "commandments, decrees, and ordinances" he has laid out, over and against those of rival deities. While this is certainly consistent with a pro-life position, it does not mandate it.

I mention these last two citations in particular because I believe that they get at the real bones of contention: what does it mean to live in and through God's care for us? What does it mean to live in covenant with God?

CHANGING THE SCRIPT ON ABORTION: THEOLOGY

Answering such questions is the theological task that Brueggemann and Hauerwas, among many others, want us to take seriously in our lives. Brueggemann relativizes partisanship, insisting that God's counterscript calls us to an altogether different path. For him, arguing scripture is natural, but when taken into public life, carries with it the risk of self-deception:

> We solemnly vote about whether we stand with Leviticus, wherein holiness has to do with sexual regulation, or with Deuteronomy, wherein holiness has to do with concern for justice for widows, orphans and immigrants. This God has spoken differently at different times in a dynamic process. As a consequence there is always something for everyone, and every position we take is readily countered with some other part of the script.[96]

Regardless of who we are, regardless of what faithful strain we claim, scripture announces God's judgment on our inability to cleanly separate ourselves from the ways of the world. More precisely, scripture reveals us to be both judge and judged at the same time, unable to integrate fully God's difference from the world into our lives. Following Reinhold Niebuhr—that other great theologian from the Evangelical and Reformed tradition—this is not a pronouncement of human nature as evil, but *ambiguous*: while we have the perspective to understand ourselves as different, we lack enough vision to see ourselves or our actions rightly.

This is more than a philosophical distinction. Too often, human fallibility is used as an excuse to do nothing or to hold back the actions of others in the name of humility. Niebuhr (and I believe Brueggemann) instead counsels action, but action taken with the knowledge of our own limitations. Brueggemann says:

> The quarrels we undertake are not only vicious; they are also convenient because they detract us from the main claims of the text, and so undermine the force of the text. Of course it matters what the church decides about sexuality, but in the long run that skirmish or a dozen like it are as nothing before the truth that the therapeutic, technological, military consumerism cannot deliver or keep its promises. All of us—conservatives who are attentive to what the Bible says about sexuality and indifferent to what it says about economics, and liberals who mumble about what the Bible says on sex but emphasize economics—all of us stand under the awareness that the primary commitments of our society amount to a choice of a path of death.

For Niebuhr, this awareness would lead to a new ethical commitment to be lived out in the paradoxical knowledge that our attempts to do good will ultimately result in evil. For Brueggemann, awareness calls us to a different way of being in the world:

> The quarrels we undertake must be kept in perspective, because none of those quarrels concerns this holy character unduly. What counts is that we were not there at the out-

set of creation and will not be there at the curfew; our life between the outset and the curfew is the gift of the One who calls us not to assault neighbor but to be on our way in wonder, love and praise.

The church announces in baptism this countercultural way of life and proclaims the good news that

> If we live, we live to the Lord, and if we die, we die to the Lord; so then, whether we live or whether we die, we are the Lord's. (Romans 14:8)

Contrary to the claims of the therapeutic script, this is the importance of our health, not whether aches and pains and discomfort and trouble can be relieved. The work of the church, then, is not to line up on one side or the other of a question like abortion, but to overcome the ambivalence and anxiety provoked by the dominant script and instill the counter-script.

Hauerwas attempts a definition of that counter-script in typically contrarian fashion. He attacks the usual frames of understanding abortion ferociously, citing first a former student's sermon:

> The first point is that the Gospel favors women and children. The second point is that the customary framing of the abortion issue by both pro-choice and pro-life groups is unbiblical because it assumes that the woman is ultimately responsible for both herself and for any child she might carry. The third point is that a Christian response must reframe the issue to focus on responsibility rather than rights.[97]

Building from this foundation, Hauerwas seeks to build a uniquely Christian perspective on abortion. He wants to step away from the language of "rights," because, he puts it, "Christians…do not believe that we have a right to do with our bodies whatever we want." Neither is life itself a right: it is the gift of a generous God. Likewise, Hauerwas disdains terms like "termination of pregnancy" because he sees *abortion* as a word properly loaded with moral content:

> One of the crucial issues here is how we learn to be a people dependent on one another. We must learn to confess that, as a hospitable people, we need one another because we are dependent on one another. The last thing that the church wants is a bunch of autonomous, free individuals. We want people who know how to express authentic need, because that creates community.
>
> So, the language of abortion is a reminder about the kind of community that we need to be. Abortion language reminds the church to be ready to receive new life as church.

For Hauerwas, this means that the church must operate as "the true family," alert to the possibility of receiving children into its midst but not enforcing marriage, much less procreation, as a norm. "It is only within that context," Hauerwas says, "that it makes sense for the church to say, 'We are always ready to receive children. We are *always* ready to receive children.' The people of God know no enemy when it comes to children."

Indeed not, but Hauerwas rejects arguments about the beginning of life and the beginning of personhood alike in considering abortion. He reminds his audience that Christian teaching does not consider life sacred in itself, but rather a good that is sometimes worth surrendering. Rather than parsing the moment life begins, Hauerwas suggests, Christians should live in *hope* that it has:

> We are not the kind of people that ask, Does human life start at the blastocyst stage, or at implantation? Instead, we

are the kind of people that hope life has started, because we are ready to believe that this new life will enrich our community. We believe this not because we have sentimental views about children. Honestly, I cannot imagine anything worse than people saying that they have children because their hope for the future is in their children. You would never have children if you had them for that reason. We are able to have children because our hope is in God, who makes it possible to do the absurd thing of having children. In a world of such terrible injustice, in a world of such terrible misery, in a world that may well be about the killing of our children, having children is an extraordinary act of faith and hope. But as Christians we can have a hope in God that urges us to welcome children. When that happens, it is an extraordinary testimony of faith.

Likewise, Hauerwas dismisses the idea that Christians should not be concerned with abortion because the aborted fetus is not yet a person. He calls the church to the practice of hospitality to life, even life that will be irrevocably handicapped or damaged, and to make sure that no child is ever truly unwanted. As a guide to public policy, Hauerwas' perspective on abortion makes an excellent challenge to the church, as he admits in response to a question:

The church is not nearly at the point where she can concern herself with what kind of abortion law we should have in the United States or even in the state of North Carolina. Instead, we should start thinking about what it means for Christians to be the kind of community that can make a witness to the wider society about these matters.

This, as always, is Hauerwas' uncompromising take on what it means to be Christian. By design, it says nothing about the responsibility of Christian citizens in pluralistic society. Even on his own terms, however, Hauerwas' read of the abortion issue leaves something to be desired. The implicit assumption behind many of his points is that abortion is undertaken for the sake of convenience, or to avoid difficult commitments. He passes over the subjects of sex education and contraception altogether—even though there is a long tradition of religious support for both—and he never addresses the health of the mother, mental or physical. Most serious, though Hauerwas discusses the disciplining of male sexuality and asserts that the church ought to create a constructive moral discourse around abortion and other social issues, he never seriously entertains the idea that abortion has something to do with the relative power of women in society. Because of that, he is naively optimistic about the counter-witness of the church. How is the body of Christ to present hope when it will not address the systems of power that create despair in the first place? How is it to present hospitality when it tolerates systemic inequalities in income, opportunity, and health care?

This is where middle ground approaches to abortion ultimately founder: they desperately seek to provide any kind of alternative to women seeking an abortion except empowering them. But hope without power is a cruel joke, or a false promise. To put matters theologically, middle ground approaches to abortion expect the greatest discipleship from those who are least able to afford it, and they refuse to understand the many ways that God's gift of life is often stolen away from women, including through the control exercised over their reproduction. The therapeutic modality of abortion by itself cannot remove the inconvenience of life. It cannot keep women safe and happy. But those who glibly dismiss the need for abortion, who view it as a selfish shortcut, misunderstand it. In many cases (but not all), abortion is not one option among many, but a tool used by those who perceive themselves to be powerless to exert power in their situation. Brueggemann's conception of the therapeutic script names the strength of this dynamic, but I believe does not condemn it in itself.

CHANGING THE SCRIPT ON ABORTION MEANS EMPOWERING WOMEN

There are some important corollaries to understanding abortion as an expression of power. Though it may seem objectionable to say so at first, it is the *perception* of powerlessness, not powerlessness itself, that is a determining factor. An upper-middle-class teenager may have more resources at her disposal than the poor mother of three, but both may feel helpless, frightened, and despairing at the prospect of bringing a new life into the world. The advocates of abortion reduction argue that the appropriate response to such a situation is to try to change the woman's feelings, in part by supplying more resources to carry the pregnancy to term. However, this is at best a temporary emotional salve. Real hope requires real choice, in the immediate situation as well as throughout a woman's life. Until women are empowered to control their own bodies through adequate access to contraception, among other means, they will always feel at the mercy of the unplanned results of sexual expression.

That last point should be of particular interest to those who claim to represent the poor, as increasingly, good reproductive options are becoming stratified by class:

> The growing disparities between richer and poorer women appeared to be the result of greater contraceptive use by the more affluent. The health statistics center, which is part of the Centers for Disease Control and Prevention, reported in 2004 that after decades of increasing contraceptive use, the trend stalled in the late 1990s and began to decline after that. The decline occurred almost entirely in poorer women.

> The overall pregnancy rate for women of child-bearing age declined slightly from 1994 to 2001, as did the abortion rate. Black and Hispanic women were considerably more likely to become pregnant than white women, and black women had by far the highest percentage of unintended pregnancies and abortions.[98]

A hope-filled approach to abortion must be a liberatory approach. It must free women to take control of their reproductive future by insuring access to birth control, including through government-funded health plans, and by redressing the causes of systemic poverty. Otherwise, "making good choices" as abortion reduction proponents such as Jim Wallis want will always be a luxury. No amount of support for pregnant women or adoption assistance will be able to change the equation until the fundamental imbalances of power are dealt with.

Progressive believers should also advocate for a responsible use of sexuality that takes into account the dimensions of power in sexual relations. This is an excellent opportunity for the church to exercise social leadership by promoting a sexual ethic based on love and mutuality which is aware of the implications individual choices have for the community as a whole. Responsible sexuality can be promoted by holding men accountable for promiscuity, as Hauerwas suggests, and by enforcing the right of women to say "no," or to use contraceptives. It can also be promoted through conversations about what it means to be sexual in the light of faith commitments. There is nothing wrong with carrying out these conversations in the public square. Even when we do not agree with the perspectives presented on such issues, we can be informed by them. However, despite the suggestions of some leading evangelicals, these discussions ought not to be led through official initiatives. The church is responsible for promoting morality among its members. There is no policy interest in discussing the "sacredness of sex."[99]

What government can do is provide comprehensive, effective sex education. In 2002, the Religious Institute on Sexual Morality, Justice, and Healing led a coalition of religious leaders in the creation of an open letter calling for educational programs to "benefit all young people regardless of income, class, ethnicity, and gender." Young people, according to the letter need help in order to develop their capacity for moral discernment and a freely informed conscience. Education that respects and empowers young people has more integrity than education based on incomplete information, fear, and shame. Programs that teach abstinence exclusively and withhold information about pregnancy and sexually transmitted disease prevention fail our young people.

Young people [also] need to know "there is a time to embrace and a time to refrain from embracing" but they also require the skills to make moral and healthy decisions about relationships for themselves now and in their future adult lives. They need help to develop the capacity for personal relationships that express love, justice, mutuality, commitment, consent, and pleasure. Our culture too often models sexuality without responsibility, and many adolescents are left on their own to struggle through conflicting sexual messages. It is with adult guidance and comprehensive information and education about sexuality—education that includes abstinence, contraception, and STD prevention—that young people will be able to make responsible decisions.[100]

Implementing age-appropriate, comprehensive sex education in public schools would meet legitimate public health concerns while guiding youth to capable, responsible maturity. However, religious believers are often uncomfortable with schools providing sexual information to their children. While the Religious Institute letter called upon "policy makers, school officials, and educators," there is no reason why the church should not provide its own education. The "Our Whole Lives" curricula, for example, were created by the United Church of Christ and the Unitarian Universalist Association to help participants make "informed and responsible decisions about their relationships, health and behavior in the context of their faith." Were conservative denominations opposed to abortion to follow suit, they might be spared headlines like "Religious school grads likelier to have abortions."[101]

The responsible use of sexuality is an important part of any plan to free ourselves from the temptation to believe that abortion can make women safe and happy. But as important as individual responsibility is, it cannot replace a systemic effort to empower women. Religious progressives need to be advocates for a responsible sexual politics, one that increases women's ability to act as social and economic agents capable of charting their own path.

This could be accomplished in a surprisingly straightforward way: the passage of the Equal Rights Amendment to the U.S. Constitution. Originally introduced in 1971, the ERA expired in 1982 when it fell five states short of ratification. However, the ERA was reintroduced in 2007 under a new name: the Women's Equality Amendment. By whatever name it is known, the amendment offers a simple guarantee to women:

> Equality of rights under the law shall not be denied or abridged by the United States or by any State on account of sex.[102]

Supporting this amendment is consistent with the announced goals of the proponents of abortion reduction. Equalizing pay and opportunities for women would do far more than any pregnancy support plan to ensure that women can afford to carry their pregnancies to term. It would marginalize extremist voices and partisan ideologues such as Phyllis Schlafly or U.S. House Representative James Sensenbrenner, whose "abortion-neutral" amendment helped end debate on the ERA in 1983.[103] Support for the new WEA would go a long way toward reassuring critics of the abortion-reduction strategy that it was not aimed at limiting women's rights. And as even advocates admit, state-level ERA's have had mixed results when it comes to government funding of abortion or same-sex marriage. Thus support for the WEA would seem to be relatively painless in political terms.[104] With Democratic congressional power likely to peak after the 2010 elections, chances for passage of the WEA could currently be their best in a generation. Support from religious progressives and moderates could contribute to an authentic advance in the status of women in this nation.

CHANGING THE SCRIPT: AGAINST FALSE CONSENSUS

Americans overwhelmingly approve of abortion being available with greater or lesser restrictions, and they rank the issue low on their list of concerns. Thus, there is no need to chart a "new conversation" on a controversy that is kept alive by a tiny minority. Besides which, conservative zealots are not interested in compromise on an issue they perceive as a literal matter of life and death, one that buoys their political fortunes and fills their institutional coffers.

Nor does finding "common ground" on abortion that at best reworks old ground and at worst moves the conversation away from the majority position contribute much to the cause of hope. Common ground is used to silence criticism with a false appeal to unity, and to help cover up the decided tilt of the abortion-reduction strategy. What women need more than persuasion or support is power: the power to make their own decisions, to control their own bodies, and to live into who they are meant to be, with all the joys and consequences that journey entails.

The discouragement of a safe and legal medical procedure gives the lie to abortion reduction's supposed support of abortion rights, and exposes the contradictions inherent in that approach. It also exposes the ways in which abortion reduction has been used to further political partisanship and advance the agenda of getting rid of legalized abortion altogether. Abortion reduction is not good politics. Neither is it good faith. There are worthwhile moral and ethical concerns about the practice of abortion that progressive believers need to engage, particularly as they develop their sense of what it means to be a religious community. But they must also consider that the issue of abortion reflects the dynamics of power in our society, particularly the kind of power used to enforce a so-called traditional vision of women's role in family and society. Without this perspective, they are liable to fall prey to political schemes based on personal discomfort with the idea of abortion.

Scripture and theological tradition alike invite us to step outside of comfortable perspectives, particularly where we might be tempted to settle for easy answers on controversial questions. Christians, among others, are called to be a pilgrim people, never resting easily but always moving forward in trust and dependence on God. Faith does not require a position one way or another on the question of abortion, but I believe that God does bless those who hunger and thirst for justice (Matthew 5:6). The way forward on the subject of abortion is not to attempt some grand scheme of reconciliation. Some things cannot be reconciled, as the Obama administration has learned in its conversations with religious leaders on the abortion issue, and as Father Hesburgh discovered in talks he led in the 1990's.

Rather than seek an artificial consensus, then, progressive believers should pursue justice in empowering women in all areas of life, including the power to control reproduction. We can be certain that some women will attempt to use that power to remedy problems that cannot be solved through therapeutic means. Abortion cannot keep women safe and it cannot keep them happy in any ultimate sense. But women always have and always will have abortions. There is ample proof that legal restrictions or official discouragement have no effect on that reality. If we truly want to change the script on abortion, we will have to write a new one in freedom, in power, and in hope.

2. A Brief History of "Big Shitpile"

Class resentment has waxed and waned in this country, but it is not typically a widespread, default emotion of the American middle class. This is at least in part because it's an article of faith here that through some combination of hard work and luck, you might get rich, too. And why abuse, soak or heap scorn upon a group you at least have a theoretical chance of joining?

The recession—with its yawning gap between the bonus class on the one hand and the foreclosed upon and newly jobless on the other—is changing that. It's not merely that Americans have, at least temporarily, abandoned the hope that they'll earn scads of money. It's the widespread sense that winners in this economy are produced by a game that's rigged.—David Segal[1]

In an April 2009 *Harper's Magazine* article, labor lawyer Thomas Geoghegan laid out the three main factors that contributed to what many bloggers colorfully refer to as "Big Shitpile," i.e. the vast financial crisis that began in 2008: the weakening of labor laws, corporate reorganization under Chapter 11, and the undermining of usury laws. The first two allowed companies to drive down wages and benefits, while the last drove capital from the production of goods and services into the financial sector. The resulting imbalance led to an economy unable to support itself under the accumulated weight of debt and derivatives.[2]

The story is more complex than that, of course, and goes back many years. Perhaps the deepest antecedent to the current crisis is the Labor-Management Relations Act of 1947, also known as "Taft-Hartley," which outlawed certain kinds of strikes, closed union shops, and federal election donations by unions.[3] Taft-Hartley also allowed for the creation of "right-to-work" laws which, combined with other economic forces, drove the transfer of jobs from the unionized north to non-union shops in the south. As a consequence, affiliation with labor unions in the American workforce, after peaking at approximately 35% in the early 1950s, fell to 12.1% in 2007, before moving up slightly to 12.4% in 2008.[4] This decline in union representation helped cause a generation-long stagnation in real wages. Geoghegan writes:

> The Economic Policy Institute reports that since 1972, the median hourly wage for men has remained basically flat, and has actually declined for the bottom fifth of workers. (Women saw more of an improvement, but that's only because women were grossly underpaid in 1972.) What is more astonishing is that in this very same period, when workers were losing financial ground, their productivity— their output per hour—nearly *doubled*. They were doing twice as much work for the same wage or less.

This is all the more confounding when one considers what happened to executive income during roughly the same time period. From the 1960s through the 1980s, the average CEO made somewhere between 30 and 40 times what the average worker made. However, by 2001, that disparity had swollen to an eye-popping 525 to 1, before settling back to "only" 317 to 1 in 2009. This fueled a similar disparity in the accumulation of wealth, as by 2005, "the top one percent claimed 22 percent of the national income, while the top ten percent took half of the total income, the largest share since 1928."[5] It doesn't take a theologian to comprehend the unfairness here, which only becomes more apparent when one remembers that in this same period, corporations used the protections of Chapter

11 bankruptcy proceedings to reorganize themselves, shedding pensions, health insurance, and other benefits in the process. Nor does it take an economist to understand that an economic system that tolerates such inequality is in the long run unsustainable.

Geoghegan locates the surprising mechanism of our financial system's demise to an obscure 1978 legal decision adjudicating a dispute between two regional banks. In *Marquette National Bank v. First of Omaha Service Corp.*, the U.S. Supreme Court held that credit card rates should be determined by the laws of the state in which the bank issuing the card was located, not that of the card holder. This left the door open for Delaware, which already allowed incorporation on friendly terms, to undermine the usury laws of other states by watering down its own banking regulations.[6]

Unsurprisingly, the credit market flourished in the wake of this decision. Banks were all too happy to lend at high interest rates, and consumers were eager to make up for lost income by borrowing. In fact, banks and other lenders became eager to give out money as interest rates climbed, finding a fat profit margin not in repaid principal, but in ongoing interest payments. This quickly became a cycle as unwary borrowers took advantage of easy credit to extend their reach, particularly in boom times.

Because the credit markets were flourishing, money that was previously invested in manufacturing began to flow instead to the financial sector. This created another cycle: as the economy pulled back from manufacturing, the United States began to run up a trade deficit with its global partners, papered over by foreign investment in the dollar. But the investments were diverted from manufacturing again, causing an even greater imbalance. The result was severe pressure on American jobs and an ever-more precarious financial position for the nation.

NAFTA AND DEPRESSIONS, OLD AND NEW
Folding layers of detail into this broad outline only strengthens the perception that Americans have been playing a rigged game for far

too long. For example, the North American Free Trade Agreement (NAFTA), implemented in 1994, was supposed to "create more high-paying jobs for American workers." In reality, the opposite happened. During the 2006 debate over a proposal to expand NAF-TA to Panama, Colombia and Peru, the Economic Policy Institute estimated that the trade pact had cost the United States a net one million jobs, while displacing another half-million into lower-paid positions. Likewise, NAFTA increased unemployment and income stagnation in both Canada and Mexico. Job uncertainty in the form of outsourcing, off-shoring and right-sizing has no doubt done much to convince the average worker that the economy has been geared to serve their bosses, not them.[7]

Similarly, a combination of unemployment, underemployment, wage stagnation, and the rising costs of education and health insurance has made a rising standard of living all but unattainable for young workers in today's economy. In 2000, the average health insurance premium for a single worker was $2,471; in 2009, it had climbed to $4,824.[8] Between 2000 and 2007, according to the Economic Policy Institute, the median wage dropped by one-tenth of one percent, and the median level of overall compensation stayed the same. These days, young workers can't afford to get sick, and they can't afford to move out of their parent's house.[9]

This rigged game extended into the financial sector as well. Robert Kuttner has detailed striking parallels between the economic atmosphere of the 1920s leading up to the Great Depression and the economy of recent years, including:

- Asset bubbles, "in which the purveyors of securities use very high leverage; the securities are sold to the public or to specialized funds with underlying collateral of uncertain value; and financial middlemen extract exorbitant returns at the expense of the real economy."
- Securitization of credit and the repackaging of loans, ostensibly to spread risk, in ways that obscured the worth of the underlying

paper, as well as maximizing revenue not through repayment of loan principle but by fees collected by the financial institution vouching for the security. Often these institutions have "structural conflicts of interest" in the sale of these instruments.

- The excessive use of leverage.
- The "corruption of the gatekeepers": "In the 1920s," Kuttner told the House Financial Services Committee, "the corrupted insiders were brokers running stock pools and bankers as purveyors of watered stock. In the 1990s, it was accountants, auditors and stock analysts, who were supposedly agents of investors, but who turned out to be confederates of corporate executives."
- Regulators' inability to keep pace with financial innovation. The practices of the 1920s led to the Pecora Commission and then the New Deal regulatory regime, such as the Glass-Steagall Act, to provide some protection against financial speculation. From the 1970s on, these laws have been chipped away piece by piece until they are either gone or unproductive.
- An ideology of capitalist triumphalism: "the nearly universal conviction, 80 years ago and today, that markets are so perfectly self-regulating that government's main job is to protect property rights, and otherwise just get out of the way."[10]

Kuttner believes that there is at least one important difference between the two eras, however: before the Great Depression, the Federal Government lacked the capacity to properly manage the crisis thrust upon it. During the recent meltdowns, he argues, it has had the tools it needed, but not always the will to use them.

A PLETHORA OF ECONOMIC SCANDAL

Kuttner does not mention parallels to the Savings and Loan Crisis of the mid 1980s, but they exist as well. S&L's were heavily invested in real estate in the early 1980s, and used "income capital certificates" to create the illusion of solvency. Fraud, the weakening of the FDIC regulatory staff under the Reagan administration, and the intervention of the "Keating Five" removed safeguards that might have protected investments in savings and loans.

Few people were held criminally liable in the S&L crisis, which roughly coincided with a period of high-profile insider trading on Wall Street. Instead, the government response to the crisis was to bail out the institutions involved in the debacle. The rescue package, which cost taxpayers nearly $179 billion,[11] fits a pattern of other financial industry bailouts: international lenders in the 1980s, Citibank and Long Term Capital Management in the 1990s, and the dot-com bust of the early 2000s.

The S&L crisis also set a pattern for corporate scandal, and often if not always, rescue at the hands of the government.[12] For example, although the collapse of the Houston-based power conglomerate Enron did not have as far-reaching economic effects as the current Wall Street crises, the similarities are instructive. At a certain point in the development of the company, executives shifted the corporate focus from the actual production of energy to creating and trading energy derivatives in various markets. Through a variety of means, Enron was able to obscure the real value of their assets while using leverage to expand the company at an astonishing rate.[13] At the same time, Arthur Andersen, Enron's accounting firm, allowed financial controls to be weakened. When federal investigators began looking into Enron's dealings, Arthur Andersen employees shredded crucial documents on the orders of managers. A 2002 *Frontline* documentary revealed that Andersen's actions with Enron were not isolated, as similar patterns were present in the accountants' interactions with Sunbeam and WorldCom.[14]

Nor was the corruption limited to a single company; Andersen's troubles came about in part because of three crucial changes in financial regulation during the 1990s. One proposal that would have required corporations to list stock options given to executives on their balance sheets was watered down after opposition in the U.S. Senate. Another, ultimately successful, piece of legislation limited the amount of damages that could be won in suits against corporations and their auditors. And a proposal to require accounting firms to avoid conflicts of interest by separating auditing and consulting clients was pushed back by congressional pressure on the Securities and Exchange Commission.

This relaxed regulatory and ideological environment led to regulators being unable to keep up with financial innovations, this time in the form of energy options and the manipulation of markets. It was not until after Enron had gone bankrupt that it was revealed that the company had played a significant role in creating artificial energy shortages in California in 2000 and 2001, activities that were made possible by the partial deregulation of the state energy market. The California blackouts cost the state billions in inflated energy prices and did irreparable damage to its economy.[15]

Similarly, WorldCom founder Bernard Ebbers was able to take advantage of the same relaxation in accounting oversight to perpetrate the fraud that brought down his company in 2002,[16] in what was at the time the nation's largest single bankruptcy.[17] WorldCom used aggressive accounting techniques to hide expenses and inflate revenues. The WorldCom board also hid hundreds of millions of dollars in loans to Ebbers, made in an attempt to forestall his cashing in on company stock and driving its value down.[18] While Arthur Andersen claimed that WorldCom hid crucial information about this wrongdoing from its auditors, it later settled a civil suit alleging malpractice.[19] The accounting giant's criminal conviction for corruption in the Enron case was later overturned,[20] but by then, the damage was done. Unaccountably, a Democratic-controlled House panel, with the blessing of the Obama administration, later watered down the independent audit requirements instituted in the wake of these scandals.[21]

THE RIGGED GAME

From these cases, a common pattern emerges: Insider dealing created astronomical but illusionary wealth, distorting markets and corrupting business practices as it did so. When the inevitable moment of reckoning came, it was the "little people" who paid the price: small shareholders, company employees and customers taken advantage of through unscrupulous practices they could not see, much less control. Often, the collapse of the paper empires took down the real production, as Enron's failure did with its gas and electricity units, or WorldCom's relentless mergers and final sale to rival Verizon.

The job losses in the examples I have cited alone are staggering. Arthur Andersen once provided 28,000 jobs in the U.S. and 85,000 around the world; today, the company is all but out of business.[22] At its height, WorldCom employed approximately 80,000 people; by the time the company (reconstituted as MCI) merged with Verizon, there were 41,000 left[23]—and its purchaser shed an additional 7,000 jobs after the merger.[24] Enron's demise displaced 20,000 employees virtually overnight.[25] As the company's stock price tanked, the savings plans of many employees were wiped out. Yet as the company unraveled, its Chief Financial Officer was cutting side deals to funnel money to businesses that he owned. And literally moments before the bankruptcy was announced, the wife of CEO Ken Lay sold 500,000 shares of Enron stock on behalf of her family foundation.[26]

Even when the companies continue on, as a reorganized World-Com did, the economic pressures created by fraud and speculation lead to yet more job cuts and increased demands for productivity to make up for lost ground. In a very real sense, the stress American workers feel today is caused by financial conditions beyond their control and sometimes created illegally.

Tilted financial policy and corporate corruption have worked hand-in-hand to create this situation, made possible by an economic climate that rewards wealth created by raising stock prices but fails to protect workers from the effects of financial speculation. As Thomas Geoghegan has pointed out, the mentality of unfair economic policy and corruption creates an environment of corporate predation, in which the profits generated by work are diverted to pay off the leverage used to buy companies. And as Simon Johnson, former chief

economist of the International Monetary Fund and currently a pro-
fessor at the MIT Sloan School of Management observes, the longer
this situation goes on, the more the American economy resembles a
developing-world plutocracy, in which economic elites compete for
slices of an ever shrinking pie.[27]

The cumulative effect of disparity and cheating has been to create what Jacob S. Hacker has called "The Great Risk Shift," in which
economic risk has been off-loaded from corporate and government
entities onto the backs of individuals. In a promotion for his book,
Hacker contends that behind the shift is what he calls the "Personal
Responsibility Crusade,"

> eagerly embraced by corporate leaders and Republican poli-
> ticians who speak of a nirvana of economic empowerment,
> an "ownership society" in which Americans are free to
> choose. But as Hacker reveals, the result has been quite dif-
> ferent: a harsh new world of economic insecurity, in which
> far too many Americans are free to lose. The book docu-
> ments how two great pillars of economic security—the fam-
> ily and the workplace—guarantee far less financial stability
> than they once did. The final leg of economic support—the
> public and private benefits that workers and families get
> when economic disaster strikes—has dangerously eroded
> as political leaders and corporations increasingly cut back
> protections of our health care, our income security, and our
> retirement pensions.[28]

Mounting economic insecurity has left a generation of Americans
not just unable to capitalize on economic opportunity, but afraid for
their jobs, their families, their health, and their future. They are in-
dentured servants not to Pharaoh, but to credit and corporate policy.

Americans have a bipartisan list of faces to blame for this rigged
game. Though not many remember the details today, Taft-Hartley
was passed by a coalition of northern Republicans and southern

Democrats. The laws allowing for Chapter 11 corporate reorganization were also a bipartisan creation, as was the failure of Congress to enact a raise in the minimum wage between 1981 and 1989 and 1997 and 2006, periods in which real purchasing power declined. And though the popular perception is that Republicans are the party of big business, NAFTA was midwived by Democratic President Bill Clinton, with the assistance of Rahm Emanuel, now Chief of Staff for Barack Obama. Likewise, the so-called "Keating Five" of the S&L crisis, who were accused of improperly influencing the investigation of Lincoln Savings and Loan, were mostly Democrats, including Senator John Glenn. (John McCain, the future presidential candidate, was the lone Republican.) In the Enron affair, the tables were turned, as the company's board and affiliates included heavyweights from the George W. Bush administration, among them the president himself, Vice President Dick Cheney, Treasury Secretary Paul O'Neill, Attorney General John Ashcroft, and White House political chief Karl Rove, who helped Religious Right leader Ralph Reed land a contract with the company. But Robert Rubin, Treasury Secretary under Bill Clinton and a member of the Citigroup board of directors, also intervened on Enron's behalf with the Treasury Department. Senators Joseph Liebermann and Christopher Dodd, both Democrats from Connecticut, led the charge against stock option disclosures and for limits on damages collected against insurance companies, respectively.[29] And there are no shortage of characters from both sides of the aisle contributing to the recent collapse of the financial markets.

The debt servitude of the American people has been revealed but not created by the recent economic collapse. The housing and finance crises and their attendant drag on the economy have served to throw into sharp relief the economic, family, health, and retirement insecurity of average Americans. It has also brought to light the rigged game, the stacking of the economic cards, whether through corruption or structure. It is a measure of where we are as a society that such a distinction increasingly seems irrelevant.

ROOTS OF THE FINANCIAL CRISIS

We can't say we weren't warned about the economic crisis of 2008. As early as 2003, William Greider was writing in *The Nation* about how the United States was "flirting with a low-grade depression, one that may last for years unless the government takes decisive action to overcome it." Greider believed that this would be a depression "with a small d, not the financial collapse and 'grapes of wrath' devastation Americans experienced during the Great Depression of the 1930s." Though conditions might not become as extreme as they were in the 1930s, Greider still believed that that the consequences of this economic calamity—"especially for the less affluent and young" would be severe: "a long interlude of sputtering stagnation, years of tepid growth and stubbornly high unemployment, punctuated occasionally with a renewed recession."

Greider belived that the coming meltdown was the end result of the"brutal unwinding" of the "delusional optimism" of the 1990s, which included "excesses like the hyperinflation in financial assets and the swollen ambitions that led investors and companies to wildly overvalue their prospects for future returns." He concluded in sobering, yet prescient fashion:

> This legacy of accumulated excesses lies across the American economy like a heavy wet blanket—overcapacity in production, overpriced financial investments, mountainous debt burdens for corporations and households, and thus a deepening reluctance to invest or to consume. Personal debt is now at an extraordinary 130 percent of disposable income, up by nearly one-third since the mid-1990s. Manufacturing is operating at only 72.5 percent of its productive capacity, greater idleness than during the 1990-91 recession and approaching the severity of the 1982 recession….That's why there is so little new investment. What company is foolish enough to build new plants when so many existing

ones are shuttered? And who would lend them the capital? If consumers run out of capacity to borrow more or can no longer refinance home mortgages, the collapse of aggregate demand will become far worse.[30]

This, of course, is almost precisely what happened. A run-up in housing prices in the 1990s turned into a full-fledged bubble as the Federal Government slashed interest rates to stimulate the economy after 9/11.[31] Simple math dictated that the situation could not last forever: housing prices rose faster than income, and homeowners turned to credit to bridge the difference. When the artificially low interest rates returned to a more natural position, the gap could no longer be sustained, and the real estate economy fell to pieces.

It is important to note here that while consumers did over-extend themselves, it was not personal irresponsibility that pulled down the economy.[32] A more accurate assessment is that sub-prime mortgages, or so-called "liar loans"—often marketed as affordability instruments to minority borrowers[33]—were symptomatic of the housing bubble. As blogger Paul Rosenberg points out,

> Indeed, the logic that justified the sub-prime boom—that those with less than conventional credit-worthiness could *rationally* buy homes with higher interest rates—was completely dependent on the pre-existing housing bubble to get itself started. Without rapidly rising house prices, none of the logic would have been even remotely plausible—and more importantly, no one beyond the usual marginal grifters would have been *motivated* to try to make such loans in the first place.[34]

Yet motivated they were, on a massive scale. A single lender, Countrywide Loans, issued *540,000* sub-prime mortgages between 2002 and 2007.[35] According to a *New York Times* analysis, these loans were often structured not in the best interest of the borrowers, but to generate interest and fees for Countrywide:

> When borrowers tried to reduce their mortgage debt, Countrywide cashed in: prepayment penalties generated significant revenue for the company—$268 million last year, up from $212 million in 2005. When borrowers had difficulty making payments, Countrywide cashed in again: late charges produced even more in 2006—some $285 million. The company's incentive system also encouraged brokers and sales representatives to move borrowers into the subprime category, even if their financial position meant that they belonged higher up the loan spectrum…For years, a software system in Countrywide's subprime unit that sales representatives used to calculate the loan type that a borrower qualified for did not allow the input of a borrower's cash reserves, a former employee said. A borrower who has more assets poses less risk to a lender, and will typically get a better rate on a loan as a result. But, this sales representative said, Countrywide's software prevented the input of cash reserves so borrowers would have to be pitched on pricier loans.[36]

As a result of these practices, Countrywide was forced in 2008 to settle predatory lending charges by paying a fine of more than $8 billion.[37]

The housing bubble also created an incentive for lenders to bring into the market borrowers who would otherwise be unsuitable for the mortgages they received.[38] The lenders found their returns not in repayment, but in secondary costs to the borrowers. They managed the financial risk by packaging the loans and selling them as financial securities. From the same *New York Times* article:

> One reason these loans were so lucrative for Countrywide is that investors who bought securities backed by the mort-

gages were willing to pay more for loans with prepayment penalties and those whose interest rates were going to reset at higher levels. Investors ponied up because pools of sub-prime loans were likely to generate a larger cash flow than prime loans that carried lower fixed rates.

In other words, the repackaging of loans created a further incentive to engage in predatory lending. It also created the opportunity to fleece institutional investors who believed the "derivatives" and "credit default swaps" to be safe investments, despite the presence of so many toxic assets. At best, these loan packages provided a form of insurance for the mortgage houses. At worst, they created a form of legalized gambling as the financial companies that sold the instruments then hedged their bets by creating new packages and reselling the debt again and again in an infinite variety. This was the "big shitpile" in a nutshell: bad loans collected and resold, amounting to an ever-larger collection of toxic assets.

THE RECKONING COMES

As mortgage defaults increased, the financial system built on their capitalization began to unwind.[39] At first, smaller companies specializing in sub-prime lending went under, but the crisis quickly spread to larger banks, financial institutions, and even Freddie Mac and Sallie Mae, the corporations chartered by the U.S. government in the 1930's to increase home mortgage lending. By early 2007, various European banks had to revise their earnings or prevent withdrawals because of the problems in the U.S. mortgage industry. In August of that year, Countrywide was forced to sell $2 billion in assets to Bank of America to stay afloat. That fall, the CEO's of Merrill Lynch and Citigroup were ousted as the scale of corporate losses became apparent.

But it was not until 2008 that the crisis fully hit. In January, Bank of America bought Countrywide; in March, a run on Bear Stearns depleted its assets in three days. The Federal Reserve infused cash while brokering a sale of Bear Stearns to rival JPMorgan Chase for only 7 percent of its market value. Washington Mutual narrowly avoided a similar buyout the next month. The summer only brought more trouble, as the U.S. government seized IndyMac Bancorp, a large mortgage lender. By September, the hits were coming hard and fast: Freddie Mac and Sallie Mae were repossessed by the government, AIG received a bailout, and Washington Mutual was unable to resist a second buyout offer from JPMorgan Chase. On September 15, Lehman Brothers filed for bankruptcy, and Bank of America bought out Merrill Lynch. Later in the month, Goldman Sachs and Morgan Stanley avoided disaster by becoming commercial banks and seeking private cash to compensate for their losses.[40] In October, Wells Fargo won a bid to acquire Wachovia, besting Citigroup. AIG was bailed out three times between September 2008 and March 2009, a program that became explosively controversial as the corporation revealed that it had paid $165 million in bonuses to the executives who had led them to the brink of catastrophe. Bank of America received a bailout in early 2009, and Fannie Mae got four over the course of the year. By summer, things had stabilized, but American taxpayers were liable for $645 billion in rescue packages.[41]

By that point, the damage had been done to the wider economy. In March 2009, the Obama administration launched a belated effort to rescue distressed homeowners. This included the staggering 48% of borrowers with sub-prime, adjustable rate mortgages who were either delinquent or facing foreclosure, and overall, 12% of all borrowers—5.1 million mortgages.[42] The bear market on Wall Street continued, with the S&P Index reaching a record low of 683.38. Meanwhile the Dow Jones Industrial Average continued a slide from 13930.01 in October 2007 to 7062.93 in February 2009. Those losses were unequalled since the start of the Great Depression. As a result of all this, credit markets froze in late 2008 and 2009, threatening to bring down the global economic system.

Closer to home, both literally and figuratively for most Americans, new construction starts dropped by 15 percent in 2008[43], creating a ripple of layoffs throughout the economy. In addition, 2.6 million jobs were lost in 2008, the highest total since 1945; from the start of the recession in 2007 through late 2009, a total of 7.6 million jobs disappeared.[44] By September 2009, 17 percent of Americans were unemployed, underemployed, or had given up looking for work.[45]

TARP AND ITS CHILDREN

Late 2008 and early 2009 were frightening economic times, a period when observers of the situation could consider seriously whether the U.S. economy was entering a self-sustaining depression. With no credit to prime the economic well and consumer demand suppressed by job losses and anxiety, there seemed to be no bottom to the hole the economy had fallen into. Without government intervention, things may well have gotten even worse.

The first government action to try and halt the economic slide was proposed by then Treasury Secretary Henry Paulson in September 2008, and was called the Troubled Asset Relief Program, or TARP.[46] Because many financial institutions were stuck with worthless assets on their books, they were unable to borrow from or lend to other corporations, as their creditworthiness could not be established. This jammed the financial machine, which in turn threatened to cut off the supply of capital to the larger economy.[47] Paulson's solution to the problem was to buy up the bonds and other instruments—the shit in the "shitpile"—thus establishing the reliability of assets used as collateral and freeing financial institutions to resume their work.

With a price tag of $700 billion[48] to be spent among the very traders and executives whose disastrous mistakes had created the problem in the first place, TARP unsurprisingly proved controversial.[49] It was initially rejected in the House of Representatives, only to be passed when a Senate version rolled in enough tax breaks and pet projects to attract the support of various lawmakers.[50] As many economists were quick to point out, TARP rewarded wealthy share-holders in financial corporations by taking bad investments off their hands, while doing nothing to relieve the burden on ordinary hom-eowners facing mounting mortgage debt. A far simpler and more equitable plan would have been to nationalize failing corporations, recapitalizing them in exchange for an equity stake.[51] After a few weeks of resisting that idea, Paulson seemed to give in, announcing in October that he would use $250 billion of TARP funds to invest in banks,[52] and then in November, scrapping the original plan alto-gether.[53]

Yet as the crisis deepened and a new administration arrived, the original TARP idea would not go away. A variation—insuring investments—was proposed in January 2009.[54] A second installment of TARP funds was released by Congress only after the incoming Obama administration pledged to detail specific uses of the money and to limit executive compensation in companies receiving aid.[55] Obama's Treasury Secretary Timothy Geithner proposed another variation in February, aimed at "legacy loans and assets that are now burdening many financial institutions."[56] At the same time, the Trea-sury pledged to "stress test" the institutions receiving funds to ensure their health. Geithner's plan led the blogger billmon to accuse the administration of trying to sell "chocolate-covered cotton."[57] Like-wise, *New York Times* columnist and Nobel Laureate Paul Krugman derided the multiple iterations of the same plan as "the big dither,"[58] referring to the administration's apparent unwillingness to nation-alize banks, the only solution many economists saw to the finan-cial crisis. Eventually, the program became what Krugman called a "zombie idea"—one that would not die.

The fourth and ultimately successful variation on TARP was a public-private partnership to buy up troubled loans and assets.[59] Geithner used a one-two combination to push the plan through, rejecting nationalization with the curt statement "We are not Swe-den"[60] while simultaneously asking for expanded powers to seize non-bank financial institutions.[61] Despite protests over the plan's effectiveness[62] and the spectacle of unseemly bonuses being distributed at the federally-rescued AIG,[63] Geithner's plan stuck.

At least it stuck in theory. In practice, the plan bogged down. One part of the project, to buy up troubled loans, was "indefinitely delayed" in June 2009 due to a lack of interest, as corporations found enough private money to clear away their problems without the need for public investment.[64] The public-private partnership to buy troubled assets, meanwhile, moved at a glacial place throughout 2009. In early October, even as other parts of the bailout package came to an end, the public-private partnership was still being finalized, and in a much smaller form. The hold-up, according to a *New York Times* report, was due to government difficulties in protecting their investments in financial institutions, and to concerns among those institutions that Congress would attempt to limit executive compensation in return for aid.[65]

WHO'S LEFT HOLDING THE BAG?

Whether or not the plan to buy troubled assets ever comes about, it is obvious that there is much to dislike about the plan that *was* carried out. Journalist Andy Kroll listed "Six Ways the Financial Bailout Scams Taxpayers," which showed, among other things, how the American taxpayer was mostly left in the dark about how their money was spent, and what if any difference that money made in repairing the economy, as well as how the government had "no coherent plan for returning failing financial institutions to profitability and maximizing returns on taxpayers' investments." Kroll also wrote how the bailout encouraged "the very behaviors that created the economic crisis in the first place instead of overhauling our broken financial system and helping the individuals most affected by the crisis."[66] In addition, journalists as diverse as Matt Taibbi[67] and Bill Moyers declared the bailout program a "takeover" of the federal government by Wall Street. Filmmaker Michael Moore called it a "financial coup d'etat."[68]

While such charges may appear alarmist, even fanciful, there is actually plenty of evidence to back them up. The independent media research program Project Censored reported that "since 2001, eight of the most troubled firms have donated $64.2 million to congressional candidates, presidential candidates and the Republican and Democratic parties," including $5.7 million given to "members of the Senate Committee on Banking, Housing and Urban Affairs, Senate Finance Committee and House Financial Services Committee" and "nearly every member of the House Financial Services Committee."[69] Furthermore, as both Taibbi and Moyers (among many others) have noted, American taxpayers have no information on how the bailout money was used, nor do they know the criteria by which its recipients were chosen. Considering that the U.S. government has "spent, lent or committed" *$12.8 trillion* in pursuit of the bailout—almost as much as the the country's GDP for 2008—this is no small matter.[70] Essentially all of American economic policy has been turned over to a small group of former Wall Street executives and their advisers still working in the financial world, with little or no oversight of any kind.[71] It would be imprudent not to greet such a situation with alarm.

It is useful here to revisit some of the parallels Robert Kuttner made between the economies leading up to the Great Depression and to today's distress. For example, Kuttner spoke of the "corruption of the gatekeepers," pointing to supposedly neutral observers of the economic system gamed by executives. He had in mind "accountants, auditors and stock analysts," and indeed there are allegations that the members of the financial system charged with protecting consumers and investors were compromised in the housing bubble.[72] But the corruption goes even farther up the chain, as there is extensive intermixing of the financial world and the government institutions that oversee it, to the extent that a favorite nickname for one financial house is "Government Sachs."[73] Hank Paulson was a former chairman of Goldman Sachs, while Robert Rubin, another former chairman, left the company to become Bill Clinton's Treasury Secretary, where he mentored Timothy Geithner and Larry Summers, the director of the White House National Economic Council under President Obama.[74] Geithner, in turn, was himself "a protégé of notorious Goldman alum John Thain, the Merrill Lynch chief who paid out billions in bonuses *after* the state spent billions bailing out his firm."[75]

This dense and bipartisan network of shared leadership is partly responsible for the woeful regulatory oversight of the financial system. As Kuttner argued, regulators were simply unable to keep pace with the financial innovation going on around them, often because of decisions made at the highest levels of government. The most obvious example is the 1999 repeal of the Glass-Steagall Act, engineered by then Texas Senator Phil Gramm, with the cooperation of the Clinton White House. The repeal allowed commercial banks to compete in the insurance and investment industry, where supervision and reserve requirements were far less stringent. These changes favored large corporations over smaller regional banks, which lacked the capital to get into the new markets.

Another Gramm-sponsored bill the next year cleared the way for unregulated trading in credit-default swaps and the other exotic instruments that led to the runaway growth in the financial industry throughout the first decade of this century.[76] According to Nobel Laureate Joseph Stiglitz, the then-head of the Commodity Futures Trading Commission had wanted to create regulations for the new devices, only to be overruled by Robert Rubin, Larry Summers, and Alan Greenspan.[77] Still another law passed at the same time actually allowed some financial institutions to choose their regulators, leaving enormous corporations like AIG to be overseen by a small and underresourced supervisory agency.[78]

Furthermore, the FDIC was unable to collect premiums for bank deposit insurance between 1996 and 2006 because Congress refused to grant it the authority to do so.[79] That left it short of cash once banks began to collapse. In 2003, as attorneys general around the nation sought to protect their states against predatory lending in the mortgage market, the Bush administration overrode their authority to do so, hamstringing oversight of the industry. In this, the administration followed precedent begun in 1998, when the Federal Reserve Board stopped enforcing fair-lending laws against subprime lenders.[80] Likewise, in 2004, the Securities and Exchange Commission, according to Stiglitz, "voted to allow big investment banks to increase their debt-to-capital ratio (from 12:1 to 30:1, or higher) so that they could buy more mortgage-backed securities, inflating the housing bubble in the process." No oversight hearings took place when this enormous change was put into effect. The S.E.C.'s idea of a counterweight to this added risk, says Stiglitz, was self-regulation among banks, a notion he derides as "preposterous" and unable to identify systemic risks.[81]

Greider names a final failure of the regulatory system:

> Likewise, banks were allowed to play these games by legislative creation of "off-balance sheet entities" where they can park their holdings—debts or assets—beyond the view of casual observers. This is essentially the same accounting trick that empowered Enron and other corporations to hide their true condition (then collapse). The biggest bankers played roughly the same game. In fact, it was the bankers who taught Enron and others these tricks. What public purpose is served by these devices except to conceal reality from public investors? For that matter, what is the public purpose of letting corporations, banks and wealthy individuals park their wealth in the Grand Cayman Islands? Everyone in Wall Street knows the answer. It allows them to evade "legally" US regulations and tax law.[82]

Project Censored amplifies the point:

> A 2008 study done by the Government Accountability Office (GAO) reported that eighty-three of the top publicly held US companies have operations in tax havens like the

Cayman Islands, Bermuda, and the Virgin Islands. Fourteen of these companies, including AIG, Bank of America, and Citigroup, received money from the government bailout.[83]

Essentially, we have socialized the risk of financial investment while privatizing the profits.[84] The public covers losses of financial firms deemed "too big to fail"—and only getting bigger as a result of government intervention—while seeing the leaders of those firms grow richer, despite the economic damage they have done, and despite the tax burden they have successfully shirked.

A FUNNY SORT OF ENTITLEMENT

This brings us back full circle to the notion of a rigged game, as well as what Robert Kuttner calls "an ideology of capitalist triumphalism," the zealous belief "that markets are so perfectly self-regulating that government's main job is to protect property rights, and otherwise just get out of the way." It was this ideology, verging on market idolatry, that drove Phil Gramm, and along with him Robert Rubin, Larry Summers and Alan Greenspan, among many others, to dismantle decades worth of prudent financial regulations. It was this ideology that led Joseph Cassano to bluster that "it is hard for us, without being flippant, to even see a scenario within any kind of realm of reason that would see us losing $1 in any of those transactions" even as his unit of AIG was losing $352 million. And it was this ideology that caused Federal Deposit Insurance Corporation Chairman Sheila Bair to say in early 2009 that her agency expected no losses from the plan to buy up toxic assets, despite the millions already sunk into cleaning them up,[85] and despite evidence later that year that financial institutions were already returning to the very same exotic instruments that had brought the system down in the first place.[86]

The people gripped by the ideology of capitalist triumph could not—and still it seems cannot—imagine that the market would some day encounter a disaster it was incapable of fixing for itself. It is, Paul Krugman argued, as if a generation of economists had forgotten the lessons of the Great Depression—because they had never read those lessons in the first place. Such is the power of the ideology that many economists make it through their graduate study without ever seriously encountering Keynsian economics, or anything that might challenge the triumph of free markets.[87]

But this ideology is more than triumphalist. It is entitlement, as illustration after illustration of self-serving deals ought to have demonstrated by now. The shenanigans continued even after the economic collapse, as AIG and other companies sought to pay out literally billions of dollars in bonuses to the very individuals who had bankrupted the company and nearly brought down the world economy,[88] sometimes with the knowledge of federal regulators.[89] When this led to the predictable public outrage, AIG executives pleaded that the law tied their hands, while the bonus recipients declared that a request that they return the money "effectively constitutes blackmail"[90] or wrote petulant, open letters of resignation published in the *New York Times*.[91]

It was this sense of entitlement that led Treasury officials to stonewall congressional questioners, in one case referring an investigator to the online TARP application form when he asked how they decided who received money from the program. It was this sense of entitlement that led the same officials to refuse to investigate how relief funds were being used, even as evidence emerged that banks were investing, paying down debt, or acquiring other banks with money given to increase lending.[92] And it was this sense of entitlement—exhibited in the midst of the most severe recession since World War II, as states continued decade-long cuts to welfare rolls,[93] as Congress debated a package of health-care reform capped at $900 billion, or less than 10 percent of what was committed to rescue troubled banks, and as millions of Americans lost their mortgages through foreclosure—that led Ohio Representativer Marcy Kaptur to tell this almost biblical story to Bill Moyers:

Let me give you a reality from ground zero in Toledo, Ohio. Our foreclosures have gone up 94 percent. A few months ago, I met with our realtors. And I said, 'What should I know?' They said, 'Well, first of all, you should know the worst companies that are doing this to us.' I said, 'Well, give me the top one.' They said, 'J.P. Morgan Chase.' I went back to Washington that night. And one of my colleagues said, 'You want to come to dinner?' I said, 'Well, what is it?' He said, 'Well, it's a meeting with Jamie Dimon, the head of J.P. Morgan Chase.' I said, 'Wow, yes. I really do.' So, I go to this meeting in a fancy hotel, fancy dinner, and everyone is complimenting him. I mean, it was just like a love fest.

They finally got to me, and my point to ask a question. I said, 'Well, I don't want to speak out of turn here, Mr. Dimon.' I said, 'But your company is the largest forecloser in my district. And our Realtors just said to me this morning that your people don't return phone calls.' I said, 'We can't do work outs.' And he looked at me, he said, 'Do you know that I talk to your Governor all the time?' He said, 'Our company employs 10,000 people in Ohio.' And I'm thinking, 'What is that? A threat?' And he said, 'I speak to the Mayor of Columbus.' I said, 'Why don't you come further north?' I said, 'Toledo, Cleveland, where the foreclosures are just skyrocketing.' He said, 'Well, we'll have someone call you.' And he gave me a card. And they never did. For two weeks, we tried to reach them. And finally, I was on a national news show. And I told this story. They called within ten minutes. And they said, 'Oh, we'll work with you. We'll try to do some workouts in your area.' We planned the first one after working with them for weeks and weeks and weeks. Their people never showed up. And it was a Friday. Our people had taken off work. They'd driven from all these locations to come. We kept calling J.P. Morgan Chase saying, 'Where's your person? Where's your person?' And they

finally sent somebody down from Detroit by 3:00 in the af-
ternoon. But our people had been waiting all morning and
a lot of people—that's how they treat our people.[94]

Despite its intricacies, the end of this story is as simple as its beginning. The wealthy in America have received decades worth of
tax breaks and policy decisions and special considerations and in
return they have helped rain devastation upon the economy. In that,
they have participated in and been abetted by corruption, legal and
otherwise. And still they do not hear the cries of the poor. In fact,
they have systematically rigged the game against them, their fellow
citizens, in the service of the bottom line. They have not so much
shut their ears to the cries of the poor as created a world in which
the poor need not be imagined. Pharaoh at least had to face Moses. But in our economy, there are no horizons or meaningful limits
on the accumulation of wealth, only the heaving and sighing of the
financial bubbles as they pass without consequence to those who
created them.

3. THE CONSUMERIST AND TECHNOLOGICAL SCRIPTS

We live in a culture that believes that the whole world and all its resources are available to us without regard to the neighbor, that assumes more is better and that "if you want it, you need it." Thus there is now an advertisement that says: "It is not something you don't need; it is just that you haven't thought of it." I use the term technological, following Jacques Ellul, to refer to the assumption that everything can be fixed and made right through human ingenuity; there is no issue so complex or so remote that it cannot be solved. —Walter Brueggemann[1]

The rabble among them had a strong craving; and the Israelites also wept again, and said, "If only we had meat to eat! We remember the fish we used to eat in Egypt for nothing, the cucumbers, the melons, the leeks, the onions, and the garlic; but now our strength is dried up, and there is nothing at all but this manna to look at."
—Numbers 11:4-6

As "Big Shitpile" has shown us, the current American economy is an immense field for critical reflection. How should—how can—progressive believers respond to a situation which has developed over the course of several decades and involves hundreds of millions of people, billions of transactions, and trillions of dollars? Closer to the question posed by the hidden scripts that dominate our lives, how can religious progressives respond to the injustice of our economy without perpetuating what Slavoj Zizek calls the "'objective,' systemic, anonymous" violence of capitalism?[2]

I want to suggest that the primary work of the religious left is to engage what Brueggemann calls "the prophetic imagination" in his book of the same name. This is to say that we are called to "nurture, nourish and evoke a consciousness and perception alternative to the consciousness and perceptions of the dominant culture around us."[3] This will no doubt seem exceptional to religious liberals raised on a diet of sermons advocating a stronger social safety net and the responsibility of believers to care for their neighbors in need. Surely our first job is to care for those wounded by the economy? To be clear, creating a "consciousness and perception" alternative to that of the dominant culture cannot replace loving acts of service. But if we are to go beyond sticking a Band-Aid on the wounds inflicted by capitalism's violence, the religious left will have to engage in "transformational politics." Though as Reinhold Niebuhr warns us, every action we undertake opens up new possibilities, including the possibility for evil, yet it is not enough for those engaged with the world to accept passively the way it works without thinking about how it could be made better. To put things in scriptural terms, God sent Moses to lead the Israelites out of Egypt, not merely to aid and comfort them where they were.

ENGAGING THE PROPHETIC IMAGINATION: CRITICISM

In his book on the subject, Brueggemann draws upon an analysis of scripture to describe the process of creating an alternative consciousness and perception as involving two broad efforts. First, prophetic speech must *criticize* the dominant understanding of the world, or as Brueggemann calls it, "the royal consciousness." But prophetic speech must go beyond simple confrontation to providing a vision that *energizes* the community.

Within these broad categories lie several smaller tasks. For example, according to Brueggemann, prophetic criticism must reject and delegitimize the current order. It must also contrast "static [religious] triumphalism and the politics of oppression" with "the religion of God's freedom and a politics of human justice."[4] Translating out of academic precision, a prophetic critique of the way the world works must point out that all is not as God has intended. Nor, despite the claims of the powerful, are things unchangeable. A dynamic God is at work to establish justice in our lives, regardless of the supposedly immutable ordering of the world declared by those whose interests it serves.

We would do well to note what an astonishing claim that is, far more daring in fact than to argue that God created the world. Yet that the peculiar God of Abraham and Isaac is an interventionist who remakes the world is a core assertion of the Jewish prophetic tradition. It is also one that carries directly into the prophetic ministry and person of Jesus. God is free, and therefore not locked into representing those whose power structures the world as we know it. Because of that there is the possibility of human freedom and human justice, all appearances to the contrary notwithstanding. Though it may seem that oppression and exploitation have the upper hand, this is only an illusion. God invites humanity into the work of reordering the world and healing its wounds, work that prophetic speech declares with confidence will succeed.

The greatest barrier to the success of this work is not those who oppose God's intentions, for evil stands no chance against God's goodness. Rather, it is human numbness and despair that hold back the remaking of the world. God is indeed free, but chooses the path of vulnerability and weakness. Until God's people are willing to act—until they realize the depth of their pain and resolve to hope and trust in God—the divine power remains in the background. It is only when the Israelites cry out that God "remembers" them and sets their liberation in motion.[5]

Brueggemann believes that lament, not confrontation, is the characteristic mode of prophetic speech:

> Prophetic criticism, as Dorothee Soelle has suggested, consists in mobilizing people to their real restless grief and in

nurturing them away from cry-hearers who are inept at listening and indifferent in response.[6]

As long as the Israelites grumble against (or to) Pharaoh, their situation will not change. It is only when they cry out to God, who hears and cares for them, that the Exodus begins.

In order to mobilize people, prophetic speech must help them understand their situation, typically through the use of symbols that allow them to grasp the truth. To borrow William S. Burroughs' terminology, prophetic speech creates a "naked lunch" moment. In doing so, it brings to light "the very fears and terrors that have been denied so long and suppressed so deeply that we do not know they are there." Prophetic speech also names "the real deathliness that hovers over us and gnaws within us." This is done not to "scold or reprimand," but to bring

> To public expression the dread of endings, the collapse of self-madeness, the barriers and pecking orders that secure us at each other's expense, and the fearful practice of eating off the table of a hungry brother or sister. It is the task of the prophet to invite the king to experience what he must experience, what he most needs to experience and most fears to experience, namely, that the end of the royal fantasy is very near. The end of the royal fantasy will permit a glimpse of the true king who is not fantasy, we cannot see the real king until the fantasy is shown to be a fragile and perishing deception. Precisely in the year of the death of the so-called king does the prophet and the prophet's company see the real king high and lifted up (Isaiah 6:1).[7]

It is only by "embracing pathos," by openly and honestly joining in the grief for what has been lost, that prophetic speech is able to criticize the royal consciousness. Without that embrace, without the candid admission of their own ambivalence and sometimes complicity, there is only the sterility of judgment. The numbness and despair will go unchallenged. That includes our own. We are at just the moment where the end of the royal fantasy has come near. The kings of Wall Street have been exposed, and by all rational standards, the end of their reigns should be at hand. Without a commitment to bring them and the government that sustains them into the experience of the end, the fantasy will quickly re-establish itself, its tyranny worse than ever. It is the business of the religious left to invite those who most fear it to experience the end of the way things have been. If we do not, no one else will.

It is also the business of the religious left to claim this as the *religious* moment that it is. This is not to suggest that Christians ought to take advantage of economic crisis to cram their beliefs down the throats of Jews, Muslims, and others. Nor is it to suggest that believers of whatever kind should use the current situation to push the agenda of their faith. As always, we must remain aware that we are part of a very diverse society. Not all of our neighbors or allies will share our religious beliefs. Yet we do speak out of a faith. A religious movement that expresses no actual religious content quickly loses its salt and becomes of no use. The religious left should be unafraid to articulate its vision of the "real king high and lifted up," not as the technical solution to a problem but as an expression of the "good reasons" citizens owe to one another in support of their positions.[8] God is free. We ought not to be ashamed to declare that.

It is finally the business of the religious left to *criticize*. To do so is not to stand in contemptuous, easy judgment, but to engage in critical thinking and to open our minds to better possibilities. Zizek says:

> When we are transfixed by something like the bailout, we should bear in mind that since it is actually a form of blackmail, we must resist the populist temptation to act out our anger and thus wound ourselves. Instead of such impotent acting-out, we should control our fury and transform it into

an icy determination to think—to think things through in a really radical way, and to ask what kind of a society renders such blackmail possible.[9]

To think critically in the prophetic sense rejects "icy determination" in favor of compassion, of standing with one's fellow citizens in their fear, doubt, and grief and helping to give voice to them. But as Zizek (an atheist) suggests, critical thought demands that we think things through in a "really radical way." This may be an unpopular suggestion, especially now that the United States has a supposedly more liberal government. We should resist the populist temptation to lash out, yes. But we should also resist the temptation to surrender to the blackmail of "we all play on the same team." God is free, regardless of who sits in office. We ought not be afraid to declare that, either.

ENGAGING THE PROPHETIC IMAGINATION: ENERGIZING

It is not enough to criticize, of course. Prophetic leadership must also energize God's people to "live in fervent anticipation of the newness that God has promised and will surely give." It must speak a word of hope, articulate new beginnings, and once again penetrate numbness and despair. But this time, rather than grieve, prophetic speech must begin to speak "the language of amazement." The people need to be energized by the "promise of another time and situation toward which the community" may move. Brueggemann stresses that this must be a true alternative, one that "avoids domestication." As the title of his book suggests, this can be an act of imagination:

> Quite concretely, how does one present and act out alternatives in a community of faith which on the whole does not understand that there are any alternatives or is not prepared to embrace such if they come along? Thus it is a practice of ministry for which there is little readiness; indeed, not even among its would-be practitioners.[10]

"Without a vision, the people will perish." (Proverbs 29:18) To work prophetically requires the ability to see possibilities that no one else has, and to be willing to embrace them in the faith of God's surprising leadership. This is a difficult task, particularly in the world of politics, where realism is a cult and the domestication of God's intentions the only safe play.

But without a sense of God's freedom and the willingness to follow where God leads, no matter how wildly unsuitable the path may be, there can be no hope and no new beginnings. To hope is to have power, for it is to think outside the limits of the present order, which is all too eager to have us believe that the ways things are is the way they always have been and always will be. Hope thus presents a future that is unmanageable by the powers that be. It instills the certainty that things are not as they should be, and in Jurgen Moltmann's terms, it summons believers to a restless impatience with the barriers to its realization.[11] To speak a word of hope therefore means both to imagine God's new possibilities and to call God's people to journey toward them.

Perhaps counterintuitively, the task of articulating new beginnings involves to a large extent getting people to understand that the present order has come to an end. Think of the common saying about rearranging deck chairs on the Titanic. Until prophetic insight is able to penetrate the "royal consciousness" enough to make the point that the ship is in fact lost, the temptation will be simply to order and reorder the situation without adaptation to the new reality breaking in all around. Brueggemann understands this desperate shuffle as a kind of despair, as with the Israelite kings who watched as exile in Babylon loomed on the horizon, yet were unable to understand that their fiefdoms were lost. Only when the depth of loss is accepted and internalized can the people be freed to reach out to the new beginnings made possible by what has ended.[12]

To penetrate the numbness and despair that protect the royal consciousness from confrontation with reality, prophetic speech can offer symbols "adequate to contradict a situation of hopelessness in which newness is unthinkable." This cannot be done by offering new symbols, says Brueggemann:

> Rather, it means to move back into the deepest memories of this community and activate those very symbols that have always been the basis for contradicting the regnant consciousness. Therefore the symbols of hope cannot be general and universal but must be those that have been known concretely in this particular history. And when the prophet returns, with the community, to those deep symbols, they will discern that hope is not a late, tacked-on hypothesis to serve a crisis but rather the primal dimension of every memory of this community. The memory of this community begins in God's promissory address to the darkness of chaos, to barren Sarah, and to oppressed Egyptian slaves. The speech of God is first about an alternative future.[13]

The prophetic task in offering symbols is to connect the past, present, and future to "mine the memory of [the] people and educate them to use the tools of hope." It is also to be alert to the power of language to create reality. The people need to be taught how their world is shaped by the dominant rhetoric, and prophetic speech itself must be attuned to its power to reshape reality.

Specifically, prophetic speech must "bring to public expression those very hopes and yearnings that have been denied so long and suppressed so deeply that we no longer know they are there." This is not talk about cautious optimism or incremental change, Brueggemann notes, but "about promises made by one who stands distant from us and over against us but remarkably *for us*."[14] God's faithful people hope and yearn for these promises rooted in relationship with us. It is the business of prophets to bring those desires to the surface and help the people to understand that they point beyond the everyday world to a life lived with God. This is more than a new stasis, however. As Brueggemann says, "Hope is what this community must do because it is God's community invited to be in God's pilgrimage."[15] To bring hope and yearning to public expression, then, is to bring the people to a new awareness of their connections to one another and to their ongoing journey with the restless, free God.

Prophetic speech must also express "the real newness that comes to us and redefines our situation." It must find in the specifics of the meeting of the present world and the memory of the community evidence of God's continued work, even against all evidence. It must in short "speak the language of amazement…a language that engages the community in new discernments and celebrations just when it had nearly given up and had nothing to celebrate." Amazement counteracts despair as grief counteracts numbness. It feels the hope in the same visceral way that grief feels loss, and it declares the new possibilities as real as the first buds of spring. Finally, it offers to God thanks and praise. Brueggemann writes:

> I believe that, rightly embraced, no more subversive or prophetic idiom can be uttered than the practice of doxology, which sets us before the reality of God, of God right at the center of a scene from which we presumed he had fled. Indeed, the language of amazement is the ultimate energizer in Israel, the prophets of God are called to practice that most energizing language.[16]

Glory to God, rightly given, is the ultimate challenge to the present order because it takes us away from the hidden scripts that promise, falsely, our independence from want and need. Giving thanks to God for providing our dinner reminds us that we are the beneficiaries of great generosity, not the entitled recipients or intrepid collectors of the bounty. It reminds us, simply, that there is a world beyond our control, one into which God calls us to meet him in hope and newness.

CRITICIZING THE ECONOMY

Living in the new world requires religious progressives to utter prophetic criticism of the current system. This must go beyond easy platitudes about "helping the poor." Specifically, it requires progressives to reject the false good news of a quick recovery from the financial collapse of 2008, a rejection that sadly is not difficult to come by. In the third quarter of 2009, 937,000 homes were in foreclosure, the highest number since 2005. Mortgage problems affected 1 in 8 American homeowners.[17] More troubling, mortgage defaults and repossessions represented "one giant wave, still building." Worse yet, these numbers excluded commercial real estate problems, including foreclosures and overbuilding. Until the problems in real estate finance are sorted out, they will present a drag on the economy, preventing a true recovery.[18]

Other indicators are equally gloomy as I write this, two years after the collapse. In August of 2009, the number of Americans receiving food stamps rose above 36 million for the first time. According to one study, nearly 1 in 4 American children have lived in a family receiving food assistance: 37% of white children, 90% of black children, and 91% of children of single parents.[19] Finally, in 2009, personal income experienced its sharpest decline since 1950. This led one pseudonymous economist to declare flatly, "Until the median wage improves relative to the cost of living, there will be no recovery."[20] The portrait that emerges from these numbers is of a largely illusionary recovery, one that may help the financial corporations but is of little or no help to the average citizen.

Again, a prophetic critique of this situation is easily made. The New Testament scholar Duane Warden writes of the Epistle of James:

> We cannot fail to notice that James is on the side of the poor people whom he addresses. His sympathy lies with them. Who are these poor? They are the hard-working people of the land. His readers are not beggars. They know about the

> waves of the sea (1:6), the farmer waiting for his fruits (5:7), the value of a spring of water (3:11), the mowing of fields (5:4), and the produce of the fruit trees (4:12). James's letter is not about charity for the destitute poor; it is about justice and equity for the working poor. James reassures his readers in words that working people understand. He appeals to no theoretical constructs. Faith means deeds; wisdom means mercy and good fruits. Doing what God says is important. Tamez is correct to see hope as a major theme in James, but the hope of James is not like that of 1 Peter. It is a strident, confrontational hope that looks to God for his judgment on the oppressors. The author of James wants to fill his readers with a sense of triumph in the face of humiliation. God is no respecter of persons. The gold and pedigree of great men mean nothing to God. God favors the poor workers who plow the fields and reap the crops.[21]

Warden might as well have been writing about today's situation. While progressives must not neglect the poor who turn up at soup kitchens and homeless shelters, they must also understand that increasingly the distinction between "beggars" and "hard-working people" is collapsing. As disparities in wages, wealth and economic opportunity continue to grow, America is becoming ever-more stratified into the privileged and the poor.

As many progressives are aware, ongoing economic injustice creates a parlous moment for their movement. The electorate is angry and discontent with half-hearted reform. Deeply conservative appeals from populists such as Mike Huckabee or from the reactionary "Tea Party" movement could provide a viable alternative to the progressive coalition. It is entirely possible that the 2010 and 2012 elections will hand setbacks to the Democratic Party, depending on their handling of the economy. Chris Hedges has written on how the Christian Right is driven not by "religiosity" but by "despair":

It is a movement built on the growing personal and economic despair of tens of millions of Americans, who watched helplessly as their communities were plunged into poverty by the flight of manufacturing jobs, their families and neighborhoods torn apart by neglect and indifference, and who eventually lost hope that America was a place where they had a future...Those in despair are the most easily manipulated by demagogues, who promise a fantastic utopia, whether it is a worker's paradise, fraternite-egalite-liberte, or the second coming of Jesus Christ. Those in despair search desperately for a solution, the warm embrace of a community to replace the one they lost, a sense of purpose and meaning in life, the assurance they are protected, loved and worthwhile.[22]

Religious progressives can hardly argue with the proposition that a community of faith ought to provide the assurance that its members are "protected, loved and worthwhile." What they can and should contest are promises that the community can be kept safe and happy by the scripts that claim to control our lives. Religious alternatives that teach conformity to or mastery over the scripts are not alternatives at all, but only reiterate false promises. I have in mind particularly the "prosperity gospel," which seeks to overcome economic struggle by reinterpreting apocalyptic texts to justify the most obscene transfers of wealth from the poor to the rich.[23] But any "faith-based" approach that preaches accommodation to consumerism is on the wrong track. The religious left should be unafraid of confronting these phony alternatives, and prepared to puncture the despair that funds them.

DELEGITIMIZING THE ECONOMIC ORDER
As Brueggemann suggests, prophetic criticism that can lift the pall of despair and numbness ought not "scold or chastise," but "consists in mobilizing people to their real restless grief" and "nurturing them

away from cry-hearers who are inept at listening and indifferent in response."[24] The task in a prophetic response to our current economy is not confrontation for its own sake, but helping our fellow citizens understand how much they have lost in this order and guiding them toward authentic leadership.

For progressives, this will mean speaking out against the economic structures that have created debt servitude and the leaders that perpetuate this condition. We must declare, first of all, that our economy is experiencing a radically disjunctive moment. The system that created "Big Shitpile" is no longer sustainable. Attempts to shuffle the pieces without fundamental, structural reform are doomed to return us to the same place. The tendency of the unregulated markets to produce bubbles creates an unstable platform for real economic growth. Corruption, entitlement, and ideology further weigh down an inherently unequal system. The bull markets of recent years have been built on the transfer of risk to the working people and their subsidization of the system through taxes. There may be economic rallies in the future, but there can be no return to the prosperity of the past without real change. The corporate kings of America and their enablers within the government have yet to understand it, but the structures that created their unprecedented wealth are dead.

If we are to find in this moment a true alternative to the economic death we have suffered, it will not be enough to declare "the poor shall always be with you." (John 12:8) As important as they are, programs aimed at poverty relief that do not challenge the systemic features that create economic inequality will forever treat the symptoms of the disease without creating true healing. This is particularly true of patronizing efforts such as a recent one that proposed financial education, matching savings accounts, and "healthy marriage and responsible fatherhood" initiatives to reduce poverty.[25] The poor do not need lectures about how better to manage their lives. They need economic fairness, opportunity, and protections for their health care, incomes, and pensions.

These things cannot be guaranteed, of course. As Brueggemann suggests, we should resist the temptation to believe that "there is no issue so complex or so remote that it cannot be solved."[26] One hundred years after the start of the Social Gospel movement, we ought to be wise enough to understand that poverty is not a problem that can be solved with enough ingenuity or bipartisan goodwill. The best we can do is strive for an approximation of justice.

The *prophetic* and the *progressive* task here are therefore the same: to declare the death of the old order, the loss of its legitimate hold over the people, and to point the way to a new order. It is to suggest, contrary to the calls of some, that we cannot do the same things, only better. Virtuous self-interest applied in the pursuit of material wealth only leads us back into the system of death. We must love our neighbors, to be sure, but we must also write fair play and opportunity into the very marrow of the structures that sustain our economic life.

There is no lack of biblical warrant for such an approach, as the Bible is rife with denunciations of oppression, and the systemic corruption that underwrote the financial crises of past years meets a clear challenge in scripture. There is also a concern for economic well-being, such as in Deuteronomy: "You shall not withhold the wages of poor and needy laborers, whether other Israelites or aliens who reside in your land in one of your towns." This may be justifiably generalized to apply to broader forms of income, such as insurance and pensions. Deuteronomy also counsels the forgiveness of debts every seven years (15:1), while the Levitical code provides for a "jubilee" once every fifty years, in which property bought and sold is returned to its original owners and slaves are set free. Jubilee is an extension of the sabbath: the Israelites are instructed to limit cultivation of their fields and forgo profits in trust that God will provide for them.

The language of jubilee has often been used in service of debt relief, as in the campaign begun in 2000 to remove the debt load of Third World nations. Given Americans' affinity for personal responsibility, it is unlikely that this symbol could be used to promote changes in the structuring of consumer debt, for example. But it might be offered as a starting point for conversations about what alternatives to a consumerist economy might look like, or to counter the script that preaches grasping and self-reliance over trust and mutuality. In that regard, Christ's prayer "forgive us our debts as we forgive our debtors"—a phrase rooted in the language of loans and contracts—is simple and powerful.[27] The Lord's Prayer is peculiarly resonant precisely because it brings to public expression the hopes and yearning of the people to anticipate somewhat the work of energizing. Religious progressives must challenge the claim of contemporary economic structures to provide for all our wants and needs because that challenge is so apparently the desire of so many people. They know intuitively that to live in love for our neighbors means not simply to live charitably, but in trust and mutual dependence on the gifts of life, whether or not those gifts are understood as divinely given.

Despite the seemingly self-evident hope and yearning for community and a simpler way of life, there is no one to bring these things to the front of the public conversation. The royal consciousness that dominates our society does an extraordinarily thorough job of proclaiming an ethic of *deserving* what we have while sharing it more or less. The alternative to this is not to argue for more sharing, but to proclaim an ethic of *receiving* what we have as a gift. In the terms of the Exodus narrative, pining for Egypt's onions, leeks, and garlic, even more equitably distributed, misses the point. It is only when the Israelites come to accept God's just-enough generosity in the manna and quail that they start to free themselves of the oppression and injustice they have internalized.

A religious progressive movement therefore will have to go beyond calling for a stronger social safety net to promoting an ethos of commonwealth to counteract the powerful idea that private wealth virtuously applied is the cure for all economic ills. That much is commonly agreed on, and is in fact a moderate position. To be truly progressive, the religious left will have to go still further to help ordinary people come to terms with the real losses of an economic system that has collapsed—losses that they are often reluctant to confront—and begin to look for real solutions to their problems. Religious progressives, in other words, must "mobilize people to their real restless grief." But they must also "nurture them away from cry-hearers who are inept at listening and indifferent in response."

This means first that a prophetic delegitimizing of the current order must not be afraid to call out the campaign finance machine dominated by corporate money that fuels the politics of economic oppression and exploitation. As Nick Baumann reported in *Mother Jones*, "Of the 535 voting members of Congress, over 44 percent of them—237 to be exact—are millionaires. Fifty members have net worths of at least $10 million, and seven are worth more than $100 million."[28] Beyond the vested interest of wealth lays the staggering access and influence bought by campaign donations. In the 2008 election cycle, commercial banks gave over $37 million dollars to congressional campaigns, nearly evenly split between Republicans and Democrats. Overall, the financial industry gave $475 million, $240 million of which went to Democrats. And the health industry gave $166 million, the majority of which went to Democrats.[29] Until the corrupting influence this money exerts on both sides of the aisle is understood and publicly expressed, "the royal fantasy" and therefore "the fearful practice of eating off the table of a hungry brother or sister" will continue.[30]

A progressive response to the current order will also build resistance to the cultural distractions used to stymie meaningful economic change. The economic system is well served by these disputes, and any meaningful delegitimization will have to address them. For example, the Stupak-Pitts Amendment to the health care reform bill passed by the House of Representatives in November 2009 threatened to derail reform by introducing tough restrictions on federal funds to keep them thoroughly segregated from any money used to pay for abortion services.[31] The amendment proved hugely controversial and prompted liberal members of the House to threat-en to vote against any reform bill that kept it.[32] Likewise, the U.S. Conference of Catholic Bishops, which had supported health care reform for decades, threatened to withdraw its approval from any bill that in its estimation required taxpayers to "pay for or participate in abortion."[33] Their interpretation of that requirement helped create Stupak's regressive measure to ban abortion coverage from any plan participating in the government "exchange," whether or not it received federal subsidy. This went considerably beyond the 1976 Hyde Amendment rules barring federal money from being spent on abortion services.[34] By some estimates, the Stupak amendment even threatened to cut off payment for the removal of dead fetuses until they directly threatened the life of their mother.[35] And as Frances Kissling has reported, Jim Wallis initially supported the Capps Amendment, an attempt to apply the Hyde Amendment to reform legislation, but then lined up with the Catholic bishops' position:

> "[The president's] commitment to these principles," said Wallis, "means we can now work together to make sure that they are consistently and diligently applied to any final healthcare legislation." For Wallis, that means that "no person should be forced to pay for someone else's abortion and that public funds cannot be used to pay for elective abortions."[36]

Asking women to surrender hard-won liberties in the name of modest economic progress transfers the burden of injustice unto their backs while doing nothing to help them address their "real restless grief." In fact, it exactly directs them back to the "cry-hearers who are inept at listening and indifferent in response." By risking reform to palliate pro-life ideology, such tactics enable both sexual and economic oppression. They should be rejected as a betrayal of progressive principles and prophetic witness alike. As it is, they are tolerated in the name of "common ground."

Another example comes from the work of American conservatives to export hardline anti-gay positions to religious allies in Africa. As Kapya Kaoma has documented, those allies then amplify the message and return it to the U.S., where it is used to divide mainline denominations in order to silence "their historic social witness." This process is fueled by, and serves the secular interests of, extremely conservative funders such as the Ahmanson and Bradley Foundations and John Mellon Scaife. It involves, among others, Rick Warren, who is held up in the United States as an example of a moderate evangelical. And not only does it keep American denominations mired in cultural divisions—which they are slowly learning to overcome—but it steers African religious leaders away from advocating for real change in their own nations.[37] Religious progressives should make such connections known and be fearless about pointing out how social conflict directs attention away from economic questions. This is an agenda item particularly suited to congregational leaders, who must often confront social and political disruptions being foisted upon their communities by outside forces.

DRAWING CONTRASTS

That the religion of the powerful reflects their interests is no surprise. The God at work in the liberation of the Israelites from Pharaoh was free, even mercurial in his temper, and called on the community to live justly. But no sooner had the Israelites settled in the promised land, Brueggemann writes, than Solomon set to work undoing the work of justice, in part by establishing a "controlled, static religion" in his courts:

> God and his temple have become part of the royal landscape, in which the sovereignty of God is fully subordinated to the purpose of the king....Now God is fully accessible to the king who is his patron, and the freedom of God is completely overcome. It is almost inconceivable that the God domiciled (sic) in Jerusalem would ever say anything substantive or abrasive.[38]

This static religion serves the royal agenda of political oppression and exploitation. It "counters the counterculture," as Brueggemann puts it, in exactly the same way that conservative operatives use religious discord to counter the counterculture of today's denominations. To outmaneuver the religion of stasis and control, prophetic criticism must be able to articulate a different vision, that of God's freedom funding a politics of human justice.

For example, we are often told by the hidden script that the greed of consumerism is inevitable. This seems intuitively correct to many if not most of us. We cannot imagine life without trips to the supermarket or the mall or the big-box retailer. Humans are acquisitive creatures, or so the argument goes, and the only thing new about their desire for material goods is modernity's ability to meet demand. In that sense, greed truly is good, because consumerism drives the economic engine, enabling prosperity for all.

Yet carefully concealed in this worldview are the signs that consumerism as it exists today is not a necessary result of history. As Jeffrey Kaplan explains, consumerism was chosen over and against competing visions:

> By the late 1920s, America's business and political elite had found a way to defuse the dual threat of stagnating economic growth and a radicalized working class in what one industrial consultant called "the gospel of consumption"— the notion that people could be convinced that however much they have, it isn't enough. President Herbert Hoover's 1929 Committee on Recent Economic Changes observed in glowing terms the results: "By advertising and other promotional devices . . . a measurable pull on production has been created which releases capital otherwise tied up." They celebrated the conceptual breakthrough: "Economically we have a boundless field before us; that there are new wants which will make way endlessly for newer wants, as fast as

they are satisfied." Today "work and more work" is the accepted way of doing things. If anything, improvements to the labor-saving machinery since the 1920s have intensified the trend. Machines can save labor, but only if they go idle when we possess enough of what they can produce. In other words, the machinery offers us an opportunity to work less, an opportunity that as a society we have chosen not to take. Instead, we have allowed the owners of those machines to define their purpose: not reduction of labor, but "higher productivity"—and with it the imperative to consume virtually everything that the machinery can possibly produce.[39]

Accepting God's freedom offered in the sabbath produces a meaningful alternative to the "gospel of consumption." As God rested from his work of creation, so humans are instructed throughout the Old Testament to rest on the seventh day, and cease from the constant struggle for economic advancement. By declaring that what we have is enough, that we do not need to undertake "work and more work" to satisfy our wants and needs, we participate in God's freedom. We also take part in a politics of human justice as we step away from the relentless pressure for "low low prices" that drives industrial and environmental exploitation around the world. Furthermore, we open up the possibility of directing our economy to different ends, such as providing for the common good. As Hubert Locke argues, the grim determinism of consumerist self-interest helps to create a political system in which government—a formidable instrument of mutual aid—is kept at an absolute minimum in the interests of "cutting the fat." This leaves society unable to respond to catastrophe, such as when Hurricane Katrina struck the Gulf Coast. This is again a choice to limit social help to the realm of charity and to diminish the role of government as inherently evil. While faith does not require a large, interventionist government, it does require us to evaluate our priorities. Is it necessary to have a nation where so many are hungry?[40]

Simply put, the economic regime we live under is more than unnecessary—it is in certain facets insane. This lack of reason is felt most acutely when the viciousness of consumerism is exposed, such as a 2008 incident in which a worker was trampled to death at a suburban New York Wal-Mart by shoppers looking for "Black Friday" savings.[41] But consumerist capitalism produces in its very structure psychological imbalance by creating expectations that by definition cannot be met, degrading the connections that sustain social identity while simultaneously fostering dependence on a distributed network of suppliers of material goods, and creating what Eric Levine calls the "pain of false hope."[42] No matter how satisfying they may be, consumer goods cannot make us happy, much less give us the joy that is the gift of God. Instead, they keep us bound to a life without future or past, only endless eternal want that can never be satisfied. God's freedom speaks against this artificial world without horizon by establishing beginnings and ends, which in turn makes real change and therefore real hope possible. By calling us to a life that means more than the fulfillment of material wants, the free God allows for the recovery of human relationships based on more than transactions. In contrast, the God who is invoked only as the guarantor of blessings bestowed through greeting cards has no power to seek a more just economy in which souls and societies are strengthened.

This gets at another characteristic of modern consumerist capitalism. As many commentators have noted, it is *idolatrous*, which is to say it seeks to displace God in our lives. The theologian Harvey Cox, for example, decries what he calls the "New Dispensation":

> Since the earliest stages of human history, of course, there
> have been bazaars, rialtos, and trading posts-all markets.
> But The Market was never God, because there were other
> centers of value and meaning, other "gods." The Market op-
> erated within a plethora of other institutions that restrained

it. As Karl Polanyi has demonstrated in his classic work *The Great Transformation*, only in the past two centuries has The Market risen above these demigods and chthonic spirits to become today's First Cause. Initially The Market's rise to Olympic supremacy replicated the gradual ascent of Zeus above all the other divinities of the ancient Greek pantheon, an ascent that was never quite secure. Zeus, it will be recalled, had to keep storming down from Olympus to quell this or that threat to his sovereignty. Recently, however, The Market is becoming more like the Yahweh of the Old Testament-not just one superior deity contending with others but the Supreme Diety, the only true God, whose reign must now be universally accepted and who allows for no rivals.[43]

Cox argues that the religion of The Market has its own liturgy, theology, even a priesthood of sorts in apologists for the free market. And as he notes, The Market certainly makes claims for divine omniscience and omnipotence, as well as for the ultimate loyalties of all people. All of this seems like something of a joke until one remembers the near-prophetic standing accorded to philosophers like Ayn Rand.

Likewise, Peter Laarman argues against what he calls "Mammonism," "a demonic and false religion" based on "the conviction that what matters most—perhaps all that matters—is money in private hands, and not money fairly distributed but money flowing ever upward to the cleverest and most aggressive." Against this, Laarman poses the alternative of "just community or commonwealth," and challenges Christian clergy to stand against the temptation to Mammonism that courses throughout society.[44] He exposes a final characteristic of modern consumerist capitalism: it is *unjust*. In an article written for *Religion Dispatches*, Laarman rejects what he calls the "'all have sinned' approach" to the financial crisis. The problems of this economy, he writes, drawing on the work of Thomas Geoghegan and Matt Taibbi, were not equally created by consumer irresponsibility and overeager lenders. Rather, as Geoghegan suggests, the problems stem from the rescinding of anti-usury regulations that have been in place since the time of Hammurabi. Laarman draws the scriptural conclusion:

> Biblical scholar and teacher Ched Myers notes how the basic liberation narrative in the Bible has everything to do with abolishing debt servitude. When God says to the newly liberated Israelites, "I am going to rain bread from heaven for you" (Ex. 16:4), God is setting a basic moral test: God is putting in place an alternative moral economy in which want is eliminated provided that hoarding, or surplus accumulation, is also eliminated. The manna reminds Israel that the purpose of economic organization is to guarantee enough for everyone, not to create opportunities for the strong to exploit the weak.[45]

Yet this is exactly the situation we encounter today in the rigged game of the economy, as working people fall further and further behind in their attempts to make ends meet, and the wealthy structure the system to suit their needs. Laarman connects the message from scripture to today's situation:

> Thus Isaiah to his bankers in the eighth century BCE: "The spoil of the poor is in your houses; what do you mean by crushing my people, by grinding the face of the poor?" (Isaiah 3:14f) And thus Jesus to his bankers—to the money changers in the Temple courtyard—"It is written, 'My house shall be called a house of prayer'; but you are making it a den of robbers." (Matthew 21:13) What will we say to *our* bankers? Obama's administration is apparently content to hope and pray that they will start lending again, once we've given them enough public subsidy. I was kind of hoping that we might begin to imagine something a little

different from the world we have known: a world of infinite debt, infinite captivity, and infinite pain.

The contrast drawn here between "debt peonage" and a "moral economy" couldn't be sharper. Indeed the entire work of prophetic criticism is nearly complete in Laarman's piece: the current order of the financial system is rejected, and its legitimacy called into question. The static triumphalism of the lenders' arrogance in believing that the housing market could expand without limit and on easy credit is exposed and contrasted to God's free initiative in the Exodus and the politics of human justice it is meant to provoke. Laarman even begins to call the people to "their real restless grief" by suggesting that the tepid response of the Obama administration to the crisis might not be enough. There remains only the "embrace of pathos" and the penetration of numbness and despair before the work of energization can begin.

AMBIVALENCE AND LAMENTATION

It is not enough to point fingers in a matter as large as economic reform, of course. We may not all be equally responsible for the mess we find ourselves in, but we are all compromised by the consumerist system in which we participate. And though we hope and yearn for something beyond that system, we are reluctant to give up its comforts and its economies. We are reluctant particularly to step off the path of consumerism to follow the difficult God of the Bible. Brueggemann writes:

> Most of us are deeply ambivalent about the alternative script. We do not want to choose decisively between the dominant script of therapeutic, technological, consumerist militarism and the counterscript of the elusive, irascible God. We are characteristically double-minded, standing between two scripts the way Elijah found Israel standing between Baal and Yahweh. And of course we know what

happens in our double-mindedness: "No one can serve two masters; for a slave will either hate the one and love the other, or be devoted to the one and despise the other. You cannot serve God and wealth" (Matthew 6:24). We are filled with anxiety: "Therefore I tell you, do not worry about your life, what you will eat or what you will drink, or about your body, what you will wear. Is not life more than food, and the body more than clothing?" (Matthew 6:25).[46]

Overcoming this ambivalence and the anxiety it provokes is a central focus of ministry, Brueggemann argues. Life in the Christian community is in large part concerned with detaching from the dominant scripts and being reformed in the counterscript. This process begins in baptism, the symbolic act of "entry into a stream of promise that is free but not cheap" in which believers renounce the dominant scripts and pledge to walk in covenant with God. Whether or not we are baptized Christians, however, the basic insight still applies: Ambivalence and anxiety are fundamental barriers to meaningful progress, and help to create the divisions that prevent us from taking the steps we need to take:

> The anxiety about our double-mindedness makes us fearful, strident and adversarial. This anxiety causes us to enlist as red or blue ministers in red or blue churches. It is our anxiety that precludes the ease of sabbath, the dalliance of birds, the leisure time of lilies: "Look at the birds of the air; they neither sow nor reap nor gather into barns, and yet your heavenly Father feeds them. Are you not of more value than they?" (Matthew 6:26).

There is, of course, an antidote, even if it is given in patriarchal form: "For it is the Gentiles who strive for all these things; and indeed your heavenly Father knows that you need all these things" (Matthew 6:32). And we are left, postanxiety, with only God's realm and God's righteousness.

Real change is difficult because it is threatening to our instincts for self-preservation and prosperity. We want to trust that we will have enough, yet we are afraid to give up Pharaoh's leeks and onions in favor of God's manna and quail. Even those who hear and accept the reassurances offered by God can't quite bring themselves to trust it. Thus, says Brueggemann,

> One of the crucial tasks of ministry is to name the deep ambiguity that besets us, and to create a venue for waiting for God's newness among us. This work is not to put people in crisis. The work is to name the crisis that people are already in, the crisis that evokes resistance and hostility when it is brought to the surface and named.

Again, while this is framed in the suppositions of Christian theology, there is an insight that is available beyond those borders. I firmly believe that one of the crucial tasks of building a sustainable progressive movement will be to name the ambiguities and crises our society are already in, and create the venue for real change. That this insight is grounded in religious thought suits this work to faithful progressives, but all liberals—believers or not—can participate in the work of transformational politics.

I insist on that point first as a reminder in the middle of this hip-deep theologizing that the religious left operates as part of a larger movement that includes diverse opinions on the subject of God. Unlike conservatives, who are dominated by evangelicals and Catholics, progressives are made up of all beliefs and no beliefs. While religious progressives need not surrender their faith to enter the public square, they must remain engaged constantly in the work of translating their insights into forms useful to those who do not share their religious commitments. The goal is to share the resources of faith, not impose religion on all people.

That needs to be spelled out because the last work of criticizing the current order is to lament it in the context of the community. This means more than marinading in the tears caused by economic hardship. It is to "bring to public expression those very fears and terrors that have been denied so long and suppressed so deeply that we do not know they are there." Prophetic lamentation also speaks "concretely about the real deathliness that hovers over us and gnaws within us." And, says Brueggemann,

> The proper idiom for cutting through the royal numbness and denial is *the language of grief*, the rhetoric that engages the community in mourning for a funeral they do not want to admit. It is indeed their own funeral….[G]rief and mourning, that crying in pathos, is the ultimate form of criticism, for it announces the sure end of the whole royal arrangement.[47]

Religious progressives walk a thin line here. They must enable the community to mourn its losses, to accept them as real, without claiming them as the special province of a particular faith. The fear, the deathliness, and the grief belong to the whole community, not just a faithful subset.

Still, this is a task the religious left is well-equipped to handle. A traditional role for religion in American society has been to insist on the human face of social pressure. In our churches, temples, and mosques, we are accustomed to providing mutual support for community members experiencing unemployment, health problems, bankruptcy, foreclosures, even homelessness. Religious organizations and individuals have advocated for solutions to these problems and many more. But their greatest power may lay simply in refusing to let their members suffer anonymously. By lifting up their voices and allowing them to be heard, religious communities bring to public expression the grief caused by economic dislocation, providing the counter-witness of lamentation against the "objective, systemic, anonymous" violence of capitalism.

Progressives of all kinds can learn from this in using individual narratives against economic oppression and exploitation. Even when such stories are not effective in changing the outcome of legislation or economic policy, they help to keep the conversation alive, counteracting ambivalence and anxiety, reducing resistance and hostility, and creating the space for newness. More generally, these narratives serve as a reminder that all is not well. To bring to public expression suppressed fear and terror involves an "honest articulation of how it is perceived when seen from the perspective of the passion of God." God cares for his people and suffers when they suffer. Allowing the reality of suffering to come to expression through the stories of real people cuts through the apathetic acceptance of misery as a necessary condition of an unchangeable system. In the same way, lamentation speaks of deathliness:

> Not the death of a long life well lived but the death introduced in that royal garden of Genesis 2-3, which is surely a Solomonic story about wanting all knowledge and life delivered to our royal management. That death is manifested in alienation, loss of patrimony, and questing for new satiations that can never satisfy, and we are driven to the ultimate consumerism of consuming each other.[48]

By revealing the costs of consumerist capitalism not with outrage but with real grief and sadness, religious progressives can invite the whole community into conversation about the hopes and disappointments of our collective economic enterprise, and the ways in which it has caused us to turn on and break covenant with one another. E.J. Dionne expresses this grief in writing about how social issues have been used to to divert attention from economic questions:

> What is so disturbing about the recent definitions of "values voters," "moral issues," and "religious concerns" is that we have continued to narrow the nature of our public moral

discourse. We have defined economic and foreign policy issues as involving something other than "moral" concerns… The narrowing of our moral and religious vision is one of the great tragedies of American politics since the late 1970s. Our traditions, most certainly Christianity and Judaism, teach us that we should not lie, cheat, or steal, and that we are supposed to love our neighbor. Shouldn't the question of how such moral rules apply to our economic and social policies be a matter of lively debate within our political system? It is simply absurd to say that religious voices can be heard on family life, but not on the economic underpinnings of the family; on personal responsibility, but not on the responsibility of great economic actors; on generosity of the spirit, but not on the economic works of mercy. "If one's faith is to infuse all parts of one's life," the economist Rebecca Blank has written, "it is hard to argue that community has meaning in one's religious life but no meaning in economic life. Religious life cannot be easily separated from religious activities."[49]

The corrosive need for profit has perverted our very sense of right and wrong, Dionne argues. By restricting the discussion of morality to the private realm, carefully walled off from anything that might subvert the dominant economic order, we have cheapened faith itself and allowed the rich to run roughshod over the rest of society without challenge. Dionne believes that the answer to this problem is create a new moral discourse:

> We do not need, and should not want, to end religion's public role. We *do* need a more capacious understanding of what that role is. We need a more demanding stand whereby religious people live up to their obligations to religious pluralism and religious liberty by making public arguments that are accessible to those who do not share their assumptions

or their deepest commitments. And we need to understand that religion offers its greatest gift to public life not when it promotes certainty, but when it encourages reflection, self-criticism, and doubt.[50]

We are meant, as I suggest in the introduction to this book, to be gadflies in the service of the Lord. But as Dionne says, this is not an end unto itself. Our grief provokes us to overcome apathy, anxiety, and ambivalence to seek a vision of social solidarity. And it is in the pursuit of that community that we are able to entertain a vision of something new. "The public articulation that we are fearful and ashamed of the future we have chosen" finally allows us to experience our pain, face the death we have sought to evade, and through our anguish, begin to hope once more.

ENERGIZING THE PEOPLE: HOPE WITHOUT SOLUTIONS

It is easy to think up possible solutions to the present financial crisis. Meaningful health care reform would be a start, as the financial security of the average person would be much more secure without the prospect of enormous medical bills hanging over their heads. According to a study published in the *American Journal of Medicine*, more than 60 percent of all bankruptcies in 2007 were due to medical costs.[51] Another significant step in the right direction would be passing the Employee Free Choice Act, which strengthens union formation, guarantee contracts after union certification and increase penalties for companies breaking the law.

Similarly, there are many options for limiting the power of Wall Street. William Greider describes two ways in particular: instituting a tax on financial transactions and breaking up large financial institutions in the same way that monopolies were busted through anti-trust laws.[52] There is also Thomas Geoghegan's caps on interest rates, and the proposed Consumer Financial Protection Agency Act. Along the same lines, the Glass-Steagall Act might be renewed, restrictions placed on corporate money in elections, or a ban imposed on the revolving door between lobbying firms and the government. We could also advocate for a more equitable distribution of wealth through economic policies directed at creating sustainable jobs, rather than the accumulation of wealth, or by the simple and direct transfer of resources through progressive taxes. There is no idol greater than that demanding ever-greater sacrifices of the common good on the altar of "reducing the tax burden." As I say, it's easy to come up with these ideas. Deciding whether or not they're practical or worth rallying around is a question for policy analysts and political operatives to decide.

What is more difficult is to "live in fervent anticipation of the newness that God has promised and will surely give" while resisting the temptation toward technical solutions. This requires us to walk one more fine line: on the one hand, the economy cannot be left to run itself. Nor can economic actors be trusted to automatically come up with a fair distribution of resources. Equity, not to mention justice, must be created through active, creative intervention that responds to the ever-changing economic environment. Even the best regulations and policies will need to be adjusted to reflect current realities.

At the same time, we must recognize that some problems are too complex to be fixed or made right by the precise application of the scientific method. "Big Shitpile" fashioned a new Tower of Babel out of derivatives and investment logarithms, all offered with the smooth lie that the bankers and insurers and hedge fund managers had solved the problem of risk. It eventually collapsed, of course, just as the original tower did. But as we pick through the rubble and consider what comes next, we must take care not to recreate the very same mistakes that led us to this point. That includes the mistake of believing that we can overcome any problem, given enough time and ingenuity, for some problems have less to do with our brains than with our hearts. If we are ever to escape the "rigged game" and come into the new life promised to us, we will have to learn to be led into new visions and new ways of life, rather than depending on our own cleverness.

A dose of Niebuhrian humility may come in handy here. That valuable concept, long a favorite of technocrats and the pundits who champion them, is often used as a call to overcome ideology in the interest of finding "real solutions." But for Niebuhr, humility involves more than a simple recognition of the human capacity for error; it is the understanding that *though we intend to do good, our actions will inevitably result in evil.* For Niebuhr, this sin was the result of both a moral overestimation of the goodness of one's cause and a technical overestimation of the human capacity for problem-solving:

> Modern technical civilization may perish because it falsely worshipped technical advance as a final good. One portion of a technical society may harness techniques to the purpose of destruction and vent its fury upon another portion, which has grown soft by regarding the comforts yielded in such great abundance by a technical age, as the final good.[53]

We will return to the subject of destructive purposes as we consider the militaristic script that opened to us the possibility of torture. But certainly "the comforts yielded in such great abundance by a technical age" has something to say to a consumerist society which possesses its material goods as the result of ever-increasing technological ingenuity allowing for the creation of cheaper products. Housing bubbles, for example, would not be possible without innovations allowing for more efficient construction. Similarly, "Big Shitpile" would also not have been possible without the temptation to believe that more and more sophisticated financial instruments can create a rising tide that raises all boats without economic cost. Mathematics can do many wonderful things, but it cannot create an evenly-distributed value.

A religious progressive movement therefore must resist the market-driven ideology that proclaims that financial inventiveness will of necessity result in the achievement of a transcendent goal: prosperity for all. Lloyd Blankfein, the CEO of Goldman Sachs, was eager to argue this ideology:

"We're very important," he says, abandoning self-flagellation. "We help companies to grow by helping them to raise capital. Companies that grow create wealth. This, in turn, allows people to have jobs that create more growth and more wealth. It's a virtuous cycle." To drive home his point, he makes a remarkably bold claim. "We have a social purpose."[54]

Blankfein claimed to be doing "God's work." His advisor, Brian Griffiths, was equally explicit: "The injunction of Jesus to love others as ourselves is an endorsement of self-interest," said Griffiths in a speech to the Britain Christian Association of Business Executive at St. Paul's Cathedral in London. "We have to tolerate the inequality as a way to achieving greater prosperity and opportunity for all."[55] But there is nothing necessary about consumerist capitalism or its distribution of wealth. Poverty cannot be "solved" by the business cycle any more than it can be by the precise application of policy, whether corporate or governmental. Progressives should labor under no illusions that a "business-friendly," "third way" model of politics such as that espoused by the Democratic Party under Bill Clinton can overcome ideological differences to achieve final economic justice.

At the same time, progressives should be cautious about rejecting out of hand technical advances. Nor should they throw over consumerist capitalism as entirely evil. Deidre McCloskey argues that

> The recessions do not come from greed .... The recessions come from hope and courage, from venturing on building railways and then overbuilding them; from founding dotcom companies, and then overfounding them; from innovating in financial services and then overinnovating. We go too far, as imperfect creatures with imperfect knowledge of the future .... But in the meantime we get better railways,

computers, banks. That's why the recovery is always greater than the decline. The trend has been startlingly upward, the second most important event in human history. The jagged rise of innovation has been disturbing, but on balance it has been immensely good for the poorest among us.[56]

And as Niebuhr was at pains to point out in *Moral Man and Immoral Society*, ideological distortion was inevitable among any group, "proletarians" no less than the "privileged classes":

> Society needs greater equality, not only to advance but to survive; and the basis of inequality is the disproportion of power in society. In the recognition of the goal of equal justice and in the analysis of the roots of present injustice the proletarian sees truly. But whether the means he intends to employ are the only possible means, as he thinks, or whether they are the most efficacious which an intelligent realistic society could devise, is another question.[57]

Progressives should not be so blinded by their commitment to the poor that they are unable to question their own motives and tactics in the search for justice. Niebuhr believed that the failure to do so was "inevitable but not necessary," yet no reason to abandon the cause of justice. He understood that the same "will to power" that led to error and indeed sin was needed to promote social and economic equality. Politics, as Jacque Ranciere has argued, may exist "when the natural order of domination is interrupted" by the poor seeking to expand the limits of the commonwealth, but this struggle should never be understood as somehow beyond the limits of human nature.[58] The economy and the politics it sponsors are not problems that can be perfectly solved, but contingent relationships that come along with all the conflicts, failings, and self-interest of any social connection. This includes our finite ability to understand our partiality, but also our tendency to equate our personal commitments to justice and equality with our ability to achieve those ends on a societal level. Goodwill and the conversion of individual hearts are not sufficient to establish the kingdom of God.

Niebuhr believed that part of the human condition was an awareness of the conflict between our potential and our limits. That awareness, he argued (and Brueggemann agrees) causes ambivalence about and anxiety for our destiny. And it is ambivalence and anxiety that hold us back from embracing true alternatives to the present order. Against this despair can only be spoken a word of hope. According to Niebuhr, "Nothing that is worth doing can be achieved in a lifetime; therefore we must be saved by hope."[59] Though we can never be sure of our own role in "the fulfillment of life," we can be confident that life will come to its appointed conclusion. Indeed, as Niebuhr says,

> The Christian hope of the consummation of life and history is less absurd than alternate doctrines which seek to comprehend and to effect the completion of life by some power or capacity inherent in man and his history.[60]

From Brueggemann's perspective, hope lays in covenant, trust, and dependence on God's leading us to a new way of life. The God who is free is free to fulfill the promises he graciously has made. This assertion leads to other conclusions, perhaps best expressed in the Exodus narrative. There are meaningful alternatives to the way things are presently: the Israelites flee Egypt in search of their own land. God will provide enough to satisfy our needs but not our avarice, in the manna that lasted only for a day and produced "neither too much nor too little." We can live with the neighbor in the forefront of our lives, as the Israelites learned to do in the desert, albeit imperfectly. And we can live justly, without oppression and exploitation, without a Pharaoh to lord it over us. It is telling that Moses the prophet only reluctantly agrees to appoint judges to ease his own workload, and that the Israelite nation lives without royalty for some time until Saul is appointed king over the prophet Samuel's objections and God's warnings that monarchy will come to no good. For when the people begin to trust the ingenuity and justice of the king over God, they are sure to go astray. This, despite the "better railways, computers, banks" that result, is our constant temptation. Hope, finally, rests in trust and relationship, not in finding better solutions to our problems.

ARTICULATING NEW BEGINNINGS, PENETRATING NUMBNESS AND DESPAIR

To have hope, the people must be able to trust that there can be meaningful change. This is precisely why the Obama campaign in 2008 ran against the policies of the Bush administration under the rubric of "hope." Modest, incremental change is simply not very inspiring. Brueggemann says that when "serious hopefulness" is locked out of the public conversation, the royal consciousness cannot be pierced, and the idea of real change cannot be entertained.

> What is most needed is what is most unacceptable—an articulation that redefines the situation and that makes way for new gifts about to be given. Without a public arena for the articulation of gifts that fall outside our conventional rationality, we are fated to despair. We know full well the makings of genuine newness are not included among these present pieces. And short of genuine newness life becomes and a dissatisfied coping, a grudging trust, and a managing that dares never ask too much.[61]

The *prophetic* task is thus to establish a vision of what can be, to accept what has come to an end, and anticipate alternatives as they emerge. As a strictly religious matter, this is helping the people understand that God has more blessings in store for them, despite all the evidence to the contrary:

> To imagine a new gift given from the outside violates our reason. We are able to believe in God's graciousness than we are in the judgment of God.

This is part and parcel of the difficult work of ministry, done on the smallest of scales over time. As Brueggemann says, to articulate real hope to those pragmatically resigned to hopelessness takes resolve. The *progressive* task in articulating hope is to assert against the forces that limit, harass, and dismiss reform that it is not only possible, but necessary. Without constant agitation for justice and equality, our economy will never move from the stasis that creates financial catastrophe. This is more than keeping politicians' feet to the fire—it is bringing into the political conversation a sense of new possibilities and alternatives, no easy task in a public realm that makes a fetish of realism and greets visions with cynicism and indifference. Without the work of articulation, though, our political life indeed becomes "a managing that dares never ask too much."

For prophets and progressives alike, the job is to establish a sense of hope that eludes the control of powerful forces. To be kept in the unchanging order of the royal consciousness only breeds despair. The people need to hear that the powers that be are not in final control of their destiny. Again, this is no easy task. Real hope is a frightening, disorienting business, as are new beginnings. They require people to let go of comfort and familiarity to reach out to unknowns. There is no guarantee that a reordered economic system could be achieved. In fact, there's every reason to expect that the current system would reestablish itself.

In order to articulate a vision of hope that will energize people to overcome their fear, prophetic speech must penetrate the numbness and despair that keeps them frozen in place.

One of the ways to do this is to offer symbols that ordinary people can take hold of to root their hope. Brueggemann cautions that offering symbols

> is not a job for a timid clerk who simply shares the inventory but for people who know something different and are prepared, out of their own anguish and amazement, to know that the closed world of managed reality is false.[62]

Prophets know what others do not: that God has a prior claim on the people. It is that claim—and God's zeal in protecting and upholding it—that constitutes reality, not the smoothly textured lies of power. "Inventing new symbols" is not equal to the challenge of instilling the hopefulness of new beginnings in the people. Brueggemann calls for mining the collective memory of the people and using their specific symbols to "educate them to use the tools of hope." It is only from speaking within a tradition that one can find effective symbols.

Prophetic speech must also name the power of language to "shape consciousness and define reality." If the royal consciousness is to be unseated, its control over our vocabulary must be contested, and its largely unseen effects exposed. This is hardly a radical insight for those who have studied political struggle, especially in the communications age. Bloggers have done a particularly good job of processing the official rhetoric of politicians and the media to expose how it supports oppression and exploitation. What should be added is that to give control over language is uniquely empowering. When the people are able to read the situation for themselves, the king is no longer in complete control. This applies not just to the official language used to describe our economy or the consumerism that sustains it, but to the very instruments used to exercise control. People who understand how mortgages and insurance and labor law can be rigged against them are people who can better resist the power arrayed against them.

Prophetic speech can also go beyond offering symbols and redefining language to "bring to public expression" the "hopes and yearnings" of the people that have been pushed back out of conscious awareness. To engage the prophetic imagination not only points the way forward, it awakens the very desire to press on. To express hope in this context is countercultural. It speaks against conventional wisdom and for the prior claim God establishes on his people:

Hope, on the one hand, is an absurdity too embarrassing to speak about, for it flies in the face of all those claims we have been told are fact. Hope is the refusal to accept the reading of reality which is the majority opinion; and one does that only at great political and existential risk. On the other hand, hope is subversive, for it limits the grandiose pretension of the present, daring to announce that the present to which we have all made commitments is now called into question...More than that, however, speech about hope must be primally theological, which is to say that it must be in the language of covenant between a personal God and a community. Promise belongs to the world of trusting speech and faithful listening. It will not be reduced to the "cool" language or the private discourse of psychology. It will finally be about God and us, about his faithfulness that vetoes our faithlessness. Those who would be prophetic will need to embrace that absurd practice and that subversive activity.[63]

The hope surpassing all hope is that God is somehow *for us* in this economic morass. To say as much is a frontal challenge to the present order which declares that all is as it should be, that God belongs in the private sphere, safely away from the social and economic order we are assured he will not upset. Hope believes that there is a better way—or more precisely, that *we can be led* to a better way and receive the fulfillment of better promises than those made by a consumerist capitalist system. This hope is rooted in the covenantal relationship between God and the people which resists the reduction of personhood to productivity or purchasing power. It insists as well that faith involves more than standing for a certain vision of sexual mores. God's people are about more than preventing abortion: they are about living in community with one another and with God, whose promises they look to in their economic life as much as anywhere else.

However, a prophetic response to the economy roots itself not in exhortations to greater charity, nor in strident denunciations of those held to blame for the crisis, but in the anticipation of what the free God intends to do for us. Whenever people yearn for a better way of life, they express the knowledge that they and their world are incomplete. There is much work to be done before we can be said to live in a truly humane system. The progressive claim is that there can be a fairer system. The *religious progressive* claim is that God is at work to create that new way of life, and to lead us into it.

I want to emphasize that this comes not from a more virtuous shuffling of the deck chairs, which leads us into the pious error of believing in our capacity to solve any problem, but from God's initiative to remake the system. Brueggemann says that

> Talk about newness in exile comes not from a happy piety or from a hatred of Babylon but from the enduring jealousy of Yahweh for his people.[64]

Proposals to make our economic system "more Christian" ultimately miss the point. Even to call for more fairness or more generosity or more concern for the poor without fundamentally altering the way the system works are mistaken. Perhaps the most radical thing that a religious left can proclaim is that God is for us, and will not tolerate dehumanization, the "'objective,' systemic, anonymous" violence of capitalism. We are "fearfully and wonderfully" made in the image of God. Our elemental connection to God, maintained by his faithfulness—by his jealous love for his people—means that by grace we are not destined to be brickmakers for Pharaoh, nor debt slaves in a post-industrial America. It is that knowledge that fully redefines our situation and gives us hope for newness in it.

SPEAKING THE LANGUAGE OF AMAZEMENT

Many readers no doubt will find it disconcerting that this proclamation does not translate into a programmatic response to the economic situation. Where is the policy? Where is the political strategy? We should recall here the position I staked out in the introduction to this book: *the religious left is meant to ask the questions, not line up behind the answers.* What I am suggesting is less an agenda than an orientation, a disposition to the "damnably disruptive questioning of the seemingly self-evident way things must be." The work of the religious left is not to produce shiny new technical solutions or to support the false equivalence of charity and justice. It is to participate in the creation of a "consciousness and perception" alternative to that of the dominant culture, to challenge the assumption that consumerist capitalism can truly make us happy, and yes, to stand in service with the poor.

This work is also about offering hope in our speech, to "speak the language of amazement" and so create the energizing alternative to the dead promises of the current order. The hope that emerges from this speech begins with the audacity to contradict the claims of the current order, to find joy where there ought to be only despair. Hence Jeremiah Wright discusses the story of Hannah from I Samuel:

> It's easy to hope when there are evidences all around of how good God is. But to have the audacity to hope when that love is not evident—you don't know where that somewhere is that my grandmother sang about, or if there will ever be that brighter day—that is a true test of a Hannah-type faith. To take the one string you have left and to have the audacity to hope—make music and praise God on and with whatever it is you've got left, even though you can't see what God is going to do—that's the real word God will have us hear from this passage... [65]

"The hope that must be spoken," says Brueggemann, "is hope rooted in the assurance that God does not quit, even when the evidence warrants his quitting."[66] This is not the hope Joe Hill famously derided as "pie in the sky, by and by," but a hope founded on realism in the current situation, and an equal realism in God's freedom. The reality of our current economy is that the oppressive, exploitative financial system appears to have made a recovery, but in truth only hangs on by its fingertips. In the long run, it is not sustainable, nor can it be maintained even in the near term without the acquiescence of the very people it crushes. The consumers upon which the predatory system depends have begun to get the idea that the system does not work for them, and that it can be changed. To say as much is to enact the hope of new possibilities. As soon as the reality is articulated, the people can begin to grasp the newness all around them.

There is also a deeper truth to be named, one that conservative perspectives on faith have been desperate to suppress for decades: that God is free, and in his freedom, he is for the poor. The reality is that God has not abandoned his people, but renews his covenant with them, even as he leads them to new life. That there is the possibility of change, that the bubble has burst and the financial certainties are on the brink of collapse, that the numbness and despair have been pierced—all of this is evidence for the faithful that God is "operating under a new plan." The plan is relational. Because God is not the agent of either the rich or the poor, he is free to be present to all of them in a new way that redefines their shared situation. Realism in our situation and realism in God's freedom create the grounds for new possibilities. Because God is faithful to our relationship, there is the strength to sing a new song: "New song time is when a new covenant inaugurates a new mode of reality."[67] We are able now to speak in a new way about the failures of consumerist capitalism and the financial predation it enables, and to imagine a reality beyond it. Even if that reality is not quite feasible politically, simply to question it changes the social construction. We are able to announce "birth to the barren," the metaphoric representation of the "opening of a future and the generation of an alternative by the miraculous power of God." Where there was no way forward, and therefore no hope, now by trust and relationship there is.

Last, we can talk about nourishment, about eating bread that satisfies, rather than robs us, of our labors. Brueggemann quotes Second Isaiah (55:1-2) thinking of the exile in Babylon:

Ho, everyone who thirsts,
　come to the waters;
and you that have no money...
Come, buy wine and milk
　without money and without price.
Why do you spend your money for that which is not bread,
　and your labor for that which does not satisfy?
Listen carefully to me, and eat what is good,
　and delight yourselves in rich food.

We should note, as Brueggemann does, the patent absurdity of these images. To speak of singing, new birth, new bread is "perfectly silly," as he says. These images by themselves cannot set us free from the current economic or political order. They cannot even hasten the inevitable. The prophetic work is to engage the imagination of the people and to reactivate their stories in the struggle to overcome despair. The poetic images offered by the prophets are therefore not technical solutions, nor are they magic words, for "prophets are not magicians":

Their art and calling are only with words that evoke alternatives, and reshaped hardware will not overcome despair in any case. That will come only with the recognition that life has not been fully consigned to us and that there is another who has reserved for himself his sovereign freedom from us and for us.[68]

To trust in God means to understand that our ability to provide material goods to answer every whim or desire is an illusion. It means to understand that despite our cleverness in solving the problems of the day, we are capable of boxing ourselves in and surrendering our capacity for new life and new possibilities. To live in relationship with God, conversely, means to receive with gratitude the gift of God's provision for us. It means to relinquish the delusion that we are at all times masters of our own destiny, and to accept the hope we are offered. That God is free and at work to do a new thing in the world seems rationally impossible:

> Those not comforted can hardly believe such a thing can be uttered. But clearly they will have no personal joy, no public justice, no corporate repentance, and no family humaneness until the community receives a newness it cannot generate for itself.

This finally is the language of amazement, and the work of a prophetic, progressive response to the rolling calamity that is the economy: to help the community to receive "a newness it cannot generate for itself" by questioning the current order and calling the people to imagine and undertake a new and better way. It is our gift to be able to offer this in religious language, and as language it may be powerful, even understood outside the framework of belief. But it can be offered only as a gift in the public square. We can call our fellow believers to find comfort in prophetic discourse, but we can only invite our fellow citizens to engage it as they will, and hope that they will find there something new.

DOXOLOGY

Progressives thus can offer praise of God not as a commandment to be followed by all citizens, whether believers or not, but as a "subversive or prophetic idiom" testifying to the real alternatives that God brings to the community. This is likely to be a stumbling block for many progressives eager to take action, whether religious or not. It certainly will confound secularists, who in all fairness cannot be expected to see how doxology presents a profound challenge to the static order.

Doxology is a testament first of all to the reality that we have run out of options. To praise God rightly is to praise the inbreaking initiative to provide us with newness. This is both a way of doing and a way of being. New energy is to be found

in receiving, and not grasping, in inheriting and not possessing, in praising and not seizing. It is in knowing that initiative has passed from our hands and we are safer for it. Obviously this becomes more than a critique of Babylon. It is also a critique of every effort to reorganize on our own, and it is a warning about settling in any exile as home.

The newness from God is the only serious source of energy. And that energy for which people yearn is precisely what the royal consciousness...cannot give. The prophet must not underestimate his or her urgent calling, for the community of faith has no other source of newness. I am aware that this runs dangerously close to passivity, as trust often does, and that it stands at the brink of cheap grace, as must always do. But that risk must be run because exiles must always learn that our hope is never generated among us but always given to us. And whenever it is given we are amazed.[69]

This is no call for simple-minded trust in the providence of God. Instead, it is the realism of those who have suffered and come to understand that to respond to their own suffering as the world responds will only increase the overall misery. It is the confidence of those who are able to imagine life outside the system, who watch and wait as it collapses around them.

Yet this is not a call to quietism either, nor for withdrawal from the world. It is very much about what happens in the same social realm inhabited by our fellow citizens. Prophetic hope is in fact an irruption into that realm reflecting God's gracious initiative in the world. Progressives can and should reach out for that hope by calling into question the legitimacy of the current order and its hold over the people. They can and should work to instill new energy, new imagination, and new consciousness into their communities. The work of activating the prophetic imagination is at the very heart of transformational politics, a slow, dedicated cultivation of minds for the sake of "better possibilities."

Therefore through doxology, progressive believers can offer a deep, if indirect, challenge to the present economic order. Praising God's generosity speaks precisely against the consumerist assumption that people can have it all without buying into the belief that want is only another technical problem to be solved. A good example might be discussions about "peak oil," where gratitude for the gift of natural resources presents a stark contrast with the squandering of those gifts, and the reality of their finiteness. As God provided manna for the Israelites, so we have had oil to sustain us, not fund our greed. It is a measure of human sinfulness that we begin to search for renewable alternatives only when it becomes apparent that our profligate use of the original gift cannot be sustained.

To put this in the terms we already have laid out, surplus wealth is a gift from God to be used to develop the community, not used to line the pockets of the already-wealthy. That precept was the justification for scriptural bans on "usury," which originally referred to charging *any* interest, not just exorbitant rates. Doxology is subversive because it accepts human limits and the political economy of easy solutions. By offering thanks and praise where they are due, doxology offers inescapable contrasts with the failures of the present order. It calls into question the promises made by consumerist capitalism: that we can have it all, without cost or consequence. And it activates the imagination of the community. God, who is good, may yet lead us to a future in which the economy is premised not on the short-term accumulation of wealth and the momentary satisfaction of material desires, but on fairness, equality, opportunity, and if not perfect security, then at least a game not rigged in favor of the rich.

Not surprisingly, to imagine such a future is to imagine a thorough upsetting of the present social order. Scripture often expresses the hope for reversal in the form of doxology. One of the greatest examples can be found in the first chapter of the gospel of Luke as Elizabeth, mother of John the Baptist, greets her cousin Mary, in words familiar to anyone who has ever prayed the rosary: "Blessed are you among women, and blessed is the fruit of your womb." Mary, herself pregnant with Jesus, responds with an ecstatic song known as the *Magnificat*:

'My soul magnifies the Lord,
    and my spirit rejoices in God my Savior,
for he has looked with favor on the lowliness of his servant.
    Surely, from now on all generations will call me blessed;
for the Mighty One has done great things for me,
    and holy is his name.
His mercy is for those who fear him
    from generation to generation.
He has shown strength with his arm;
    he has scattered the proud in the thoughts of their hearts.
He has brought down the powerful from their thrones,
    and lifted up the lowly;
he has filled the hungry with good things,
    and sent the rich away empty.
He has helped his servant Israel,
    in remembrance of his mercy,
according to the promise he made to our ancestors,
    to Abraham and to his descendants for ever.' (Luke 1:46-55)

Here is hope and joy realized, trust in God's covenant thoroughly intertwined with the reversal of the social hierarchy.

Mary's doxology is based on the earlier Song of Hannah (1 Samuel 2:1-10), in which the mother of the prophet Samuel gives thanks and praise to God for providing her a son. The level of trust

Mary expresses is remarkable. Hannah—a beloved wife—offers doxology for the gift of a child to provide her with financial security, even as she promises to dedicate her son to God's service. Mary does not have even that much reassurance. She is not yet married to Joseph, whom Luke advises us would be well within his rights to break the engagement, and her son will die young, commending her to the care of his friends. There is no indication that Mary understands how the story will end as she praises God, yet she accepts God's initiative willingly. She announces herself as the recipient of God's gracious activity, rather than its initiator: "the Mighty One has done great things for me." Her song emphasizes God's initiative with the refrain, "he has…" This is the religion of God's freedom, the worship of a God who does not forget the people, astonishingly at work "right at the center of a scene from which presumed he had fled." God, who keeps the promises made to Abraham and through him to the Israelite nation, blesses the lowly servant Mary. Through God, the powerful have been brought down, the hungry fed, and the rich sent away.

It is clear from Mary's song that it is praise given for God's gift to her and to the entire community: "his servant Israel" is metonymic for the people of Israel, and the promises kept are to the descendants of Abraham. The gospel message articulated here is social at its very core: Membership in the community that receives God's promises creates an obligation to uphold the covenant requirements instituted by God. Ethnicity is not sufficient, as John the Baptist preaches:

> John said to the crowds that came out to be baptized by him, "You brood of vipers! Who warned you to flee from the wrath to come? Bear fruits worthy of repentance. Do not begin to say to yourselves, 'We have Abraham as our ancestor'; for I tell you, God is able from these stones to raise up children to Abraham. Even now the ax is lying at the root of the trees; every tree therefore that does not bear good fruit is cut down and thrown into the fire." (Luke 3:7-9)

God is still free. He can deliver his promises to this people, or create another to inherit them if they choose not to uphold their end of the bargain. While that is an eschatological reality—it reflects the truth of future judgment—it also has very much to do with life today. John explains the ethics of this proclamation just before Christ's ministry begins:

> And the crowds asked him, "What then should we do?" In reply he said to them, "Whoever has two coats must share with anyone who has none; and whoever has food must do likewise." Even tax-collectors came to be baptized, and they asked him, "Teacher, what should we do?" He said to them, "Collect no more than the amount prescribed for you." Soldiers also asked him, "And we, what should we do?" He said to them, "Do not extort money from anyone by threats or false accusation, and be satisfied with your wages." (Luke 3:10-14)

The gospel is social. It is also *economic*, the creation of a more generous, more equitable community. To hear the good news is to participate in the imagination of a new life, one that is based on social solidarity and the assurance of God's provision rather than the false promises of financial safety and consumerist happiness. Even before Christ can promise the Kingdom of God, it begins to become a reality in the alternative consciousness and perceptions of those who hear John's message. The vision of that reality can only be caught by those who have lost everything, even their illusions. Only when the kingdoms of this world have come to an end can the people begin "to think things through in a really radical way."

As the kingdom of consumerist capitalism that brought us Big Shitpile continues its death throes, progressives have the opportunity to wake the people to the reality of their situation, spark their imagination, and energize them to take hold of new possibilities. Faithful progressives in particular have the opportunity to ask questions of the present order rooted in God's freedom and a "politics of human justice." There is no guarantee that those questions will be heard, much less receive a response. Likewise, there can be no guarantee that the *answers* will not succumb to self-interest and the limits of insight. We are in constant threat of hubris and partiality. But the alternative to the risk-filled enterprise of activating the prophetic imagination is surrender to "the consciousness and perceptions of the dominant culture." It is to inure ourselves to the death, exploitation, and oppression all around us, to surrender as the creators of Big Shitpile reorganize one more time secure in the knowledge that the debt slaves who work for them will be unable to resist yet another raid on the public treasury should they fail. Without leadership prophetic enough to help the people understand that another way is possible and give them the energy to journey toward it, they may well be proved correct.

The crisis sparked by the worldwide financial meltdown brings the failed promises of the current economic order and the possibilities for new life into sharp focus. The end of consumerist capitalism is here, whether or not its death is visible from within the consciousness of it sponsors. It is time for progressives, religious or not, to announce its end and call the people to grieve its loss as they enter into the hope-filled future given by the God who will not quit his children.

4. THE MILITARIST SCRIPT: TORTURE

*The militarism that pervades our society exists to protect and main-
tain the system and to deliver and guarantee all that is needed for
therapeutic technological consumerism. This militarism occupies
much of the church, much of the national budget and much of the
research program of universities.*—Walter Brueggemann[1]

*When feelings of insecurity develop within those holding power,"
reads one CIA analysis of the Soviet state applicable to post-9/11
America, "they become increasingly suspicious and put great pressures on the secret police to obtain arrests and confessions. At such
times police officials are inclined to condone anything which produces a speedy 'confession' and brutality may become widespread.*—
Alfred McCoy[2]

Why did they do it? It's not as though they didn't know it was wrong:
there is a long trail of precedent that says as much. In British law,
prohibitions on torture appear as early as the twelfth century.[3] The
phrase "cruel and unusual punishment" for criminal acts predates
the American Constitution, first appearing in the English Bill of
Rights in 1689.[4] European nations banned waterboarding in the
1800's,[5] and a U.S. soldier was sanctioned for using the technique
during the Spanish-American War.[6] The third Geneva Convention,
barring "outrages upon personal dignity, in particular humiliating
and degrading treatment" against prisoners of war went into effect in
1929.[7] Members of the German and Japanese militaries were con-

victed of war crimes during World War II for using torture, including waterboarding.[8] In 1968, another American soldier was court martialed for waterboarding a Vietcong prisoner;[9] in 1983, a Texas sheriff was sentenced to ten years in prison for doing the same thing to his inmates.[10] The *U.S. Army Field Manual* prohibits torture, as does federal law and international treaty.[11] Even Ronald Reagan— no shrinking violet—called torture "an abhorrent practice unfortunately still prevalent in the world today."[12]

So why did they do it? After all, it's also well-known that torture doesn't work. As far back as 1631, a Jesuit opponent of torture complained, "It is incredible what people say under the compulsion of torture, and how many lies they will tell about themselves and about others; in the end, whatever the torturers want to be true, is true."[13] More recently, in 1963 the CIA concluded after exhaustive research that the use of torture creates unreliable information, a conclusion shared by virtually every expert to have studied the question.[14] Even more recently, the FBI repeatedly warned, based on past experience, that abusive interrogation methods were counterproductive and would make terror suspects unsuitable for later prosecution. Yet their warnings were ignored.[15]

And there are alternatives to the practice. Sherwood F. Moran, a Marine interrogator of Japanese prisoners during World War II, counseled the use of humane interview strategies to elicit information. Among them: a "human-to-human attitude," "speaking the language of the captive," "short-circuiting patriotic defensiveness" by resisting the temptation to gloat, and "breaking recalcitrant prisoners" not through the use of force but by playing on their feelings of indebtedness to their captor's kindness. Moran was legendary for his ability to get information from prisoners; a memo he wrote on the subject was still in circulation in 2005.[16] His principles were shown to be correct in 2000 when the FBI was able to extract inside information without torturing an Islamic radical charged with helping to bomb the U.S. embassy in Nairobi, and again in 2004 when Ali Soufan, then an FBI interrogator, revealed that Osama Bin Laden's bodyguard, Abu Jandal "opened up about the 9/11 terror attacks only after being offered sugar free cookies." Apparently, Abu Jandal was a diabetic, and Soufan noticed that he wouldn't eat the cookies he had been served with his tea. So, one day Abu Jandal was given sugar-free cookies, which hepled to calm his anger toward his interrogators. "We had showed him respect, and we had done this nice thing for him," Soufan told *Time Magazine*, "So he started talking to us instead of giving us lectures."[17]

They—I am speaking of the leaders of the United States government in the years after the attacks of September 11, 2001—had to know all of this. They had to know that torture was a criminal act. They had to know that it was ineffective, counterproductive, a waste of time, effort and humanity. Yet they chose to do it anyway. Why?

We will consider several theories in this chapter, none of which are exclusive of other explanations. Before we consider the question of why, however, it will be useful to remind ourselves of what exactly happened.

THE BEGINNINGS OF THE TORTURE REGIME

After the 9/11 attacks, the Bush administration was quick to lay the groundwork for torture. As early as September 16, 2001, Vice President Dick Cheney pledged to use "any means at our disposal" in the War on Terror. In a *Meet the Press* interview with Tim Russert, Cheney said that the U.S would have to

> work, though, sort of the dark side, if you will. We've got to spend time in the shadows in the intelligence world. A lot of what needs to be done here will have to be done quietly, without any discussion, using sources and methods that are available to our intelligence agencies, if we're going to be successful. That's the world these folks operate in, and so it's going to be vital for us to use any means at our disposal, basically, to achieve our objective.

When Russert asked if restrictions that had been placed "on the United States intelligence gathering, reluctance to use unsavory characters, those who violated human rights, to assist in intelligence gathering," would be relaxed, Cheney responded, "Oh, I think so," adding that in order to penetrate al-Qaeda, "You need to have on the payroll some very unsavory characters if, in fact, you're going to be able to learn all that needs to be learned in order to forestall these kinds of activities. It is a mean, nasty, dangerous dirty business out there, and we have to operate in that arena."[18]

Cheney set out to do exactly what he had told Russert he would do. Largely (but not entirely) under his sponsorship, the Bush administration undertook a series of decisions, expressed in executive orders, legal memoranda, and signing statements, designed to expand the scope of actions taken against those deemed "enemy combatants." This matched the president's determination: according to Richard Clarke, on the night of September 11, Bush told his staff: "I want you all to understand that we are at war and we will stay at war until this is done. Nothing else matters. Everything is available for the pursuit of this war. Any barriers in your way, they're gone. Any money you need, you have it. This is our only agenda." When Secretary of Defense Donald Rumsfeld pointed out the legal restrictions on military efforts, Bush responded, "I don't care what the international lawyers say, we are going to kick some ass."[19]

With such a cowboy mentality, it is hardly surprising to find that the resulting policies set few if any limits on what interrogators could do. It began with a "Memorandum of Notification" signed by President Bush on September 17, 2001, giving the CIA "operational flexibility" in its fight against al-Qaeda. The memo authorized the creation of a CIA paramilitary force in Afghanistan, and allowed the intelligence agency to "kill, capture and detain al-Qaeda operatives" around the world.[20] Administration figures were clear about the breadth granted: "After 9/11 the gloves came off," CIA Counterterrorism Operations Director Cofer Black later coyly suggested to Congress.[21] Indeed they did: on September 25, John Yoo of the Office of Legal Counsel presented the first of several notorious memos, which argued that the administration could undertaken preemptive action against anyone it deemed a threat:

> In both the War Powers Resolution and the Joint Resolution, Congress has recognized the President's authority to use force in circumstances such as those created by the September 11 incidents. Neither statute, however, can place any limits on the President's determinations as to any terrorist threat, the amount of military force to be used in response, or the method, timing, and nature of the response. These decisions, under our Constitution, are for the President alone to make.[22]

On November 13, President Bush signed an executive order asserting his authority to try terror suspects in military commissions.[23] And in December, the Department of Defense began researching interrogation methods reverse-engineered from the survival techniques taught to U.S. service personnel.[24]

Early in 2002, the first detainees arrived in Guantanamo Bay. Their collection on the battlefields of Afghanistan and elsewhere was both cause and symptom of a systemic failure in American security. Many of the prisoners were needlessly detained, either peripheral to the operations of al-Qaeda and the Taliban, or simply uninvolved, rounded up to collect bounties from American forces. According to a former Army interrogator, military officials were aware of this, but chose to keep to a broad sweep:

> In talking to some of the officers at Kandahar and Bagram…they all talk about how there was a great fear among them, those who were going to be putting their signatures to the release of prisoners, great fear that they were going to somehow manage to release somebody who would later turn out to be the 20th hijacker. So there was real concern

and a real erring on the conservative side, especially early in the war. [25]

The collection of so many prisoners overwhelmed the detention system at Guantanamo. It also led to the perverse pressure to justify their detention, as Lawrence Wilkerson, a former U.S. Army Colonel and Chief of Staff to Secretary of State Colin Powell, reported:

> Several in the US leadership became aware of this improper vetting very early on.... But to have admitted this reality would have been a black mark on their leadership from virtually day one of the so-called Global War on Terror and these leaders already had black marks enough: the dead in a field in Pennsylvania, in the ashes of the Pentagon, and in the ruins of the World Trade Towers. They were not about to admit to their further errors at Guantánamo Bay. Better to claim that everyone there was a hardcore terrorist, was of enduring intelligence value, and would return to jihad if released. [26]

This produced an incentive to interrogate *all* prisoners as if they were hardened terror suspects. That incentive, in turn, was amplified by the Bush administration's determination to do "whatever it takes" to protect the nation. In February 2002, the president issued another executive order exempting terror suspects from the protections of the Geneva Conventions.[27] In December, Defense Secretary Donald Rumsfeld approved new methods for use at Guantanamo Bay, including the use of "stress positions." In the margins of one memorandum, he wrote: "I stand for 8-10 hours a day. Why is standing limited to four hours?"[28] In approving these techniques, Rumsfeld overruled objections raised by staff in all five branches of the military as well as the Criminal Investigation Task Force at Guantanamo.[29] He did so with the assistance of Joint Chiefs of Staff Chairman Richard Myers, who intervened to quash a legal review that threatened to derail the new policy.[30] Around the same time, the CIA asked for even more leeway in its treatment of prisoners, apparently with the concurrence of some leaders within the FBI and Department of Justice, even though they had previously objected to such treatment.

At first, harsh interrogations were meant to be used only on "high-value" detainees, those believed to hold critical information needed to save American lives. Rumsfeld's approval of these techniques, for example, were limited initially to a single detainee, Mohammed al-Kahtani, often referred to as "the 20th hijacker" after his presumed role in the 9/11 attacks.

Likewise, the CIA at first asked for administration approval of "alternative interrogation methods, including waterboarding," for just one prisoner, Abu Zubaydah, whom it believed to be a senior al Qaeda operative. A later memo notes that the CIA based its request on the ticking time-bomb scenario, "because the CIA believed that Abu Zubaydah was withholding imminent threat information during the initial interrogation sessions."[31] President Bush himself defended the decision in 2006: "We knew that Abu Zubaydah had more information that could save innocent lives, but he stopped talking.... And so the CIA used an alternative set of procedures."[32] CIA interrogators would later apologize to Zubaydah, admitting that they had overestimated his involvement in terror cells:

> They told me, 'Sorry, we discover that you are not Number 3, not a partner, not even a fighter,' " said Abu Zubaida, speaking in broken English, according to the new transcript of a Combatant Status Review Tribunal held at the U.S. military prison in Guantanamo Bay, Cuba...Intelligence, military and law enforcement sources told *The Washington Post* this year that officials later concluded he was a Pakistan-based "fixer" for radical Islamist ideologues, but not a formal member of al-Qaeda, much less one of its leaders.[33]

Permission for Zubaydah's interrogation was granted in July 2002, first by National Security Advisor Condoleezza Rice, then by Attorney General John Ashcroft. In August, an internal decision known as the "Bybee Memo" defined torture as "acts which result in pain equivalent to organ failure, impairment of bodily function, or even death."[34] With the guidelines set so broadly, virtually no technique was off-limits. As a result, Zubaydah was waterboarded more than eighty times in August 2002. He later told Red Cross investigators of horrific beatings, sleep deprivation, being shackled with his hands above his head for days or to a chair for weeks on end, and confinement in a wooden box, among other techniques. The Red Cross summarized the program of "alternative interrogation techniques" as it developed:

- Suffocation by water poured over a cloth placed over the nose and mouth...
- Prolonged stress standing position, naked, held with the arms extended and chained above the head...
- Beatings by use of a collar held around the detainees' neck and used to forcefully bang the head and body against the wall...
- Beating and kicking, including slapping, punching, kicking to the body and face...
- Confinement in a box to severely restrict movement...
- Prolonged nudity...this enforced nudity lasted for periods ranging from several weeks to several months...
- Sleep deprivation...through use of forced stress positions (standing or sitting), cold water and use of repetitive loud noises or music...
- Exposure to cold temperature...especially via cold cells and interrogation rooms, and...use of cold water poured over the body or...held around the body by means of a plastic sheet to create an immersion bath with just the head out of water.
- Prolonged shackling of hands and/or feet...
- Threats of ill-treatment, to the detainee and/or his family...

- Forced shaving of the head and beard...
- Deprivation/restricted provision of solid food from three days to one month after arrest...[35]

Eventually this mistreatment would spread from the "high-value" detainees to the population at large. As the historian Alfred McCoy notes, this reflects a pattern in the use of torture. McCoy cites counterintelligence programs used by the United States in Vietnam and Great Britain in Northern Ireland. In both cases, what was originally intended to applied to a few, selected individuals soon devolved "toward the torture of the many and into a paroxysm of brutality towards specific individuals."[36] This certainly fits the emerging history of Guantanamo and the network of "black sites" in nations like Afghanistan, Thailand, Poland, Romania, or the British territory of Diego Garcia, where torture was carried out in the early days of the War on Terror. As it happened, though, the use of torture would soon broaden even beyond the confines of Guantanamo Bay.

FROM GUANTANAMO TO ABU GHRAIB AND BEYOND

In late 2002, at least three prisoners died as the result of abuse, while new, unauthorized techniques—including waterboarding—were used on a fourth.[37] At the same time, the CIA, which had been taping the interrogations of some high-profile detainees, stopped its monitoring. These developments set internal investigations in motion.[38] In January 2003, Navy General Counsel Alberto Mora raised objections to the interrogation techniques being used at Guantanamo with his supervisor, Department of Defense General Counsel Jim Haynes.[39] In response to Mora's concerns, Defense Secretary Rumsfeld suspended the abusive practices at Guantanamo. But in a complex piece of bureaucratic infighting, Rumsfeld also ordered a "Working Group" to write new standards for interrogations. While Mora participated in this group, its conclusions were dominated by John Yoo, who wrote in one of his brief: "Just as statutes that order the President to conduct warfare in a certain manner or for specific goals would be unconstitutional, so too are laws that would prevent the President from gaining the intelligence he believes necessary to prevent attacks upon the United States."[40] Mora would later claim not to have seen the Working Groups' final guidelines before they were put into action.

In May 2003, FBI field agents expressed concerns about interrogation tactics used by the Department of Defense in a memo written to counterintelligence supervisors and legal counsel. While the agents conceded that harsh interrogation methods might produce battlefield intelligence, "the reliability of information obtained using such tactics is highly questionable, not to mention potentially legally inadmissible in court." Despite the warnings, the military continued the practices—including stress positions and sleep deprivation—for at least three years. It is unclear if senior legal advisors ever took the FBI memo into consideration as they drafted later interrogation guidelines.[41]

A month later, the 9/11 Commission requested information collected through the interrogation of various detainees, including Zubaydah.[42] As the administration worked on its interrogation policies, President Bush flatly declared that torturers would be prosecuted,[43] prompting CIA Director George Tenet to seek legal cover for the the agency's use of waterboarding.[44] A summer meeting of senior leaders to hash out the details ended in disagreement, as Attorney Geenral Ashcroft expressed doubts about the CIA program.[45]

Events quickly overran the administration's planners. As had happened in Afghanistan, the military had been flooded with detainees that it struggled to process. To hold the prisoners it collected, the Joint Command retrofitted the Iraqi prison at Abu Ghraib. The facility—staffed with 450 American reservists—eventually held over 8,000 detainees picked up in security sweeps, nearly double its intended capacity. It has been estimated that up to ninety percent of those jailed at Abu Ghraib had no connection to terrorist groups or resistance units fighting the American-led coalition forces; sixty percent posed no danger to Iraqi society and should have been released, according to one official report.[46]

In June 2003, U.S. Army Reserve Brigadier General Janis Karpinski was put in charge of the American prison system in Iraq. Unfortunately, neither Karpinski nor many of the soldiers she commanded had any prior experience dealing with prisoners. *New Yorker* journalist Seymour Hersh, drawing on the "Taguba Report" on prisoner abuses at Abu Ghraib, reported that

> During Karpinski's seven-month tour of duty…there were at least a dozen officially reported incidents involving escapes, attempted escapes, and other serious security issues that were investigated by officers of the 800th M.P. Brigade. Some of the incidents had led to the killing or wounding of inmates and M.P.s, and resulted in a series of "lessons learned" inquiries within the brigade. Karpinski invariably approved the reports and signed orders calling for changes in day-to-day procedures. But Taguba found that she did not follow up, doing nothing to insure that the orders were carried out. Had she done so, he added, "cases of abuse may have been prevented."

According to Taguba, Karpinski was also "rarely seen at the prisons she was supposed to be running." In addition, the report discovered a "wide range of administrative problems, including some that he considered 'without precedent in my military career.' The soldiers, he added, were 'poorly prepared and untrained . . . prior to deployment, at the mobilization site, upon arrival in theater, and throughout the mission.'"[47]

In an overcrowded and understaffed prison like Abu Ghraib, these issues alone could have caused serious problems. But as the Iraqi insurgency exploded and the Global War on Terror expanded, the military police running the prison came under constant pressure from military intelligence officers, civilian contractors, and CIA operatives to "set physical and mental conditions for favorable interrogation" of the detainees in their care. Hersh, again drawing on the Taguba Report, describes the results of this pressure:

> Specialist Sabrina Harman, one of the accused M.P.s, testified that it was her job to keep detainees awake, including one hooded prisoner who was placed on a box with wires attached to his fingers, toes, and penis...Another witness, Sergeant Javal Davis, who is also one of the accused, told C.I.D. investigators, "I witnessed prisoners in the MI hold section . . . being made to do various things that I would question morally. . . . We were told that they had different rules."

Once again, what was initially limited to a few prisoners eventually broadened. Between October and December of 2003, many of the practices used at Guantanamo became widespread at Abu Ghraib. The Taguba Report also disclosed a list of newer techniques that were perverse and often simply depraved. Among them were American soldiers videotaping and photographing naked detainees, often in sexually explicit positions or otherwise humiliating situations; piling them naked into pyramids and then jumping on them; and turning dogs on them. Taguba could not corroborate some incidents, but found them "credible based on the clarity of their statements and supporting evidence provided by other witnesses." According to these reports, detainees had chemical lights broken on them, were threatened with loaded pistols, were threatened with rape or were actually sodomized "with a chemical light and perhaps a broom stick."[48]

The horror in these incidents is perhaps not a coincidence. In the summer of 2003, Major General Geoffrey Miller, the overseer of the detention facility at Guantanamo Bay, made an extended visit to Abu Ghraib. Miller, according to General Karpinski, announced his intentions to "'Gitmoize' the detention operation." Thus, Miller trained the American staff in Iraq in "intelligence integration, synchronization, and fusion; interrogation operations; and detention operations," using Guantanamo "procedures and interrogation authorities as baselines." It was Miller who suggested that military police guards work for intelligence operatives in "setting the conditions for successful exploitation of the internees." And it was Miller, according to the former head of military intelligence at Abu Ghraib, who "introduced the use of dogs and other harsh tactics at the prison."[49]

Miller's role in the abuses at Guantanamo and Abu Ghraib underscores the involvement of senior leaders in the torture regime. Miller had been ordered to Abu Ghraib by Undersecretary Douglas Cambone "after a conversation with Secretary of Defense Donald H. Rumsfeld." The prison itself was visited several times by Iraq forces commander Ricardo Sanchez, though Sanchez denies approving any of the exceptional techniques.[50] Certainly senior members of the Bush administration knew what was going on: The President himself approved of harsh techniques such as waterboarding, stress positions, and sleep deprivation for use on particular individuals. Such techniques were discussed more broadly by Vice President Dick Cheney, Secretary of State Colin Powell, Secretary of Defense Donald Rumsfeld, National Security Advisor Condoleezza Rice, Attorney General John Ashcroft, Director of Homeland Security Michael Chertoff, FBI Director Robert Muller, and then-White House Counsel Alberto Gonzales, as well as by staff and lawyers within the administration. Ashcroft famously declared after one meeting, "Why are we talking about this in the White House? History will not judge this kindly."[51]

Between 2003 and 2005, administration officials also briefed several members of Congress about the interrogation practices, both Democrats and Republicans. Then House Minority Leader Nancy Pelosi was informed of at least some parts of the interrogation program. Later in 2005, as the Senate considered legislation to restrict the treatment of detainees, selected Republican Senators were briefed on the use of torture, apparently in an attempt to weaken the bill.[52] Vice President Cheney attempted to persuade Arizona

Senator John McCain to give up on the legislation,[53] and other members of the administration briefed Tennessee Senator Bill Frist. In December 2005, Congress passed the Detainee Treatment Act barring "cruel, inhumane, or degrading" behavior toward prisoners. President Bush signed the bill into law, while simultaneously issuing a "signing statement" of his intent to disregard key elements of the legislation.[54]

However, the administration's efforts to reach out seem to have paid off. In 2006, Congress passed the the Military Commissions Act, which endorsed the CIA's torture regime and retroactively pardoned interrogators for suspected abuse. Some progressives have argued that the passage of the MCA represents political malpractice on the part of Democratic lawmakers. According to Glenn Greenwald, among others, Democrats in Congress had a duty to oppose the torture regime in legislation. That point can be debated. What seems harder to refute is Greenwald's argument that the failure of Democrats to vigorously oppose torture under Bush set them up for greater difficulties in changing interrogation policy later on. In a typically stinging blog post, Greenwald singled out West Virginia Senator Jay Rockefeller, head of the Senate Select Committee on Intelligence and asked, "How [can] Senate Democrats pretend to be outraged at such policies when the leader they chose supports them?"[55]

After the abuses at Abu Ghraib emerged in mid-2004, however, the torture regime was finished for the most part. There is some reason to think that the CIA continued to waterboard prisoners after 2005, and recent investigations into the deaths of three detainees at Guantanamo Bay in 2007 strongly suggests that they were tortured to death, rather than committing suicide as was reported at the time.[56] But objections to the treatment of detainees at Guantanamo raised in 2003 and Abu Ghraib in 2004 seems to have basically ended the interrogation programs in those locations. At the same time, there is a tremendous amount of information that has yet to come to light about what happened under the Bush administration.

More disturbing, much of the legal apparatus that administration created to justify its use of torture survives under President Obama.[57] For example, the legal framework that allowed for torture has not been dismantled,[58] though the current administration has signaled that torture is not its policy.[59] Similarly, though Obama ordered CIA black sites closed soon after taking office, his orders carefully exempted secret prisons run by the military. As late as 2009, the *New York Times* was reporting on detainees who had been held incommunicado at one such prison in Afghanistan. Those prisoners alleged that beatings and sleep deprivation were used on them as part of the interrogation strategy.[60]

Worse, the Obama administration has established a preference for not pursuing investigations into Bush-era misdeeds. After a former Guantanamo Bay guard raised questions about the 2007 suicides there, his allegations essentially dropped into a bureaucratic black hole, [61] and though President Obama has expressed qualified support for a "truth commission" to look into the Bush administration enhanced interrogation program, so far, nothing has come of the idea.[62] A separate probe into wrongdoing in the CIA is ongoing.

The Obama administration has also refused to release all the photographic and video evidence of prisoner abuse at Abu Ghraib and other locations, claiming that making these materials public would endanger American troops.[63] This has stymied full disclosure of what happened under the torture regime. As many as one hundred detainees may have been killed by torture, according to Human Rights First, and many more abused.[64] As a result of this suppression of information, Americans do not know what was done in their name, nor what continues to be done.

TO KEEP AMERICA SAFE

I have only sketched out the barest thumbnail of the coercive detention and intelligence policies carried out under the Bush administration. There is much more that could be said about "extraordinary rendition," black prisons, prisoner abuses in Iraq, Afghanistan and elsewhere, indefinite detention, domestic espionage, even a proposed assassination squad. We will touch on some of this material presently. But I think this outline is sufficient for us to begin to consider the "why" questions about torture and related subjects. Why, at long last, did they do it?

The most generous explanation is the one offered by the Bush administration itself: that they were doing whatever it took to keep the nation safe.[65] This justification is consistent with the enormous effort undertaken after 9/11: the invasion of Afghanistan, the creation of the Department of Homeland Security, preventative detention of suspected terrorists, extraordinary rendition, wiretapping, torture. Even the invasion of Iraq can be understood (very charitably) as an attempt to prevent the next "smoking gun" that "could be a mushroom cloud," as Condoleezza Rice argued.[66] That the Bush administration was acting to keep the nation safe through its use of torture is also consistent with the lavish spending that reflects the U.S. commitment to military might. America will do "whatever it takes" to maintain its security.

What torture was not consistent with, however, was the actual result of making America safe. No security plan, no matter how good, can stop every attack. But even with that caveat, the Bush administration's program was a failure. Torture produced little, if any, actionable intelligence and a good deal of false information.[67] Interrogators decided that Abu Zubaydah was not the man they thought he was, for example. And after being waterboarded 183 times in a single month, Khalid Sheikh Mohammed gave up no "ticking time bomb," but only mistaken information on the whereabouts of Osama bin Laden.[68] According to Lawrence Wilkerson:

> It has never come to my attention in any persuasive way—
> from classified information or otherwise—that any intelligence of significance was gained from any of the detainees
> at Guantánamo Bay other than from the handful of undisputed ring leaders and their companions, clearly no more

than a dozen or two of the detainees, and even their alleged contribution of hard, actionable intelligence is intensely disputed in the relevant communities such as intelligence and law enforcement.[69]

To collect that much information, the torture regime had to incur significant costs. The most obvious of these is to American prestige, but of course the privilege of being a nation that does not torture is the assumed reciprocity for service personnel captured by other countries. Thus, the Bush administration arguably put its military men and women at greater risk for abuse by indulging in torture. In addition, as Glenn Greenwald, among many others, has argued, torture not only cedes moral ground to the very people who claim that American values are nothing but a sham[70], it actually provokes extremists to undertake terror operations.[71] Little wonder that even the conservative columnist David Brooks would eventually come to denounce the fetish of security at all costs as "the God that fails."[72] The militaristic script in general cannot keep its promise to keep us safe. In particular, torture has done if anything the exact opposite: it has made us *less* safe and *more* afraid. It may have actually brought us more war, rather than peace.[73]

BECAUSE IT'S WHAT THE UNITED STATES HAS ALWAYS DONE

Unfortunately, the metastasis of torture fits the historical pattern of the United States. As Alfred McCoy points out, torture—and hypocrisy about torture—have been a part of American intelligence operations for decades:

> The CIA's torture experimentation of the 1950s and early 1960s was codified in 1963 in a succinct, secret instructional booklet on torture—the "KUBARK Counterintelligence Interrogation" manual, which would become the basis for a new method of torture disseminated globally over the next three decades. These techniques were first spread through

the U.S. Agency for International Development's Public Safety program to train police forces in Asia and Latin America as the front line of defense against communists and other revolutionaries. After an angry Congress abolished the Public Safety program in 1975, the CIA worked through U.S. Army Mobile Training Teams to instruct military interrogators, mainly in Central America.[74]

Torture has long been deployed by the United States to defend itself against the enemies of Brueggemann's scripts. As developed by the CIA, it is a highly *technical* effort to solve a security problem, used by the military and other forces to defend the *therapeutic, consumerist* society. When the War on Terror came around, the CIA was ready to implement these same techniques, as it did in Abu Ghraib and other locations. Political leaders, perhaps eager to cover up for their failures to prevent the 9/11 attacks (as Mark Danner suggests),[75] were willing, even eager, to allow torture to return to its place on the "dark side" of American operations. McCoy argues that because the American government has never directly confronted its own complicity in torture, the practice continues to cause the nation moral and political problems:

> At the Cold War's end, Washington resumed its advocacy of universal principles, denouncing regimes for torture, participating in the World Conference on Human Rights at Vienna in 1993 and, a year later, ratifying the UN Convention Against Torture. On the surface, the United States had resolved the tension between its anti-torture principles and its torture practices. Yet even when Congress finally ratified this UN convention it did so with intricately-constructed reservations that cleverly exempted the CIA's psychological torture method. While other covert agencies synonymous with Cold War repression such as Romania's Securitate, East Germany's Stasi, and the Soviet Union's KGB have

disappeared, the CIA survives—its archives sealed, its officers decorated, and its Cold War crimes forgotten. By failing to repudiate the Agency's propagation of torture, while adopting a UN convention that condemned its practice, the United States left this contradiction buried like a political land mine ready to detonate with such phenomenal force in the Abu Ghraib scandal.[76]

Darius Rejali, an Iranian-American historian, points out torture's "migration":

> Everyone knows waterboarding, but no one remembers that it was American soldiers coming back from the Philippines that introduced it to police in the early twentieth century. During the Philippine Insurgency in 1902, soldiers learned the old Spanish technique of using water tortures, and soon these same techniques appeared in police stations, especially throughout the South, as well as in military lock-ups during World War I. Likewise, the electrical techniques used in Vietnam appeared in the 1960s appeared in torturing African Americans on the south side of Chicago in the 1970s and 1980s....And the techniques of this war are likely to show up in a neighborhood near you. Likewise, the techniques that appeared in the War on Terror were already documented in INS lockupin Miami in the 1990s. There is no bright line between domestic and foreign torture; the stuff circulates.[77]

In this light, torture begins to make sense as "business as usual" for the United States, an extreme form of the same "militarism that pervades our society...to protect and maintain the system."

Without the resolve to address this history, the country will never be able to come to terms with torture. Forgoing investigation into "enhanced interrogation techniques" leaves torturers and their patrons essentially above the law. It denies justice to the victims of torture, and leaves many of them in legal limbo: detainees who have been tortured cannot be tried, and therefore cannot clear their names in open court. Even when they are believed to be innocent, other nations are reluctant to accept potentially dangerous individuals, leaving detainees incarcerated for lack of a better place to go. Simply put, the inability to address the history of torture forecloses justice and healing.[78]

As McCoy and Rejali agree, failing to address the use of torture is toxic in a liberal democracy. It creates a difficult political problem that cannot be resolved even as it undermines democratic values such as dignity and freedom. It also perpetrates a fraud on the citizens as the government struggles to conceal the awful truth it dare not name. And it leaves a trail of devastation behind it—not just in those who are tortured, but in those who torture. Torture makes plain what should be obvious: the promise of militarism to provide for ultimate safety and security cannot be fulfilled. Torture cannot make us safe, and it cannot make the geopolitical system stable.

This is no small point in a nation as committed to militarism as the United States. Fueled in part by inflationary monetary policy, total U.S. military expenditures in 2008 amounted to approximately $623 billion, taking up nearly half the annual revenue of the federal government.[79] That is more than the $500 billion the rest of the world *combined* spent on its militaries, and nearly ten times what the next largest spender, China, spent. Furthermore, it is almost double what the U.S. spent in 1996, and "29 times as large as the combined spending of the six 'rogue' states (Cuba, Iran, Libya, North Korea, Sudan and Syria)."[80] Yet U.S. military spending is nearly sacrosanct, as Glenn Greenwald points out, even as it threatens to choke out the American economy.[81] Still, with all this expense, the Bush administration would have had us believe that "homeland security" would have been imperiled without the use of torture, a practice that has been suspect for nearly 2,000 years. Clearly something more than history must have motivated them.

AUTHORITARIANISM

It is possible to say without exaggeration that the Bush administration possesed at least some of the characteristics of an authoritarian regime.[82] For example, their decision-making process was almost completely opaque, made behind closed doors, and often with unclear motivation or origin. In addition, administration leaders were certainly not afraid to work around or outside of formal bureaucratic structures, had few if any meaningful limits on the exercise of political power, particularly against their opponents, and often seemed contemptuous of the norms of civil society. They also seeded ideologues throughout the government, particularly in the Department of Justice, and successfully politicized national security for at least five years.

However, it is hyperbolic and unhelpful to conclude from this that the Bush administration was totalitarian, as some have charged. Though they may have been of an authoritarian mindset, they were authoritarians more in Robert Altemeyer's psychological sense of the term, requiring deference to authority within the government and endorsing "high levels of aggression in the name of their authorities."[83] Christopher L. Blakesley and Thomas B. McAffee suggest that the willingness to accept force led to some of the worst parts of the Bush administration. They argue that the administration found in the 9/11 attacks virtually unlimited justification for their tactics. This, coupled with the administration's belief that it had to take aggressive, pre-emptive action to keep the nation safe, led to a "self-justifying self-defense" that permitted the government to go to the "dark side" to protect the nation against its enemies, internal or external. Indeed, Blakesley and McAffee argue, the administration may have felt *compelled* to take aggressive action in order to preserve "good order" in American society.[84]

Again, this is not to suggest that the Bush administration was out to create some kind of "police state." As Darius Rejali argues, democratic states do use torture. In fact, that Americans used so-called "clean techniques" that minimize or obscure the effects of torture suggests that the administration was concerned enough about public opinion that it did not engage too openly in the practice of torture.[85] But the fact is that they reacted in strikingly aggressive ways to perceived threats after 9/11, and their response can be understood through the lens of authoritarianism. With weak internal controls, deference to power, and a commitment to the use of force to achieve security, it seems almost inevitable (if not necessary) that the Bush administration would engage in violations of accepted norms.

In that, they seem to have been both product and producer of the authoritarian mindset. Product, in that like the wider conservative movement, the administration seemed to understand terrorism as part of a broader existential threat facing the United States and American values. President Bush, for example, famously named an "axis of evil" threatening global democracy.[86] Vice President Cheney, meanwhile, saw many threats to American security, even going so far as to argue for a pre-emptive strike against Iran.[87]

At the risk of psychologizing, the rush to torture may have reflected an inability to sit with unpleasant emotions in the face of threat. As a Daily Kos diarist pointed out in response to a tirade from conservative talk show host (and former Congressman) Joe Scarborough: "Joe wants to take his anger, frustration and sense of helplessness about terrorism out on people who he's sure deserve it, just for the hell of it, and is throwing a temper tantrum at being told no."[88] Even without applying this point to government leaders, the diarist's larger point stands: the reason our society endorses the rule of law is precisely to avoid the consequences of governing through inflamed emotions.

Likewise, Glenn Greenwald argues that American security policy has been infected with a particular pathology. He chastised *Washington Post* columnist Jo-Ann Armao for criticizing President Obama for not returning from vacation after a failed terror attack in December 2009:

Many people are addicted to the excitement and fear of Terrorist melodramas. They crave some of that awesome 9/12 energy, where we overnight became The Greatest Generation and—unified and resolute—rose to the challenge of a Towering, Evil Enemy. Armao is angry and upset because the leader didn't oblige her need to re-create that high drama by flamboyantly flying back to Washington to create a tense storyline, pick up a bullhorn, stand on some rubble, and personally make her feel "safe." Maureen Dowd similarly complained today that Obama "appeared chilly in his response to the chilling episode on Flight 253."

Again, we need not pathologize any particular person to understand that the political system encourages a perverse incentive for leaders to react to perceived threats in an authoritarian fashion. As Greenwald writes, the desire expressed here is for reassurance that all is safe by means of the leader expressing a "clear and unambiguous authority."[89] The Bush administration may have responded to that desire by producing an authoritarian mindset, or at least using it to further their political ends.

It is probably not an accident that the Americans most likely to support the use of torture are conservative evangelicals,[90] who form the backbone of the Republican Party. Conservative evangelicals score the highest on indexes of authoritarian belief such as "negative racist stereotyping, a belief in biblical inerrancy, a preference for simple rather than complex problem-solving, and low levels of political information," according to political scientist Tom Schaller.[91] The Bush administration almost certainly did not torture in order to garner the political support of this demographic, but they were at pains to communicate to it that they were doing everything they could to "impose order on an otherwise disordered world" in waging the War on Terror. According to one study,

The majority of evangelical respondents self-identified as

Republicans and were strong backers of President Bush. Their reasons were based on the righteousness of the cause in Iraq, trust in the commander-in-chief, potential for a Christian mission in a Muslim country, and the need to name evil and deter it at whatever price. It was at times inspiring to listen to them as they would say that, as parents, they felt that it was their duty to send their sons and daughters for this cause. As one evangelical pastor said, "In the evangelical world, patriotism is still a high value, sacrificial patriotism." Indeed, while several liberals spoke about the "real reasons" the United States went to war in Iraq as having to do with "oil and war-profiteering," evangelicals were certain and glad that the commander-in-chief was leading them to pay the "ultimate price" for the sake of "liberating an oppressed country from an evil dictator." Many evangelicals were dedicated to the idea that the United States had a "God-given" responsibility to "give itself" for the sake of others in the world.[92]

While the Bush administration acted in sync with this worldview, it was also happy to exploit it. As Jonathan Weiler and Marc J. Hetherington demonstrate,

> The same type of person who is attracted by the Republicans' position on "moral values" is also attracted to their position on terrorism. Both positions place a premium on order, strength, established norms and suspicion—if not outright hostility—toward those who are different.[93]

Authoritarianism is a strong predictor of party affiliation. Authoritarians vote Republican, non-authoritarians vote Democratic. Furthermore, when the perceived level of threat (whether social or terror) is high, those who are only moderately authoritarian tend to drift to the preferences of those who are score high on the scale.

This obviously gives Republicans a structural incentive to elevate public fears, whether through color-coded terror alerts or campaigns against same-sex marriage. It also gave them, under the Bush administration, an incentive "to name evil and deter it at whatever price." That price may have been terrible indeed.

DEHUMANIZATION

It may be prudent to stop here and remind ourselves that there seems to have been little or no strategic intent behind the torture regime. As far as we know, the only purpose behind the use of "enhanced interrogation methods" was the stated one: to extract information from enemy combatants. Even supposing that the American use of torture began as a way to link al Qaeda and Saddam Hussein, das some have argued, nothing has emerged to suggest that Bush administration leaders genuinely did not believe that such a connection could be found. Again, there is much left to uncover about this story. Perhaps new evidence will come to light. But at the moment, it appears that there was no greater purpose to torture than the tactical desire to gain intelligence.

Whatever the intended purpose of torture, its function is the same as any other form of violence. William Cavanaugh writes,

> So what is torture for? Torture has a formative effect on the collective imagination of a society. It is, in the strict sense, a taboo. Its name must not be spoken, but its presence must be widely known, because it generates a special kind of collective imagination about us and about our enemies. Torture does not merely respond to enemies; it helps make them.[94]

Torture, according to Cavanaugh, delineates and enforces a strict separation between "us" and "them." And it justifies the separation it has created:

> Torture tells us about them: the procedure is so extreme

that they must have done something to deserve it. As the Abu Ghraib photos illustrate, torture reduces them to what they are in our imagination: depraved sub-humans. Torture also tells us about us: we are willing to go to heroic lengths to save the world from evil. The threat must be terribly severe if we are forced to use such extreme measures; torture is therefore invested with the highest moral seriousness. Only the most righteous nation on earth could be trusted to use torture for good.

If we understand torture in Cavanaugh's paradigm of "taboo," it becomes part of a larger existential drama, in this case the Global War on Terror declared by the Bush administration. There is no question that senior leaders in the administration understood the War on Terror as a fight for survival, or that they manipulated that perception to accomplish strategic and political goals. Their use of rhetoric to depict their own willingness "to go to heroic lengths to save the world from evil" has been extensively documented. Torture takes root when such self-justification meets with opponents who are seen as being somehow less than human. The initial setting of the War on Terror may have provided the opportunity for just such a perception to arise. There are disturbing reports—still under investigation—that U.S. forces in Afghanistan may have turned a blind eye to the massacre in 2002 of about 1,000 al-Qaeda and Taliban fighters in Dasht-e Leili by forces belonging to Abdul Rashid Dostum, an Afghan warlord and American ally. The method used to kill these prisoners is stunning in its simplicity and brutality: the men were locked in abandoned shipping containers and left to die in the sun.[95]

Horrors take place in war all the time, of course. The point here is that such atrocities made it easy to plead that America, "the most righteous nation on earth," was dealing in a dirty business in a very dirty part of the world, an arena we had to operate in, according to Vice President Cheney.[96] That the American government was prepared to do just that can be seen in the lengths it went to neutralize two of its own citizens. John Walker Lindh, later called "the American Taliban" by Attorney General John Ashcroft, was captured in Afghanistan after a prison uprising was brutally suppressed by General Dostum's forces. Lindh had survived being shot, bombed, starved, and very nearly drowned in a week-long siege. When American forces took custody of him, he was given some medical treatment, though a bullet lodged in his leg was not removed until weeks later.[97] Michael Teitelman summarizes what happened next:

> Lindh was taken to Camp Rhino, a U.S. base near Kandahar. The conditions of his confinement were abysmal. He was stripped, fastened to a stretcher with duct tape, and enclosed in a windowless metal shipping container. He was fed starvation-level rations. When he needed to urinate, the stretcher was lifted into a vertical position so that he was forced to wet himself. Guards heard him crying and talking to himself inside the box. He was exposed to the frigid weather. His wounds were inspected by medical personnel but not treated; shackles cut blood flow to his hand and caused excruciating pain, which his captors refused to relieve; he was taunted by guards who cocked a gun to his head and threatened him with death. Foreshadowing Abu Ghraib, photographs circulated with salacious slogans ("shithead") written on his blindfold.[98]

It would later emerge that Defense Department officials had approved of this treatment, relaying instructions to Lindh's interrogators to "take the gloves off."[99]

Jose Padilla, accused of attempting to manufacture a "dirty bomb" for al Qaeda, was subjected to even worse treatment. NPR detailed the conditions of his imprisonment:

> According to court papers filed by Padilla's lawyers, for the

first two years of his confinement, Padilla was held in total isolation. He heard no voice except his interrogator's. His 9-by-7 foot cell had nothing in it: no window even to the corridor, no clock or watch to orient him in time. Padilla's meals were delivered through a slot in the door. He was either in bright light for days on end or in total darkness. He had no mattress or pillow on his steel pallet; loud noises interrupted his attempts to sleep…When he was transported, he was blindfolded and his ears were covered with headphones to screen out all sound. In short, Padilla experienced total sensory deprivation. During length interrogations, his lawyers allege, Padilla was forced to sit or stand for long periods in stress positions. They say he was hooded and threatened with death. The isolation was so extreme that, according to court papers, even military personnel at the prison expressed great concern about Padilla's mental status.[100]

After years of this treatment, Padilla was left so damaged that his personality began to disintegrate, and his lawyers questioned his ability to assist them at his own trial. As the blogger Digby pointed out when this story came out in 2007, the point of this treatment is chilling:

> Indeed, there are even some within the government who think it might be best if Padilla were declared incompetent and sent to a psychiatric prison facility. As one high-ranking official put it, "the objective of the government always has been to incapacitate this person."

Digby goes on to point out that this is exactly the kind of treatment used in Soviet psychiatric hospitals "to not only break prisoners' will and minds, but also to warehouse and torture political prisoners."[101] It is also precisely the kind of behavior that might be used to remove the humanity of a person deemed a traitor and wholly "other." As

Cavanaugh argues, it is an attempt to "reinforce a social imagination often called American exceptionalism," indeed an attempt to divide the righteous from the unrighteous.[102]

In Brueggemann's terms, torture can be understood as a cancerous outgrowth of the militarist script that requires Americans to secure their therapeutic technological consumerism through the use of force. Torture is like that broader militarism in kind, but different in degree of brutality and violation. If Cavanaugh is correct, torture is also different in that it is not an instrumental form of violence, but one that seeks its own justification. In its very infliction of suffering, torture asserts the moral superiority of the torturer over the victim, who is deemed to be a threat to the duly constituted order of society. In other words, torturers and those they work for may want not just "to obtain arrests and confessions," but also the security of knowing that theirs is a virtuous cause.

That, it should go without saying, is an impossibility. The lengths that powerful regimes will go to in chasing it, and the amount of damage they are willing to sustain to their own values, only underscores torture's importance by its own perverse logic. The greater the exception to the rule being applied to the hapless prisoner, the more important the issue at stake. And so the torture regime continues, feeding on its own desperation. It is possible that the feelings of insecurity that prompted the Bush administration to endorse the use of torture ran much deeper than simple military matters. Much of their national security agenda consisted of long-term goals left unaccomplished under previous administrations. "Taking the gloves off" in the face of a security threat may have provided them with the means to check long-desired items off their list, or it may have distracted from their failure to prevent the 9/11 attacks. They may have felt the need to legitimate their own rule after the bitterly contested election of 2000. Perhaps they wanted to vindicate the broader philosophy of conservative authoritarianism that they represented in the political realm.

Whatever the reasons, it is unlikely that we will get a firm answer to what happened, and it is impossible to receive a simple one. The American security apparatus and its leaders are dauntingly complex, with innumerable motivations, self-understandings, and moral reasonings. Moreover, the Bush administration was never known for addressing openly or honestly its reasons for doing things. What can be said is that the administration wanted to be safe, and it had the power to pursue its deluded vision of security—and now the nation is left to atone for its sins.

If we go back and ask our original question again, "Why did they do it?" other questions are then forced upon us: "Why didn't we stop it?" and "What do we do now?" More precisely, it forces us to ask why the opposition to torture has not been more effective. After all, there have been many attempts to put this particular genie back in the bottle. Among religious groups, major efforts have been led by the National Council of Catholic Bishops, the National Religious Coalition Against Torture, and Evangelicals for Human Rights. There have been many more initiatives among secular organizations. Yet though the Obama administration has forsworn the use of "enhanced interrogation," much of the legal apparatus enabling torture remains in place. And while the Bush administration was notoriously indifferent to dissenting opinion, the fact remains that they felt confident enough to implement the torture regime. The controversy that erupted after it was revealed only barely stopped it, piecemeal, and no successful pressure has yet been applied to cause the current administration to disclose fully what happened under its predecessor.

Objectively, religious opposition to torture has failed. I say this not to blame the religious activists who have opposed torture, many of whom have worked very hard and in some cases risked their public reputations, but to state what should be obvious: In an ideal world, torture would be so reprehensible that our government would never consider using it. In a slightly less ideal situation, religious opprobrium would be enough to bring the practice to an end immediately, and produce an immediate reckoning for sins.

Neither of these scenarios fits the current reality. What has actually happened is that the American government broke one of the basic norms of civilized nations. When it was called on the carpet by religious leaders, it essentially shrugged its shoulders and made slim, grudging changes in its policy. Meanwhile, some of the people in the pews were the strongest supporters of torture. What went wrong? And where do we go from here?

AGAINST HUMAN RIGHTS

The readiest answer to the question of how things came to such an awful pass is that the Bush administration was uniquely resistant to all but the most overt, and partisan, political pressure. Without the oversight imposed on them by the loss of Congress to the Democrats in 2006, the torture regime would have continued for far longer, and perhaps in even worse form.

Thus, an easy, if cynical, strategy would be to mobilize religious progressives in support of candidates and political parties opposed to torture, making political fortunes dependent on a strong condemnation of torture in its many forms. That looks straightforward enough. But if it were easy, it would have been done already. The religious progressive movement, as we have seen, is not nearly as organized or as united as its counterpart in the conservative realm. Nor is it as interested in partisanship. It may be faulted for these characteristics, or applauded; either way, it means that a frontal assault on torture led by religious progressives is unlikely to materialize.

Beyond the practical question of whether such a response could be organized, however, there are problems with a strategy of applying pressure to political leaders. First, as John Howard Yoder asks, who is really in charge, the tyrants or the citizens? To focus on leaders diverts attention from the power that ordinary people hold, and from their complicity in systems of violence. To put things in Brueggemann's terms, the militarist script only plays to the extent that we allow such a thing. This is particularly true in democratic nations like the United States, where we cannot blame a far-off Caesar for oppressive policy, but even authoritarian states derive some part of their legitimacy from public consent. Yoder writes,

> In any society the greatest room for change is subject to the discretion and initiative of voluntary associations, intermediate organizations, and subsidiary institutions (to use the technical buzz-phrases of several different recent schools of social thought). People at the top in repressive governments can seek to prevent important social change, but they cannot do even that thoroughly or permanently. Even less can they implement successfully the most urgent or wholesome change, even if they want to...It is therefore an unnecessary and illegitimate narrowing of the available room for mental maneuver, and a retreat from the courage and creativity which the gospel (or plain civil creativity) enables, when social critics grant to the oppressors that "they have the key." Of course: *if* the oppressors should choose to permit peaceful social change, at less cost to the initiators of that change, they could do so, and that would be fine. Then they would not be oppressors. That option is part of the gospel promise which we should offer to them. We will not do so, we will not summon them to be less oppressive, if we agree with them that they are totally in control, or if we agree that they have the last word in the choice of the weapons for our conflict with them.[103]

Petitioning political leaders to change their policies is not wrong. Nor is calling on them to live up to presumably shared values. Yoder, for example, sees nothing wrong with attempting to produce a conversion in leaders, in order to create disciples who act in accordance with scriptural norms of non-violence. Though this theme is never fully developed in Yoder's work, it is a major theme of more evangelical writers like Jim Wallis, who want to instill a more liberal, but still recognizably Christian, ethos in society. Others, myself included, have doubts about a strategy based on individual conversion, preferring systemic change.

More to the point, to count on leaders to produce change deals away our power at the outset, and it is not faithful to the gospel claims that the God of peace sets reality. It is God and God alone who can keep us safe. Bargaining with the worldly powers who cannot keep their promises of safety only denies that truth. Yoder suggests that a better alternative is to make those powers irrelevant through our own action. For that reason among others, he warns against entering into "consequentialist" arguments. As soon as we abandon our ideals to evaluate the costs and benefits of particular actions, we entertain the notion that evil can be justified if it produces a greater good. Yoder finds such outcomes repulsive. For example, he writes that though it can be argued that "non-violent direct action" may produce better security results than militarism, making such calculations leaves room open for the inevitable exception: *in this case, war is the most practical option.* Yoder believes that war is *always* wrong. Therefore he is not interested in evaluating possible justifications for breaking the rule.

We see the analogous problem with the issue of torture. Many pundits and thought leaders have been eager—sometimes disturbingly eager—to justify torture because "it works." In the case of a ticking time bomb, they argue, there may be no alternative but to torture a terror suspect. This is a ridiculous argument, of course. As many people have pointed out, the ticking time bomb scenario only exists on television. Torture does *not* work, and in fact, may do more harm than good. But pursuing such arguments allows the proponents of torture to keep alive a phony debate. Torture is wrong, always. Even its advocates tacitly admit as much when they speak of having to go to "the dark side," or getting involved in "mean, nasty, dangerous dirty business." They want to offset their evil with a greater good, a notion Yoder would have been quick to scoff at. Returning evil for evil only produces more suffering, not good, he might say.

Yet even articulating and standing by ideals can create difficulties. Religious objections to torture are often premised on concern for the dignity of the individual, which is expanded into the principle of human rights. Thus, the "Evangelical Declaration Against Torture" begins:

1.1 The sanctity of human life, a moral status irrevocably bestowed by the Creator upon each person and confirmed in the costly atoning sacrifice of Christ on the Cross, is desecrated each day in many ways around the globe. Because we are Christians who are commanded by our Lord Jesus Christ to love God with all of our being and to love our neighbors as ourselves (Mt. 22:36-40), this mistreatment of human persons comes before us as a source of sorrow and a call to action.

1.2 *All* humans who are mistreated or tormented are *somebody's* brothers and sisters, sons and daughters, parents and grandparents. We must think of them as we would our own children or parents. They are, by Jesus' definition, our neighbors (Lk. 10:25-37). They are "the least of these," and so in them and through them we encounter God himself (Mt. 25:31-46)...

1.3 However remote to us may be the victim of torture, abuse, or mistreatment, Christians must seek to develop the moral imagination to enter into the suffering of all who are victimized... Commitment to a transcendent moral vision of human dignity which is rooted in the concrete reality of particular suffering human beings motivates the signers of this statement as well.[104]

All of this is true, and absolutely correct in naming basic Christian values. However, it does not take into account the way torture functions as a taboo in our society, as William Cavanaugh suggests. Such statements may thus actually help to produce the very thing they oppose, by enabling the construct of torture as a tragic but necessary exception to the general rule. As Cavanaugh understands, the exception is itself evidence of its own necessity: that such horrible things are done demonstrates the need for strong and violent action by authorities.

Neither does the human rights strategy confront the ambivalence provoked by the military script. As Brueggemann writes in response to the idea of creating a new social confession,

> It is my judgment that before we get very far toward a confession, we have an enormous task of preaching, teaching, witness, and interpretation, in order to show that the urgency of confession is powerfully intrinsic to our faith, and not an "extra" about which there is an option. Thinking about confession, so it seems to me, does not fit our concern about "being prophetic" in any conventional way. It concerns core matters. But such a claim would be an immense surprise to many of our church people, precisely because we have, for the most part, cast our preaching and teaching and witnessing in other categories.[105]

If the groundwork has not been laid, even the most eloquent statement of conscience will wither like seeds cast on rocky soil. It will take careful preparation to recover the proclamation of inalienable human rights as central to faith. In a nation where half the citizens say that it is "sometimes" or "always" justified to torture a terror suspect,[106] this is likely to be slow, painful and very necessary work, particularly in those religious traditions that lean toward the authoritarian.[107]

Last, statements like the Evangelical Declaration (among many others) give an easy out to their supporters. Having signed the petition for redress, we can carry on with our day, confident that we have done what we can to end the practice of torture. This is how such efforts become politically irrelevant: everyone—including those who authorize torture—agrees with them. But because they have no mechanism for producing a future different than the past, no hook to connect to the motivating core of faith, they are ignored and quickly forgotten. If consequentialist arguments can be defeated by finding the inevitable exception to the rule, idealist arguments can be defeated by acceptance without follow-through. Unfortunately, this is the case no matter how basic or important the ideal is.

IF NOT IDEALS, THEN WHAT?

I offer this critique not out of mean spiritedness, but simply to explain the apparent failure of the religious response to torture. There is no evidence that religious voices were able to change the policies of the Bush administration, nor that they have had any significant influence on the Obama administration. The most we can say is that religious opposition may have prevented worse abuses, or helped to ensure that the policies were not continued, but this is really argument from absence. What we know is that torture took place under Bush, Obama seems content to sweep things under the rug for the most part, and Dick Cheney can go on national television to defend torture with impunity.[108]

If we are to be serious about making sure that the United States government does not engage in torture again, we will need a more effective strategy. Such a strategy, I believe, will need to offer a word of hope to both the victims and perpetrators of torture. But it will also have to speak to those average citizens made complicit in the actions of their government. If torture is not to become an entrenched part of our security policy, the tortured will need freedom, the torturers accountability, and the people a new situation. This will require a delegitimization of the government's claim to secure the needs of therapeutic, technical consumerism through the use of torture. It will also require a confrontation with the religious authoritarianism that funds torture. The church (and other religious institutions) must nurture its members away from the national security state and the lie that only military might can keep us safe, and toward the hope-filled safety of the heavenly city.

In brief, it may be that the most effective *social* and *political* response to torture that the religious left can offer is a *religious* one. That is to say, a response aimed not at changing the behavior of political or security leaders, but at transforming the beliefs and attitudes of religious believers so as to deny the implied social permission for torture and to provide an alternative witness to the work of the state.[109] This is an enormous task. However, it may be the only plausible alternative. If we have learned nothing else from the Bush administration, we should have learned that moral suasion of government officials does not work. As Cavanaugh argues convincingly, the modern nation-state by its very design cannot be the guarantor of the common good. Rather it exists to provide for the needs of the market, which includes securing the social order. The Bush administration, for all its proclaimed deference to "Christian values" and "limited government," was always an unapologetic advocate for the work of the state in advancing values deeply at odds with authentic Christian teachings, or true conservatism, for that matter.[110]

This is why we cannot rely on bare statements of principle to carry the day. By the logic of the nation-state, the Bush administration was acting rationally. Indeed, they were acting *ethically*: the highest priority for the nation-state is the stability of the marketplace, not human rights, nor the professed social ethics of the citizens it nominally represents. To counter these priorities, a steady, patient, and long-term effort to shape, strengthen, and embed progressive values in the society will have to be carried out. The purpose of such an effort will be not to call on political leaders to live up to shared values, but to increase social capital so that the community can resist misdirection by its political leaders. Thus the effort will have to be pragmatically grounded in the social realities of community, but challenging enough to motivate people to action. In short, it will look less like idealist activism and more like the mundane work of ministry.

There is a framework available for such an effort. Earlier, I suggested that Americans would have to atone for the use of torture by their government, to find a way to put things right in the wake of what has been carried out in their name. In order to do that, we will need to engage actively, prophetically, and imaginatively in discerning a new path forward for the nation that does not include torture. Again, this is not a task for officials, but for citizens. As Yoder argues, "the greatest room for [social] change is subject to the discretion and initiative of voluntary associations, intermediate organizations, and subsidiary institutions."[111] Power resides in the hands of the people, and in the hands of the God who goes before them to lead them from death into life, and from oppression into freedom. We must act without mediation to make our community a better place.

The role of an effective religious left will be to facilitate this process without controlling it or taking it out of the hands of ordinary people. Creativity is essential. The religious left, as we have often said, is not geared for the application of raw partisan power. The alternatives to that power that the religious left has so far been able to muster have not worked. There needs to be some fresh approach. I suggest that we take the idea of atonement seriously. Americans need to make amends. But they must also pursue the work of reconciliation: they need to be at one with one another, and with the community, writ large, that surrounds them.

REDEMPTION

In theology, atonement refers to theories about how Jesus saves humanity from sin. Timothy Gorringe derives four "metaphors" for atonement from the works of Paul: redemption, justification, sacrifice, and reconciliation. To these, he adds two: forgiveness and solidarity.[112] Each of these provides a helpful image in understanding the work before us. Though they describe the work of Jesus, Christians at least are called to live in imitation of Christ, and thus these categories can guide our action.

Gorringe locates the metaphor of redemption in two political roots: the Exodus narrative (the freeing of the Israelites from slavery in Egypt) and the purchase of Christians "at a great price," which he takes as a literal statement about slaves being bought out of the market. Meanwhile, Esther Reed sees three essential elements to redemption:

> God's solidarity with humankind and especially those in need; deliverance from all that prevents life being lived to the full; transformation from imperfection to perfection, from loss of potential to its fulfillment.[113]

In a sense, this brings us full circle to the Uighur prisoners mentioned in the introduction to this book, and really to all the terror suspects caught up in the American security net. Progressives at a minimum ought to be agitating against indefinite detention without charges, and pushing for a speedy close to Guantanamo and any other secret facilities that can be uncovered. Their prisoners should be freed, repatriated, or held on formal charges.

More radically, we might ask questions within our own communities about what it means to say that God stands "with humankind and especially those in need." We might ask, as Jim Wallis does, whether outlandish military expenditures can be justified in a time of economic downturn.[114] We can work to humanize terror detainees and especially those who have been the victims of torture, and reflect on what it means that God would stand in solidarity with those treated so brutally. What has God imagined for such people? What would it mean for God to lead them—and us—into freedom?

Even more broadly, we might wonder with Glenn Greenwald about the factors that drive young men and women to join terror networks.[115] Could a comprehensive Middle East peace plan, or a step back from aggressive military involvement in nations like Yemen and Sudan, rob terrorists of their fuel? What loss of potential keeps prospective terrorists from living their lives in a more fulfilled, and more peaceful, way? How is it that Christ has bought even these people at a great price? What does it mean that God intends to bring them—and us—from imperfection to perfection? What does it mean that God leads us as a nation out of danger into safety, as he did the Israelites? What indeed does it mean to be safe? To be free?

The purpose of these conversations is first to open a critical discourse around security issues, to ask those damnably disruptive questions about the seemingly obvious way things must be. As Brueggemann says, we are not safe, and we are not happy. Even to think outside the militarist script challenges its automatic rehearsal and is in a sense to be redeemed from it. This is the case both in the challenge posed to assumptions about the size, shape, and purpose of the national security apparatus, and about the enemies it is deployed against. Particularly in the humanization of the nameless, faceless, terrorist other, it counters the silence and passivity that allow torture to take place.

To that end, we can imagine certain bold acts of witness. A Christian church might seek out an intentional partnership with a Muslim community in the United States or abroad. Such relationships are fraught with social, cultural, and political difficulties, but that is of course why they are needed. Or a religious group might offer to resettle a detainee released from U.S. custody. What greater testimony to the possibility of redemption could be offered than a community willing to work for healing alongside its supposed enemy?

JUSTIFICATION

Protestants typically understand justification as a legal metaphor, where Christ pays the debt of sinful humanity in order to establish a righteous relationship with God. "I am charged and found guilty, but when it comes to sentencing the Judge takes my place," Gorringe explains. On the surface, this legal metaphor matches Paul's language in Romans 5, among other places, but the apostle may have been repurposing Old Testament ideas:

> If any judge is in mind in this imagery it seems most likely
> to be the Hebrew kind, not operating in a court but vindi-

cating the poor, and dealing with the oppressor. Righteousness here delivers shalom, a concrete situation of peace and justice in which the rich are put in their place and the poor lifted up. This Hebrew idea is a vital, though neglected, aspect of the biblical meaning of salvation.[116]

Still, legal metaphors for salvation have been the primary reading of justification since the time of Luther. Christ is understood as having "paid the price" for believers by suffering in their place. As Gorringe points out, such a view is ironic at the very least. It seems to validate the actions of the human court against Jesus, which is "almost certainly the opposite of its original sense, to reaffirm rather than deconstruct the power of human law." Gorringe prefers to view justification in what he sees as Luther's original sense, "being crucified with Christ" in a way that "embraces suffering."

Later theologians take these ideas in different directions. Some draw out Luther's idea of Christ's presence within believers to talk about "being incorporated into Christ's humanity, joined to his divinity and made a sharer in God's own triune life." Scholars of Paul point to his concern for community life and the ways Christians are "grafted onto" Jewish righteousness before God to suggest that justification has to do with covenant and communal identity. The early Anabaptists expanded upon Luther's opposition to "works righteousness" to seek a countercultural "kind of polity in which people did not deal with each other in adversarial ways, but rather learned forgiveness." That is, they pressed for a community that went beyond the letter of the law to keeping its spirit.[117]

I realize that this must seem terribly abstruse. The underlying point is fairly simple, however. If we understand justification as a legal metaphor, we have to ask about the basic fairness of a legal or security system that would recreate the abuses that killed Jesus. Crucifixion, after all, is a form of lethal "stress position" that slowly suffocates its victims, and Jesus was executed as a threat to the security of the Roman state.

If justification is about more than simple substitution, then the Christian community is about much more than the privatized salvation of individual believers. This opens the door to rebuilding the identity of the church around the work of creating peace and (primarily) economic justice.

Again, this is likely to be very long term, difficult work. It challenges believers to accept responsibility for torture, rather than shunt the blame onto political leaders. It also calls them into a new way of being in the world that goes against the cultural grain. It will therefore provoke a good deal of hostility, resentment, and resistance. But I am convinced that it is both the work of the gospel and the strongest possible response to torture. Only a community that will not sponsor brutality can hope to prevent the reappearance of torture as a tool of national security. For Christians at least, that means allowing the imagination of a new future into which God is leading us to reshape the community in the present.

SACRIFICE

In some ways an extension of the concept of justification, sacrificial atonement emphasizes Jesus' salvific action as the paschal lamb. This is taken from common New Testament imagery: Jesus is referred to as "the lamb of God" (John 1:29), "our Passover lamb" (1 Corinthians 5:7), and "like a lamb without blemish or spot" (1 Peter 1:19).[118] Some contemporary theories have focused on sacrifice as a ritual cleansing or as a symbolic means of releasing guilt, blame, and thus violence. But perhaps the most famous exponent of sacrificial atonement was the medieval theologian Anselm, who developed the idea that Christ paid for the enormous "debt" of sin with the only possible sacrifice capable of providing satisfaction, his own life.

Modern ideas about sacrifice consider whether Christ's death was as necessary as theories of sacrificial atonement believe. For example, Franz Hinkelammert believes that sacrifice is demanded by a "reality uninterested in reconciliation" but instead focused on punishment and adversarial legalism. As an alternative, Hinkelammert points to the Lord's Prayer, where "our debts" are forgiven "as we forgive our debtors." Gorringe, meanwhile, turns the tables on Anselm. Sacrifice, he argues, depends on the notion that forgiveness is too costly to be accomplished any other way. But what if the real cost of forgiveness is what it takes "not to be consumed by bitterness, resentment, and rage, in the face of injustice"? What, Gorringe wonders, "did it cost Jesus, or better, what life practices enabled Jesus to say, on the cross, while being tortured to death, 'Father forgive them, they do not know what they are doing' (Luke 23:34)?"[119]

This opens up new ground. Understanding sacrifice not as an impartial demand imposed from the outside but as our willing gift makes it possible to offer it as a way of keeping covenant by imitating the God who pours out his own life on our behalf. This may seem a bit soft-headed or unrealistic, but generosity in the interest of maintaining relationship was the value behind the Marshall Plan and the American occupation of Japan. As the very realistic security leaders of the day realized, a return to the punitive measures imposed after the Armistice at the end of World War I would only cause more destabilization and violence. This history might spark religious progressives to question what Americans are doing to help alleviate poverty or provide for economic opportunity in potentially violent areas of the world.

Sacrifice seen as a gift also allows us to articulate in religious terms the principle that jettisoning American values in the name of upholding them is complete madness. Terrorists win when they are able to lock their opponents into a cycle of "bitterness, resentment, and rage." The very purpose of terrorism is to undermine the legitimacy of powers who cannot be defeated through military means. Sacrifice frees us of that power by denying the terrorists the fight they so covet and by refusing to be willing participants in the loss of our shared humanity.

More broadly still, we may be called to sacrifice the prerogative of control. Yoder "observes that no Christian accepts war because they like it or think war is a good thing, but 'because they assume that the church is called to run society in collaboration with the state."[120] Against this assumption, he calls on the church to be "a different kind of human community in the midst of the world" and on Christians to be "more relaxed and less compulsive about running the world." It is a delusion to think that we can be kept safe by the precise application of violence, as the militarist script promises. But so too is the idea that the precise application of a particular religious ethic of the state or military or the use of force will make things more just or more secure.

In a sense, what I am saying here is that religious ethics are for religious communities. It is true that very few people live solely within the discrete boundaries of a religious community, and so the values that are preached in church make their way into broader discourse. But we may do well to heed Yoder's advice to stop thinking of democracies as equitable producers of the good, and start thinking of them as an imperfect, uneven, but still preferable means to hold back the bad.[121] Giving up the illusion that we can and should run the world in collaboration with the government and instead taking up the work of providing an alternative witness may in the long term be the most effective sacrifice religious progressives can offer.

RECONCILIATION

Where other metaphors borrow from legal terminology, the idea of reconciliation is rooted in the marketplace. Paul's root word (it appears only in his letters) refers to currency exchange, and by extension correcting variances in tally sheets. Generally, it means to be reunited with another, or to have differences resolved. As Gorringe notes, Paul sees reconciliation as "'breaking down the dividing wall' between different groups (Ephesians 2:13-16)."[122] The ground of reconciliation in the New Testament is the emerging hostility between Jews and the new Christians. Paul sees the divide bridged "by the cross," that is, by God's reconciliation with humanity through Christ, which radiates outward to human relationships, both individual and on the level of communities. Reconciliation opposes false community with real community. Put differently, it finds common ground in muddled human relationship rooted in the love of God for humanity, rather than the clean lines of ideology, beliefs, and values that define a social group. The God of reconciliation transcends all the partial understandings of divinity used to fuel fear and mistrust of the outsider. Gorringe here draws on the work of Kosuke Koyama, who

> found faith in the midst of the ruins of Tokyo at the end of World War II. He saw that the devastation around him was the result of a false "center symbolism," the idolatry of Japanese power. The cross, he realized, was a critique of all such idols. Following Luther, he understood a true theology of the cross to imply a necessary brokenness, for him the critical dividing line between theology and ideology. The theologically instructed community is necessarily broken, necessarily contains a moment of sharp self-criticism, as opposed to the community governed by ideology, which knows no such necessity...Such brokenness protects me against an idolatrous center symbolism, and in this way makes reconciliation possible.[123]

Likewise, Jan Lochman is careful to oppose reconciliation to the "false ideology" that surrounds it. Reconciliation "cannot be identified...with a desire for appeasement, with facile and vain promises, with a spurious peace which avoids conflicts, conceals real tensions, glosses over real injustices." Reconciliation is costly because it is accomplished in Jesus' sacrificial death. Therefore it cannot be held as a value sentimentally or without critical thought about the powers that oppose and subvert it:

> Above all, a Christian ministry of reconciliation refuses to capitulate to these powers, refuses to abandon the field to them. Although the Christus Victor approach provides no

optimistic explanation of the world, it does open up the eschatological hope, in which all of these powers have been demythologized, stripped of their fateful character, and forfeited all right to be regarded as ultimately decisive factors and can and should, therefore, be constantly challenged and called into question.[124]

The business of believers is not to proclaim a triumphalist vision that God has won every final battle with evil in the world, but to live in hope with the assurance that God is slowly but steadily peeling back the power of evil and moving the world to its appointed end. This may seem like an overly subtle distinction, but it is vital. If atonement has already been accomplished in Christ's death on the cross, then those who resist the Christian message can be read as willful enemies of the message of salvation. Faith is reduced to the ideology of a particular social group anchored by the knowledge that Christ died for them and their values, and without obligation to those outside the walls of their community. But if the work of reconciliation continues, the essential task is to challenge the forces that would separate and divide humanity from itself, to bring hope to an ever-expanding circle of community.

This may take the concrete form of furthering individual efforts of reconciliation, such as that of Brandon Neely, a former Guantanamo Bay prison guard who sought out Ruhal Ahmed and Shafiq Rasul, two of his former charges, to apologize for their interment.[125] It may also take place by establishing international partnerships, as previously suggested, or in the creation of interfaith groups specifically dedicated to reconciling religious differences. Such programs should not be mistaken for religious universalism, however, and particularly not for ill-considered, nebulous attempts to get at "the truth behind all religions." Authentic differences in faith are a gift, and even conflict is a given. The work is to find a way to live without allowing conflict, violence, and injustice to control us.

FORGIVENESS

To that end, religious progressives must participate in the active work of forgiveness, the necessary condition of reconciliation. The reconciliation accomplished by Christ begins with his forgiveness of those responsible for his death and continues as his Spirit moves graciously among those it inspires. Forgiveness is thus part of the spiritual path Christians travel and of the working out of God's purposes through the people of God. Gorringe discusses the political ramifications:

> Perhaps the most interesting example of this in the twentieth century is the way Gandhi's practice of fasting to make atonement for communal violence, and to try to bring it to an end, was understood. The American missionary Stanley Jones felt that Gandhi's insistence that people can joyously take on themselves suffering for the sake of national ends "put the cross into politics."…It may be objected that such readings turn the cross into a "principle," but perhaps rather they are a recognition, firmly grounded in the Gospel, of the cross as a way on which the disciple has to tread.[126]

Like reconciliation, forgiveness is no easy out, but an imitation of the costly example of Christ's sacrifice. Forgiveness is sustained by "life practices" that enable the freedom to forgo retribution, and allows Christians to be in a countercultural way that seeks peace rather than violence.

The former Iranian hostage Terry Anderson demonstrated what this meant in the days after 9/11:

> "We have every reason to be terribly angry at these people. They have every need to be punished," former hostage Terry Anderson told a rapt St. Andrew's School audience about last week's terrorist attacks. "But forgiveness is a willingness not to hate."[127]

It is not only a willingness not to hate, but the willingness not to be controlled by hatred and violence. Had Anderson's view been internalized by the American government, the torture regime would never have been implemented. Almost certainly, there would have been no invasion of Iraq.

As it is, voices like Anderson's were ignored or marginalized. (Anderson lost an Ohio State Senate campaign to an opponent who criticized him as "soft on terrorism.")[128] But forgiveness can still suggest a path forward in the wake of torture. Walter Wink notes the work of the Catholic church in Guatemala:

> In late 1994 the church decided to establish its own "alternate truth commission," funded largely by the governments of Sweden and Norway. Names will be named, not to submit the perpetrators to judicial processes but to encourage them to admit their sin and ask for pardon. Most disturbing to the military, perhaps, the study will not only present a historical record but develop an interpretation of the incidents and their causes and suggest measures to prevent their repetition. Those who are being trained to do the research are bracing themselves for government harassment and violence. There is something fitting in the church publishing the names of torturers as a basis for forgiveness. Since the church has no authority to prosecute, and the military is not likely to allow prosecutions anyway, the matter has effectively been circumscribed.[129]

If full disclosure of what happened under the Bush administration is not forthcoming from successive presidents, religious progressives should follow this model, resisting the temptation to soft-pedal the results of the investigation.

Religious progressives should also continue to speak out against the hatred of Muslims and other minorities. The need for a counter-witness on this score is particularly acute because so much of the dehumanizing rhetoric about the "Clash of Civilizations" comes from conservative religious voices. If progressives ever hope to reclaim the mantel of normative faith from the religious right, they must provide some alternative to its dominant, and hate-filled, understanding of Christianity as the American ideology.

SOLIDARITY

In Christ, God chose to keep covenant with the poor, the suffering, and the dispossessed. Paul's hymn in Philippians 2:5-8 demonstrates the radical nature of this act:

> Let the same mind be in you that was in Christ Jesus,
> who, though he was in the form of God,
>   did not regard equality with God
>   as something to be exploited,
> but emptied himself,
>   taking the form of a slave,
>   being born in human likeness.
> And being found in human form,
>   he humbled himself
>   and became obedient to the point of death—
>   even death on a cross.

Gorringe quotes Martin Hengel's interpretation of this passage as an expression of the "solidarity of the love of God with the unspeakable suffering of those who were tortured and put to death by human cruelty." As Hengel and Gorringe note, the Philippian hymn connects slavery with the cross. Jesus was crucified as the lowest sort of person, not even important enough to be afforded the mercy of beheading. Yet God chose to remain in solidarity with him, and through him all those beaten down by the power of the world.[130] Where for Kosuke Koyama the cross calls into question all totalizing ideologies, here God's solidarity with the poor and powerless challenges the divisions enforced by power in human society. To remember Christ's life and death, as in eucharistic prayers, produces a "dangerous memory" alternate to that of the powerful. Johann Baptist Metz writes that

> the dominion of God among us is revealed by this, that dominion of men over men has begun to be thrown down, that Jesus declared himself to be on the side of the invisible, the oppressed and exploited, and thus proclaimed the coming dominion of God as the liberating power of an unconditional love.[131]

William Cavanaugh has written extensively on this issue. He cites the example of religious opposition to torture in Chile, where Catholic bishops "issued a declaration of excommunication for anyone involved, directly or indirectly, in facilitating torture," and where a religious activist group would "appear in front of torture centers and government buildings, block traffic, pass out leaflets, and perform ritual actions denouncing torture." These actions, among many others, spoke truth to counter the lies of the Pinochet regime, and evoked the Body of Christ to stand in solidarity with those the government wanted to isolate and break.[132] For Cavanaugh, "the Church is the politics of Jesus," a community formed in the image of its Savior and challenging national divisions and "the politics of the world when it brings death instead of life." The communal nature of the church comes to fullest expression in rituals, especially the eucharist. To celebrate the eucharist in this light is a deeply political act that reenacts the fundamental solidarity of God with humanity and calls the church to live united within its own body. Moreover, it prods the church to live with love and compassion for the world outside its borders. In eucharistic liturgy, the church claims a hope and a reality that points beyond the death-dealing limits of the nation-state. In ritual, the church rehearses God's presence in all of life, including the public square, thus relativizing the nationalist ideologies which lay claim to our life, death, and ultimate loyalty.

At least, this is what the church should be doing. The truth, as Cavanaugh points out, is that the church has allowed its imagination to shrivel into a privatized faith with nothing to say to the "real" world. It is a measure of Christianity's ineffectiveness that its adherents continue to dwindle in the United States even as real freedom, equality, and peace are threatened by the ever-increasing violence of the American political imagination. If Christians cannot voice the radical alternative their faith presents to the seemingly obvious way things must be, why should anyone listen to us? Likewise, a religious left that prefers moral suasion of the powerful and easy reconciliation cheapened even further by a refusal to address real differences of power cannot hope to find traction in the public realm. Nor can it offer hope to "the invisible, the oppressed and exploited."

So it is that I want to close with what may seem like a strange response to torture. We know that authoritarians are generally socially intolerant, that authoritarianism runs very high among Biblical literalists, and that authoritarians—particularly evangelicals—are the strongest supporters of torture. We know, finally, that fear tends to activate authoritarianism, and to flatten distinctions between mild and strong authoritarians. As Jonathan Weiler and Marc J. Hetherington note,

> The same type of person who is attracted by the Republicans' position on "moral values" is also attracted to their position on terrorism. Both positions place a premium on order, strength, established norms and suspicion—if not outright hostility—toward those who are different. When Republicans talk about one, they might as well be talking about both. Reference to the social agenda and security issues tap into the same worldview, which is embodied by authoritarianism. The same can be said for flag burning and illegal immigration—two issues that trigger authoritarians' aversion to social dissensus and potential unruliness.[133]

Republicans tend to benefit from increasing fear, while Democrats do well when they can allay fears, say Weiler and Hetherington. More important for our purposes, the same holds true for torture policies. Torture is a practice of the frightened, not of those who are confident in their own position. Thus, a very effective response may be for religious progressives to proclaim the radical solidarity of God with the marginalized: dissenters, immigrants, religious and racial minorities, the poor, the handicapped, the mentally ill and challenged. Above all, women and sexual minorities, such as gays, lesbians, bisexuals, and transgendered persons, must be brought fully into the life of the church, because their difference has been for so long the fault line that divides the righteous from the stranger in the identity politics of the religious right.

By proclaiming Christ's liberation of all people, the religious left can call into question the degradation and dehumanization of the current reality. In the same way, that Christ paid the debt for all opens the possibility of a new and forgiven community based on mutual accountability, unafraid of equality and freed from the domination and violence that control our society. By facing into the storm surrounding sexual mores and putting a human face on those who are different—much more by meeting them as equals before God—the religious left can seek true reconciliation and at the same time defund the authoritarianism that sponsors torture. It can make real in present community the future hope of liberation from the control of fear and hate, and so defund the suspicion and hostility that drive torture.

It can, at long last, give up on the delusion that the powers of this world can make us safe and happy, and begin to steer the people of God into a life of trust and hope.

POSTSCRIPT

As Walter Brueggemann assures us, God cares very much about what happens to us in all aspects of our lives, public, private, and otherwise, refusing to remain silent about the social, economic, and political dimensions of human existence, scandalously taking sides in historical struggles. Moreover, God, who is free and sovereign in creation, is constantly at work, constantly on the move: to upset too-tidy human orders, break the chains of oppression, spark imagination, and call all his people into what John F. Haught calls God's "gracious, extravagant and surprising future."[1]

We catch glimpses of God at this work even in the political world. It matters very much to God what happens to pregnant women trapped by circumstance and the control of others. It matters to God what happens to millions of working people caught up in the bland, automatic oppression of consumerist capitalism. It matters to God what happens to prisoners of all sorts, especially the tortured and victims of abuse. We see consistent patterns of this elusive character God, as Brueggemann sometimes refers to him, taking the side of the poor and the powerless in all these issues and more. God is free, and wants his people to be free. God hears the cries of the people that otherwise go unheard, and expects those in power to do likewise.

Yet those who say with smooth confidence they know that "God want us to do this or that" are liars. The God who emerges from

Brueggemann's encounters with scripture is mercurial, restless, and undomesticated. In some ways, as Brueggemann tells it, the God of Exodus is paradigmatic. He is present to the Israelites each night in the pillar of fire that leads them forward, and he provides for them each morning in the manna and quail. Yet he baffles his people's desires for an easy, unthinking return to settlement. Until the Israelites learn to depend on him more than on Pharaoh, they remain wanderers in the desert.

God is likewise bound to frustrate those who would depend on him to provide a foundation for partisan agendas. He escapes human politics, even and especially those that claim to speak for the people of God. For that reason, we must be suspicious of politics that seek the moral renewal of the public realm. Though faithful people are certainly called to struggle with what is just and how to implement it, they always must be aware that God relativizes and works outside all our perspectives, liberal, conservative, or non-partisan. That is not a call to declare "a pox on both houses" in politics, however. Nor is it a call to a mush-mouthed centrism, nor again to eschew partisanship in favor of "God's politics." As Reinhold Niebuhr keenly understood, there is no higher morality available to humanity that allows us to lift ourselves out of conflicted interests, partiality, and the tendency to do wrong even as we seek the right. To put it another way, "you can't take the politics out of politics," even if you claim to represent God.

What I mean to suggest is that the Religious Left must forever be seekers, without being so arrogant as to assume they have found God's answers. To be true to our faith and our politics, we must continually question the assumptions that undergird the structures of social power. We must ask if controlling women's sexuality and denying them control of their reproductive future keeps them safe or happy? Or does it serve the interests of patriarchal power that claims to know better than women themselves what will be therapeutic for them? Can God lead us into a new way forward that preserves life (or potential life) while giving women hope and freedom? We must ask if an economy structured to make the rich richer while the vast majority sink into debt bondage makes anyone safe or happy? Or is there perhaps a new way forward that provides equity, opportunity and fair play without falling prey to the delusion that we can secure prosperity for ourselves without thought or effort? We must ask, finally, what safety we are promised in a military society. What does it mean that those promises lead to brutality and death in our name? How are we implicated in those promises, and how do our social structures sustain them beyond our awareness?

To take part in the counter to these scripts means not so much to accept a particular political agenda—though again there is no easy escape from politics—as it is to live with a sense of God leading us forward into new life. That requires imagination, a willingness to question all assumptions, even our own, and perhaps most difficult but most important, a sense of grateful dependence on God. For it is gratitude, more than anything else, that allows us to ask the questions, rather than provide the answers. Gratitude subverts the scripts that lay claim to our lives and our ultimate loyalties. When we affirm with glad thanksgiving what God has done for us and look with hope and trust to the future into which God leads us, we offer a powerful, if quiet, challenge to the scripts that dominate our lives.

In this light, even the simplest actions take on great significance. Brueggemann cites as an example "the observation of Mark Douglas that regular table prayers of thanksgiving are a primal way in which to challenge the market view of the supply and movement of valuable goods." I honestly believe that to be true. In giving thanks each day for the food we receive, and for all God's goodness, we proclaim our freedom from consumerism, militarism, therapy, and technology, and we call into question the failed promises they have made. In this way, we are slowly remade. The future we yearn for comes closer to being a reality in the present.

I want to conclude then with an embarrassingly simple suggestion. Why not begin (or continue) the journey of the Religious Left not with polls or positions but with a prayer? A common table grace may not mobilize "people of faith" to vote a certain way, nor does it have immediate policy implications. It does not even provide an obvious alternative to conservative religious perspectives. But to pray in this way engages in the most transformational politics of all. I often use some variation of this prayer at our house:

> Gracious God, loving Father (or Mystery):
>> You are our hope.
> We know that only you can keep us safe.
>> Only you can bring us joy.
> We give you thanks for all your gifts to us,
>> and we pray that you lead all people into your future
>> and fulfill the promise of your love for us.

This is how the scripts are countered: one small prayer at a time offered at one dinner table at a time. In this slow, difficult way that resists programs and agendas, we set ourselves on the open-ended journey toward "where God may yet lead us." We give voice to the questions that must be asked and so open ourselves to better possibilities, or so we hope. There is nothing perfect about it, but it is faithful, more or less. It is a way of walking with God. Only in that way can a movement that calls itself religious find and articulate the meaningful alternatives it has to offer to a nation starved of possibility and locked out of its own future.

ACKNOWLEDGMENTS

Every author has too many people to thank for kindness and assistance in the production of their writing. I want to mention in general all the people who helped me to get to this place, in particular my parents. For their help on this specific project, these people deserve thanks: Evan Derkacz and the staff at *Religion Dispatches*; Sara Posner, Frederick Clarkson and Peter Laarman, all of whom made suggestions, pointed to resources, and offered encouragement; Diane Von der Horst, who proofed the manuscript; Ig Publishing; and Walter Brueggemann, without whose ideas this book would not have been possible. I would also like to thank the readers of Street Prophets, where I developed many of the ideas found here, and the people of Salem United Church of Christ, Wayne Wiscomsin, for their generosity with my time.

NOTES

INTRODUCTION

1. Amy Sullivan, "The Good Fight," *Washington Monthly*, March 3, 2005, http://www.washingtonmonthly.com/features/2005/0503.sullivan.html.

2. Mike Lux, "Chicago Politics," OpenLeft, July 24, 2008, http://openleft.com/showDiary.do?diaryId=7121.

3. Charles Taylor, "Two Books, Oddly Yoked Together," Social Sciences Research Council's Immanent Frame blog, July 24, 2008, http://www.ssrc.org/blogs/immanent_frame/2008/01/24/two-books-oddly-yoked-together/.

4. Walter Brueggemann, "Counterscript: living with the elusive God," *The Christian Century*, November 29, 2005.

5. Eric Schneiderman, "Transforming the Liberal Checklist," *The Nation*, March 10, 2008, http://www.thenation.com/doc/20080310/schneiderman.

6. Nathan J. Russell, "An Introduction To the Overton Window of Political Possibilities," Mackinac Center for Public Policy, January 4, 2006, http://www.mackinac.org/article.aspx?ID=7504.

1. THE THERAPEUTIC SCRIPT: ABORTION

1. Stanley Hauerwas, "Abortion, Theologically Understood," Lifewatch, http://www.lifewatch.org/abortion.html.

2. NES and GSS data from John Sides, "Has the Public Become More Opposed to Abortion?" The Monkey Cage, May 16, 2009, http://www.themonkeycage.org/2009/05/has_the_public_become_more_opp.html.

3. The Pew Forum on Religion and Public Life, "A Slight but Steady Majority Favors Keeping Abortion Legal," September 16, 2008, http://pewforum.org/docs/?DocID=350.

4. Pew Forum, "Pragmatic Americans Liberal and Conservative on Social Issues," August 3, 2006, http://people-press.org/report/283/pragmatic-americans-liberal-and-conservative-on-social-issues.

5. Fabrizio McLaughlin & Associates, "The Elephant Looks In The Mir-

ror 10 Years Later: A Critical Look at Today's Grand Old Party," Survey of Republican voters conducted May 28-June 3, 2007; Jeffrey M. Jones, "GOP Losses Span Nearly All Demographic Groups," Gallup, May 18, 2009, http://www.gallup.com/poll/118528/gop-losses-span-nearly-demographic-groups.aspx.

6. Lydia Saad, "More Americans Pro-Life than Pro-Choice for the First Time," Gallup, May 15, 2009, http://www.gallup.com/poll/118399/More-Americans-Pro-Life-Than-Pro-Choice-First-Time.aspx.

7. Pew Forum, "Public Takes Conservative Turn on Gun Control, Abortion," April 30, 2009, http://people-press.org/report/513/public-takes-conservative-turn-on-gun-control-abortion.

8. Ed Kilgore, "More About the Unbearable Lightness of Abortion Polls," FiveThirtyEight, May 15, 2009, http://www.fivethirtyeight.com/2009/05/more-about-unbearable-lightness-of.html.

9. Chip Berlet and Frederick Clarkson, "Culture Wars, Evangelicals, and Political Power," *The Public Eye*, vol. 23, no. 4, Winter 2008, http://www.publiceye.org/magazine/v23n4/culture_war_2008.html; Pew Research Center, "A Look at Religious Voters in the 2008 Election," February 10, 2009, http://pewresearch.org/pubs/1112/religion-vote-2008-election.

10. Frederick Clarkson, "The Culture Wars Are Still Not Over," *The Public Eye*, vol. 23, no. 4, Winter 2008, http://www.publiceye.org/magazine/v23n4/the_culture_wars_are_still_not_over.html.

11. Randall Balmer, *Thy Kingdom Come*; George Packer, "The Fall of Conservatism," *The New Yorker*, May 26, 2008, http://www.newyorker.com/reporting/2008/05/26/080526fa_fact_packer.

12. National Abortion Federation, "NAF Violence and Disruption Statistics," available at http://www.prochoice.org/pubs_research/publications/downloads/about_abortion/violence_statistics.pdf.

13. Joe Battaglia, Randy Brinson, Dr. Robert P. Jones and Rachel Laser, "Come Let Us Reason Together: A Fresh Look at Shared Cultural Values between Progressives and Evangelicals," Third Way, October 2007, http://www.thirdway.org/subjects/27/publications/87.

14. Aspen Institute, "Religious Voices in Divisive Moral Debates: A Statement on Faithfulness, Dialogue and Common Ground," quoted in Deborah Haffner, "Ground We've Already Covered," RH Reality Check, June 17, 2009, ttp://rhrealitycheck.org/commonground/2009/06/17/ground-weve-already-covered.

15. "The America We Seek: A Statement of Pro-Life Principle and Concern," First Things, May 1996, quoted in Frederick Clarkson, "Where Did the Abortion Reduction Agenda Come From?" RH Reality Check, http://

www.rhrealitycheck.org/blog/2009/02/13/where-did-abortion-reduction-agenda-come-from.

16. Susan Brooks Thistlethwaite, "Who Are You Calling A Religious Centrist?" On Faith, *Washington Post*, April 2, 2009, http://newsweek.washingtonpost.com/onfaith/panelists/susan_brooks_thistlethwaite/2009/04/who_are_you_calling_a_relgious_centrist.html.

17. John Gehring and Simone Campbell, "What Makes Liberals and Conservatives Angry? Abortion Reduction," God's Politics Blog, March 25, 2009, http://blog.sojo.net/2009/03/25/what-makes-liberals-and-conservatives-angry-abortion-reduction/.

18. Michelle Goldberg, *The Means Of Reproduction: Sex, Power, and the Future of the World*, (New York, Penguin Group (USA), 2009).

19. Jim Wallis, "Response to Readers," God's Politics Blog, August 2008, http://blog.beliefnet.com/godspolitics/2008/08/response-to-readers-by-jim-wal.html.

20. Galatians 3:28-4:7.

21. Robin Toner, "Abortion Foes See Validation for New Tactic," *New York Times*, May 22, 2007, http://www.nytimes.com/2007/05/22/washington/22abortion.html.

22. Jill Filopivic, "Because respecting women means making all their decisions for them," Feministe, May 21, 2007, http://www.feministe.us/blog/archives/2007/05/21/because-respecting-women-means-making-all-their-decisions-for-them/.

23. Jill Filopivic, "We know what's best for you," Brilliant at Breakfast, May 2007, http://brilliantatbreakfast.blogspot.com/2007/05/we-know-whats-best-for-you.html.

24. Robin Toner, "Abortion Foes See Validation for New Tactic," *New York Times*, May 22, 2007, http://www.nytimes.com/2007/05/22/washington/22abortion.html.

25. Reva Siegel and Sarah Blustain, "Mommy Dearest?" *American Prospect*, September 17, 2006, http://www.prospect.org/cs/articles?articleId=12011.

26. *Associated Press,* "South Dakota governor signs abortion ban," March 7, 2006.

27. Ballotpedia, "2008 ballot measure election results," http://ballotpedia.org/wiki/index.php/2008_ballot_measure_election_results#South_Dakota

28. Zita Lazzarini, "South Dakota's Abortion Script — Threatening the Physician–Patient Relationship," *New England Journal of Medicine*, November 20, 2008, summarizing South Dakota Codified Laws 34-23A-10.1.

29. Scott Lemieux, "Why the 'Golden Mean' Position on Abortion is Unreasonable," Lawyers, Guns and Money, February 2006, http://lefarkins.

blogspot.com/2006/02/why-golden-mean-position-on-abortion.html.

30. Ross Douthat, "Not All Abortions Are Equal," *New York Times*, June 8, 2009, http://www.nytimes.com/2009/06/09/opinion/09douthat.html, cited in Jodi Jacobson, "Note to Women: Don't Think! Ross Douthat Is Here to Do It For You" RH Reality Check http://www.rhrealitycheck.org/blog/2009/06/09/note-women-dont-think-ross-douthat-will-do-it-for-you.

31. Real Abortion Solutions, http://www.realabortionsolutions.org/inspiration/ See, for example, David Gushee, Samuel Rodriguez, and Jim Wallis, among others.

32. Catholics United, "Republicans Embrace Failed Abortion Policies," e-mail Press Release, September 2, 2008.

33. Guttmacher Institute, "An Overview of Abortion in the United States," http://www.guttmacher.org/presentations/ab_slides.html, cited in Jodi Jacobson, "Looking for Common Ground on Abortion? You're Standing On It," RH Reality Check, March 18, 2009, http://www.rhrealitycheck.org/blog/2009/03/18/looking-common-ground-abortion-youre-standing-on-it.

34. Third Way, "Reducing the Need for Abortion and Supporting Parents Act: A Summary" http://www.docstoc.com/docs/10218758/MM-Template.

35. Digby (Heather Parton), "Pragmatic Princples," Hullabaloo, April 12, 2009, http://digbysblog.blogspot.com/2009/04/pragmatic-princples-by-digby-greenwald.html.

36. Pew Forum, "How The Faithful Voted," November 10, 2008, http://pewforum.org/docs/?DocID=367.

37. tmatt (Terry Mattingly), "Obama, Democrats and young evangelicals" GetReligion, July 1, 2007, http://www.getreligion.org/?p=2515.

38. Dan Gilgoff, "Ralph Reed Launches New Values Group: 'Not Your Daddy's Christian Coalition'" God & Country Blog, June 23, 2009, http://www.usnews.com/blogs/god-and-country/2009/06/23/exclusive-ralph-reed-launches-new-values-group-not-your-daddys-christian-coalition.html.

39. Pew Forum "A Religious Portrait of African-Americans" January 30, 2009, http://pewforum.org/docs/?DocID=389; see also Pew Forum and Pew Hispanic Project, "Changing Faiths: Latinos and the Transformation of American Religion," April 25, 2007 , http://pewforum.org/surveys/hispanic/.

40. Damon Linker, "How to End the Culture War" The New Republic blog, January 29, 2009, https://www.tnr.com/blog/damon-linker/how-end-the-culture-war; Fred Clarkson, "The Culture Wars Are Still Not Over",

Public Eye Magazine, Winter 2008, Vol. 23, No. 4.

41. Laurie Goodstein, "For a Trusty Voting Bloc, a Faith Shaken," *New York Times,* October 7, 2007.

42. Bob Unruh, "Dobson says 'no way' to McCain candidacy" World Net Daily, January 13, 2007, http://www.worldnetdaily.com/news/article. asp?ARTICLE_ID=53743.

43. Tara Wall, "Commentary: Why VP choice is crucial for values voters," CNN, August 22, 2008, http://www.cnn.com/2008/POLITICS/08/22/ wall.faith/index.html.

44. pastordan (Daniel Schultz), "Did John McCain Choose Palin?" Street Prophets, September 2, 2008, http://www.streetprophets.com/story/2008/9/2/122125/6878.

45. *Associated Press,* "Man who ousted Senate leader was supported by churches and activists," May 28, 2006, http://chestertontribune.com/ Politics%20and%20Elections/man_who_ousted_senate_leader_was.htm; *Associated Press,* "Political confrontation in Buffalo church for NY lawmaker," January 24, 2007, http://www.disciplesworld.com/newsArticle. html?wsnID=10732.

46. Jennifer Mesko, "Dr. Dobson: 'I'm Struggling over the Path the Nation Has Taken,'" CitizenLink, November 6, 2008, http://www.citizenlink. org/content/A000008622.cfm.

47. Michelle Vu, "Rick Warren: Obama not clear enough on abortion," *Christian Post,* August 19, 2008, http://www.christiantoday.com/article/ rick.warren.obama.not.clear.enough.on.abortion/21251.htm.

48. Paul Raushenbush, "What Rick Warren Should Ask Obama & McCain On Abortion," Progressive Revival, August 4, 2008, http://blog.beliefnet.com/progressiverevival/2008/08/what-rick-warren-should-obama. html.

48. Dana Goldstein, "Women's Issues And The Democratic Platform," Tapped: The Group Blog of American Prospect, August 12, 2008, http://www. prospect.org/csnc/blogs/tapped_archive?month=08&year=2008&base_ name=draft_womens_issues_in_dem_pla.

50. Robert Novak, "A Pro-Choicer's Dream Veep," *Washington Post,* May 26, 2008, http://www.washingtonpost.com/wp-dyn/content/article/2008/05/25/AR2008052502275.html.

51. Adelle Banks, "Biden provides Catholic link, but renews abortion debate," *Religion News Service,* August 25, 2008, http://www.usatoday.com/ news/religion/2008-08-25-catholic-biden_N.htm.

52. Amy Sullivan, *The Party Faithful: How and Why Democrats Are Closing the God Gap* (New York: Scribner, 2008), p.78ff.

53. Jamison Foser, "The Hill peddles Bob Casey convention myth," Media Matters, January 6, 2009, http://mediamatters.org/blog/200901060002.

54. Robert Casey, "A New American Compact: Caring about Women, Caring for the Unborn" found at Catholic Online, http://www.catholic.org/printer_friendly.php?id=28241&section=Cathcom.

55. Jamison Foser, "The Hill peddles Bob Casey convention myth."

56. Robert Casey, "A New American Compact: Caring about Women, Caring for the Unborn."

57. digby (Heather Parton), "Two Front War," Hullabaloo, August 22, 2008, http://digbysblog.blogspot.com/2008/08/two-front-war-by-digby-as-anyone-who.html.

58. Dan Gilgoff, "God & Country: As White House Readies Abortion Plan, Packaging Emerges as Major Issue," U.S. News & World Report, June 29, 2009, http://www.usnews.com/blogs/god-and-country/2009/06/29/as-white-house-readies-abortion-plan-packaging-emerges-as-major-issue.html.

59. Dan Gilgoff, "God & Country: White House Discerns 'Need for Abortion,' But Some Disagree," U.S. News & World Report, June 30, 2009, http://www.usnews.com/blogs/god-and-country/2009/06/30/white-house-discerns-need-for-abortion-but-some-disagree.html.

60. Ed Pilkington and Matthew Weaver, "Man charged with murder of 'late-term' abortion doctor in US," Guardian UK, June 1, 2009, http://www.guardian.co.uk/world/2009/jun/01/us-abortion-doctor-shooting-murder.

61. citizenlink.com, "Pro-Life Leaders: Murder is Always Wrong," June 1, 2009, http://www.citizenlink.org/content/A000010144.cfm.

62. Jaura Bauer, and Judy L. Thomas, "Operation Rescue adviser helped Tiller suspect track doctor's court dates," Kansas City Star, June 3, 2009.

63. Daniel Starling, "Operation Rescue: Terrorizing Kansans since 1991," KCTribune, June 5, 2009, http://kctribune.com/article/KC_News_Features/Daniel_Starling/Operation_Rescue_Terrorizing_Kansans_since_1991/18879.

64. Jill Filipovic, "Who killed George Tiller?" Guardian UK, June 1, 2009, http://www.guardian.co.uk/commentisfree/cifamerica/2009/jun/01/george-tiller-abortion-doctor-murder.

65. Randall Terry, "George Tiller was a Mass-Murderer, says Randall Terry—We Grieve That he Did Not Have Time to Properly Prepare his Soul to Face God," Press Release, May 31, 2009, http://www.christian-newswire.com/news/8967610531.html.

66. Joe Rodriguez, Tim Potter and Stan Finger, "Suspect in shooting death of abortion provider George Tiller may be charged today," Wichita

Eagle, June 1, 2009, http://www.kansas.com/2009/06/01/834444/suspect-in-shooting-death-of-abortion.html.

67. Dan Gilgoff, "Rick Warren on His Saddleback Summit with McCain and Obama," BeliefNet, http://www.beliefnet.com/News/Politics/2008/08/Rick-Warren-On-His-Saddleback-Summit-With-Mccain-And-Obama. aspx.

68. Media Matters, "O'Reilly hosts Coulter to discuss the "reaction" of "the left-wing media" to "our reporting" on Tiller," June 22, 2009, http://mediamatters.org/mmtv/200906220035.

69. Gabriel Winant, "O'Reilly's campaign against murdered doctor," *Salon,* May 31, 2009, http://www.salon.com/news/feature/2009/05/31/tiller/.

70. *Washington Post,* "Tucker Carlson and Ana Marie Cox: Abortion, Affirmative Action, More," May 29, 2009, http://www.washingtonpost.com/wp-dyn/content/discussion/2009/05/29/DI2009052902325.html.

71. Robert W. Finn, "Kansas City Bishop to pro-lifers: 'We are at war!'" *National Catholic Reporter,* April 28, 2009, http://ncronline.org/news/faith-parish/kansas-city-bishop-pro-lifers-we-are-war?page=1.

72. Thomas Frank, "Red State Story: How a murder fed conspiracy theories about the liberal media," *Wall Street Journal,* June 10, 2008, http://online.wsj.com/article/SB124459106205300065.html.

73. John Buchanan, "Pro-choice perspective," *The Christian Century,* June 30 2009, http://www.christiancentury.org/article.lasso?id=7229.

74. Faith in Public Life, "Faith leaders condemn murder of Dr. George Tiller, call for common ground...," June 3, 2009, http://faithinpubliclife.org/content/feature/faith_leaders_condemn_murder_o.html.

75. Tim Rutten, "The choice on abortion: rhetorical recklessness or civil expression," *Los Angeles Times,* June 3, 2009, http://articles.latimes.com/2009/jun/03/opinion/oe-rutten3.

76. Bill Berkowitz, "Hate Speech Leads to Violence: In Wake of Abortion Doc Murder, Religious Leaders Skirt the Issue," *Religion Dispatches,* June 2, 2009, http://www.religiondispatches.org/blog/sexandgender/1520/hate_speech_leads_to_violence%3A_in_wake_of_abortion_doc_murder%2C_religious_leaders_skirt_the_issue.

77. Barb Shelley, "Operation Rescue turns its sights on Nebraska abortion doctor," Midwest Voices, June 27, 2009, http://voices.kansascity.com/node/4961.

78. Hunter (Michael Lazzaro), "Tiller Suspect Known By Friends as Believer in "Justifiable" Murder of Doctors," Daily Kos, May 31, 2009, http://www.dailykos.com/story/2009/6/1/737417/-Tiller-Suspect-Known-By-Friends-as-Believer-in-Justifiable-Murder-of-Doctors.

79. Think Progress, "DHS Report: After Obama's Election, Right-Wing Extremists 'May Be Gaining New Recruits,'" April 14, 2009, http://thinkprogress.org/2009/04/14/dhs-report-right-wing/.

80. Peter Wallsten and Robin Abcarian, "Doctor's slaying a setback for common ground on abortion," *Los Angeles Times*, June 3, 2009, http://articles.latimes.com/2009/jun/03/nation/na-tiller3.

81. Brueggemann, "Counterscript: living with the elusive God."

82. Christian Smith with Melinda Lundquist Denton, *Soul Searching: The Religious and Spiritual Lives of American Teenagers*, (New York: Oxford University Press, 2005).

83. Hauerwas, "Abortion, Theologically Considered".

84. First Things, "The America We Seek: A Statement of Pro-Life Principle and Concern," May 1996, http://www.firstthings.com/article/2007/10/005-the-america-we-seek-a-statement-of-pro-life-principle-and-concern-16.

85. Russell Shorto, "Contra-Contraception," *New York Times*, May 7, 2006, http://www.nytimes.com/2006/05/07/magazine/07contraception.html.

86. Jacob Alperin-Sheriff, "New Evidence: Palin Had Direct Role In Charging Rape Victims For Exams" Huffington Post, September 11, 2008, http://www.huffingtonpost.com/jacob-alperinsheriff/sarah-palin-instituted-ra_b_125833.html.

87. Dante Atkins, "WHY would Palin refuse to fund rape kits? Here's your answer," Daily Kos, September 17, 2008, http://www.dailykos.com/story/2008/9/17/175430/636/888/601186.

88. President George W. Bush Receives 'International Medal Of Peace' That Coincides With Pepfar Milestone On World Aids Day Press release, Rick Warren News, December 1, 2008, http://www.rickwarrennews.com/081201_forum.htm.

89. David Savage, "Broader medical refusal rule may go far beyond abortion," *Los Angeles Times*, December 2, 2008, http://articles.latimes.com/2008/dec/02/nation/na-conscience2.

90. Noam Levey, "Obama administration may rescind 'conscience rule'" *Chicago Tribune*, February 9, 2009, http://www.chicagotribune.com/news/politics/obama/chi-conscience-rulefeb27,0,1515759.story.

91. David Brody, "Obama and the Abortion Conscience Clause," The Brody File: CBN News, http://blogs.cbn.com/thebrodyfile/archive/2009/02/27/obama-and-the-abortion-conscience-clause.aspx.

92. Jacqueline L. Salmon, "Obama Reaches Out Before Vatican Trip," *Washington Post*, July 3, 2009, http://www.washingtonpost.com/wp-dyn/content/article/2009/07/02/AR2009070202451.html.

93. James Dobson, *Emotions: Can You Trust Them?* (Wheaton, IL: Tyndale House Publishers, 1992), p. 68 and *When God Doesn't Make Sense* (Wheaton, IL: Tyndale House Publishers, 1993) p. 184-185, cited in Albert J. Menendez, "The world of James Dobson," *Public Eye*, August 1996 http://www.publiceye.org/ifas/fw/9608/dobson.html.

94. John D'Emilio, and Estelle B. Freedman, *Intimate Matters: A History Of Sexuality In America,* 2nd ed. (Chicago: University Of Chicago Press, 1998), p. 140.

95. For warnings against pharmakeia, see Galatians 5:20, Revelation 9:21, 18:23, 21:8, 22:15.

96. Brueggemann, "Counterscript: living with the elusive God."

97. Hauerwas, "Abortion, Theologically Considered."

98. Marc Kaufman, "Unwanted Pregnancies Rise for Poor Women," *Washington Post,* May 5, 2006.

99. David Gushee, "Should Sex Be Sacred?" RH Reality Check, June 16, 2009, http://www.rhrealitycheck.org/blog/2009/06/16/should-sex-be-sacred.

100. Religious Institute on Sexual Morality, Justice, and Healing, "Open Letter To Religious Leaders About Sex Education," 2002, http://www.religiousinstitute.org/sites/default/files/open_letters/sexeduopenletter.pdf.

101. "Religious school grads likelier to have abortions," LiveScience.com, June 1, 2009, http://www.msnbc.msn.com/id/31048153/.

102. Roberta W. Francis, "The History Behind the Equal Rights Amendment," The Equal Rights Amendment, http://www.equalrightsamendment.org/era.htm.

103. The Phyllis Schlafly Report, "A Short History of E.R.A.," http://www.eagleforum.org/psr/1986/sept86/psrsep86.html.

104. Juliet Eilperin, "New Drive Afoot to Pass Equal Rights Amendment," *Washington Post*, March 27, 2007, http://www.washingtonpost.com/wp-dyn/content/article/2007/03/27/AR2007032702357_pf.html.

2. A BRIEF HISTORY OF "BIG SHITPILE"

1. David Segal, "Windfalls for Bankers, Resentments for the Rest," *New York Times*, July 19, 2009, http://www.nytimes.com/2009/07/19/weekinreview/19segal.html.

2. Thomas Geoghegan, "Infinite Debt: How unlimited interest rates destroyed the economy," *Harper's Magazine*, April 2009, http://www.harpers.org/archive/2009/04/0082450.

3. Taft-Hartley Act, http://vi.uh.edu/pages/buzzmat/tafthartley.html.

4. Sam Hananel, "Union membership rises for a second year," *Associ-*

ated Press/USA Today January 29, 2009, http://www.usatoday.com/money/workplace/2009-01-28-union-membership_N.htm.

5. Don Monkerud, "Wealth Inequality Destroys US Ideals," *Consortium News*, July 4, 2009, http://www.consortiumnews.com/2009/070409a.html.

6. Fred Clark, "Printing the legend," Slacktivist, August 20, 2009 http://slacktivist.typepad.com/slacktivist/2009/08/print-the-legend.html.

7. Jeff Faux, Carlos Salas and Robert E. Scott, "Revisiting NAFTA: Still not working for North America's workers," Economic Policy Institute Briefing Paper #173, September 2006, http://www.epi.org/publications/entry/bp173

8. John Fritze, "Average family health insurance policy: $13,375, up 5%," *USAToday*, September 15, 2009, http://www.usatoday.com/money/industries/health/2009-09-15-insurance-costs_N.htm

9. Lawrence Mishel, Jared Bernstein and Heidi Shierholz, "Economic Policy Institute presents...The State of Working America 2008/2009," http://www.stateofworkingamerica.org/

10. Robert Kuttner, "Testimony before the US House Financial Services Committee," October 2, 2007, reprinted as "1929 Redux: Heading for a Crash?", *AlterNet* October 8, 2007, http://www.alternet.org/economy/64684/

11. FDIC, "The S&L Crisis: A Chrono-Bibliography," http://www.fdic.gov/bank/historical/s&l/.

12. Pro Publica, "What Happens After a U.S. Gov't Bailout?" September 25, 2008, http://www.propublica.org/special/bailout-aftermaths.13. *Houston Chronicle*, "The Fall of Enron: Timeline," January 17, 2002, http://www.chron.com/news/specials/enron/timeline.html.

14. PBS Online, "Accounting Lessons," *Frontline*: Bigger Than Enron, http://www.pbs.org/wgbh/pages/frontline/shows/regulation/lessons/.

15. Paul M. Healy and Krishna G. Palepu, "The Fall of Enron," *Journal of Economic Perspectives* 17, Spring 2003, http://www-personal.umich.edu/~kathrynd/JEP.FallofEnron.pdf.

16. Dennis Moberg and Edward Romar, "WorldCom," Santa Clara University Markkula Center For Applied Ethics, http://www.scu.edu/ethics/dialogue/candc/cases/worldcom.html.

17. Christopher Tkaczyk, "The 10 largest U.S. Bankruptcies," *Fortune Magazine*, May 20, 2009, http://money.cnn.com/galleries/2009/fortune/0905/gallery.largest_bankruptcies.fortune/index.html.

18. Luisa Beltran, "WorldCom files largest bankruptcy ever," CNN/Money, July 22, 2002, http://money.cnn.com/2002/07/19/news/worldcom_bankruptcy/.

19. Office of the New York State Comptroller Alan Helvesi, "Arthur Andersen, Final WorldCom Defendant, Settles," Press Release, April 26, 2005, http://www.osc.state.ny.us/press/releases/apr05/042605.htm.

20. *Arthur Andersen LLP V. United States* (04-368) 544 U.S. 696 (2005), Cornell University Legal Information Institute, http://www.law.cornell.edu/supct/html/04-368.ZS.html.

21. Shahien Nasiripour, "Obama Administration Helps House Democrat Gut Post-Enron Reforms," Huffington Post, November 3, 2009, http://www.huffingtonpost.com/2009/11/03/obama-administration-help_n_344042.html.

22. BBC News, "Andersen guilty in Enron case," June 15, 2002, http://news.bbc.co.uk/2/hi/business/2047122.stm.

23. Yuki Noguchi, "MCI Calls Qwest's Latest Bid 'Superior'," *Washington Post*, April 24, 2005, http://www.washingtonpost.com/wp-dyn/articles/A11647-2005Apr23.html.

24. Ken Belson, "WorldCom's Audacious Failure and Its Toll on an Industry," *New York Times*, January 18, 2005, http://www.nytimes.com/2005/01/18/business/18ebbers.html.

25. CNN/Money, "Enron cuts jobs in Europe," November 30, 2001, http://money.cnn.com/2001/11/30/companies/enron/.

26. Carrie Johnson, "Stock Sale by Lay's Wife Investigated," *Washington Post*, November 18, 2001, http://www.washingtonpost.com/wp-dyn/articles/A58825-2004Nov17.html.

27. Simon Johnson, "The Quiet Coup," *Atlantic Monthly*, May 2009, http://www.theatlantic.com/magazine/archive/2009/05/the-quiet-coup/7364/.

28. Jacob S. Hacker, *The Great Risk Shift: The Assault on American Jobs, Families, Health Care and Retirement (And How You Can Fight Back)* (New York: Oxford University Press, 2006).

29. PBS Online, "Accounting Lessons."

30. Greider, William, "Deflation," *The Nation*, June 12, 2003, http://www.thenation.com/doc/20030630/greider.

31. Dean Baker, "The Run-Up in Home Prices: Is it Real or Is it Another Bubble?" Center For Economic And Policy Research, http://www.cepr.net/documents/publications/housing_2002_08.pdf.

32. Les Christie, "Subprime lenders push back," CNNMoney.com, March 22, 2007, http://money.cnn.com/2007/03/22/real_estate/subprime_lenders_deny_responsibility/index.htm.

33. Michael Gimein, "Inside the Liar's Loan," *Slate*, April 24, 2008, http://www.slate.com/id/2189576/.

34. Paul Rosenberg, "Who Could Have Foreseen The Housing Bubble Collapse? Dean Baker, That's Who--In 2002" OpenLeft, August 29, 2009, http://www.openleft.com/diary/14839/who-could-have-foreseen-the-housing-bubble-collapse-dean-baker-thats-whoin-2002.

35. Michael LaCour-Little and Jing Yang, "Taking the Lie out of Liar Loans," Federal Housing Finance Agency, http://www.fhfa.gov/webfiles/15048/website_lacour.pdf.

36. Peter Goodman, "Lucrative Fees May Deter Efforts to Alter Loans," *New York Times*, July 29, 2009, http://www.nytimes.com/2009/07/30/business/30services.html.

37. Consumer Affairs, "Countrywide Settles Predatory Lending Charges for $8.68 Billion," October 6, 2008, http://www.consumeraffairs.com/news04/2008/10/countrywide_settlement.html.

38. Gretchen Morgenson, "Inside the Countrywide Lending Spree," *New York Times*, August 26, 2007, http://www.nytimes.com/2007/08/26/business/yourmoney/26country.html.

39. BBC, "Timeline: Credit crunch to downturn," August 7, 2009, http://news.bbc.co.uk/2/hi/7521250.stm.

40. ProPublica, "History of U.S. Gov't Bailouts," http://www.propublica.org/special/government-bailouts.

41. Chris Dolmetsch, "Subprime Collapse to Global Financial Meltdown: Timeline," *Bloomberg.com*, October 13, 2008 , http://www.bloomberg.com/apps/news?pid=20601208&sid=aleqkSjAAw10.

42. *Associated Press*, "Foreclosures now affect 1 in 8 U.S. Homeowners," March 6, 2009, http://www.allbusiness.com/government/government-bodies-offices-legislative/11959368-1.html.

43. Robert Murray, "New Construction Starts in December Retreat 5%; Annual Total for 2008 Slides 15% to $543 Billion," Construction.com, January 21, 2008, http://construction.com/ResourceCenter/forecast/2008/Jan.asp.

44. Bureau of Labor Statistics, "Employment Situation News Release," October 2, 2009.

45. Bureau of Labor Statistics, "Table A-12. Alternative measures of labor underutilization," October 2, 2009.

46. "Legislative Proposal For Treasury Authority To Purchase Mortgage-Related Assets," *Washington Post*, September 2, 2008, http://www.washingtonpost.com/wp-dyn/content/article/2008/09/20/AR2008092002376.html.

47. Paul Krugman, "Bailout questions answered," *New York Times*, September 29, 2008, http://krugman.blogs.nytimes.com/2008/09/29/bailout-

questions-answered/.

48. Nouriel Roubini, "Is Purchasing $700 billion of Toxic Assets the Best Way to Recapitalize the Financial System? No! It is Rather a Disgrace and Rip-Off Benefitting only the Shareholders and Unsecured Creditors of Banks," Nouriel Roubini's EconoMonitor, http://www.rgemonitor.com/roubini-monitor/253783/is_purchasing_700_billion_of_toxic_assets_the_best_way_to_recapitalize_the_financial_system_no_it_is_rather_a_disgrace_and_rip-off_benefitting_only_the_shareholders_and_unsecured_creditors_of_banks.

49. Nomi Prins, "Why the Bailout Sells America Short," *Mother Jones*, September 29, 2008, http://www.motherjones.com/politics/2008/09/why-bailout-sells-america-short.

50. Paul Kiel, "Prospects for Big-Bailout-Rural-School-Aid-Mental-Illness Bill Seem Good," Pro Publica, October 2, 2008, http://www.propublica.org/article/prospects-for-big-bailout-rural-school-aid-mental-illness-bill-seem-good-10.

51. Paul Krugman, "The good, the bad, and the ugly," *New York Times*, September 28, 2008, http://krugman.blogs.nytimes.com/2008/09/28/the-good-the-bad-and-the-ugly/.

52. US Department of the Treasury, "Statement by Secretary Henry M. Paulson, Jr. on Capital Purchase Program," October 20, 2008, http://www.ustreas.gov/press/releases/hp1223.htm.

53. Paul Kiel, "Paulson Scraps Original Bailout Plan," Pro Publica, November 12, 2008, http://www.propublica.org/article/paulson-scraps-original-bailout-plan-1112.

54. David Cho, "A Multi-Pronged Bank Plan," *Washington Post*, January 31, 2009, http://www.washingtonpost.com/wp-dyn/content/article/2009/01/30/AR2009013003742.html.

55. Paul Kiel, "Senate Votes to Release Bailout Money," Pro Publica, January 15, 2009, http://www.propublica.org/article/senate-votes-to-release-bailout-money-090115.

56. Timothy Geithner, "Remarks Introducing the Financial Stability Plan," February 10, 2009, http://www.cfr.org/publication/18514/remarks_by_treasury_secretary_timothy_geithner_introducing_the_financial_stability_plan.html.

57. billmon (Bill Monroe), "Chocolate Covered Cotton," Daily Kos, February 19, 2009, http://www.dailykos.com/storyonly/2009/2/19/05524/5446/499/699191.

58. Paul Krugman, "The Big Dither," *New York Times*, March 5, 2009, http://www.nytimes.com/2009/03/06/opinion/06krugman.html.

59. Kevin G. Hall, "Toxic Assets Plan, Take 2: Will Geithner get it right this time?" *McClatchy Newspapers*, March 22, 2009, http://www.mcclatchy-dc.com/homepage/v-print/story/64565.html.

60. "Visconti," "Timothy Geithner Press Briefing – PPIP – Toxic Asset Bailout," March 23, 2009, All That Natters, http://allthatnatters.com/2009/03/23/transcript-timothy-geithner-press-briefing-pipp-toxic-asset-bailout-march-23/.

61. Binyamin Applebaum and David Cho, "U.S. Seeks Expanded Power to Seize Firms," *Washington Post*, March 24, 2009, http://www.washington-post.com/wp-dyn/content/article/2009/03/23/AR2009032302830.html.

62. Joseph E. Stieglitz, "Obama's Ersatz Capitalism," *New York Times*, March 31, 2009, http://www.nytimes.com/2009/04/01/opinion/01stiglitz.html.

63. Sam Stein, "Geithner's Leaked Talking Points: In The Private Investor We Trust," Huffington Post, March 23, 2009, http://www.huffington-post.com/2009/03/23/geithners-leaked-talking_n_178074.html.

64. Pro Publica, "Bailout Timeline: Another Day, Another Bailout," http://bailout.propublica.org/main/timeline/index.

65. Deal Book blog, "Program to Buy Bad Assets Nearly in Place, U.S. Says," *New York Times*, October 5, 2009, http://dealbook.blogs.nytimes.com/2009/10/05/program-to-buy-bad-assets-nearly-in-place-us-says/.

66. Andy Kroll, "The Greatest Swindle Ever Sold," Tom Dispatch, May 26, 2009, http://www.tomdispatch.com/post/175075.

67. Matt Taibbi, "The Big Takeover," *Rolling Stone*, March 19, 2009, http://www.rollingstone.com/politics/story/26793903/the_big_takeover/print.

68. Bill Moyers, *Bill Moyers' Journal*, PBS, October 9, 2009, http://www.pbs.org/moyers/journal/10092009/transcript4.html.

69. Project Censored, "US Congress Sells Out to Wall Street," http://www.projectcensored.org/top-stories/articles/1-us-congress-sells-out-to-wall-street-sources/.

70. Mark Pittman and Bob Ivry, "Financial Rescue Nears GDP as Pledges Top $12.8 Trillion," *Bloomberg.com*, March 31, 2009, http://www.bloomberg.com/apps/news?pid=20601087&sid=armOzfkwtCA4.

71. Matt Taibbi, "The Big Takeover."

72. Kevin G. Hall, "How Moody's sold its ratings - and sold out investors," *McClatchy Newspapers*, October 18, 2009, http://www.mcclatchydc.com/2009/10/18/77244/how-moodys-sold-its-ratings-and.html.

73. Julie Creswell and Ben White, "The Guys From 'Government Sachs'", *New York Times*, October 19, 2008, http://www.nytimes.com/2008/10/19/

business/19gold.html.

74. Michael McKee and Matthew Benjamin, "Stiglitz Says Ties to Wall Street Doom Bank Rescue," *Bloomberg.com*, April 17, 2009, http://www.bloomberg.com/apps/news?pid=20601087&sid=afYsmJyngAXQ.

75. Eliot Spitzer, "Fed Dread," *Slate*, May 6, 2009, http://www.slate.com/id/2217811/.

76. Matt Taibbi, "The Big Takeover."

77. Joseph Stiglitz, "Capitalist Fools," *Vanity Fair*, January 2009, http://www.vanityfair.com/magazine/2009/01/stiglitz200901.

78. Matt Taibbi, "The Big Takeover."

79. Michael Kranish, "Now-needy FDIC collected little in premiums," *Boston Globe*, March 11, 2009, http://www.boston.com/news/nation/washington/articles/2009/03/11/now_needy_fdic_collected_little_in_premiums/.

80. Binyamin Applebaum, "As Subprime Lending Crisis Unfolded, Watchdog Fed Didn't Bother Barking," *Washington Post*, September 27, 2009, http://www.washingtonpost.com/wp-dyn/content/article/2009/09/26/AR2009092602706.html.

81. Joseph Stiglitz, "Capitalist Fools."

82. William Greider, "Obama's False Financial Reform," *The Nation*, June 19, 2009, http://www.thenation.com/doc/20090706/greider2.

83. Project Censored, "Bailed out Banks and America's Wealthiest Cheat IRS Out of Billions," http://www.projectcensored.org/top-stories/articles/8-bailed-out-banks-and-americas-wealthiest-cheat-irs-out-of-billions1/.

84. Matt Taibbi, "The Big Takeover."

85. Matt Taibbi, "The Big Takeover."

86. Kevin Drum, "Wall Street's Latest Trick," *Mother Jones*, September 30, 2009, http://motherjones.com/kevin-drum/2009/09/wall-streets-latest-trick; Jenny Anderson, "Wall Street Pursues Profit in Bundles of Life Insurance," *New York Times*, September 5, 2009, http://www.nytimes.com/2009/09/06/business/06insurance.html.

87. Paul Krugman, "How Did Economists Get It So Wrong?", *New York Times Magazine*, September 2, 2009, http://www.nytimes.com/2009/09/06/magazine/06Economic-t.html.

88. Mark Decambre, "'Damage' control: Goldman chief drowning in record $16B bonus pool," *New York Daily News*, September 24, 2009, http://www.nypost.com/p/news/business/damage_control_wMcWJrGnm5en-lZYGHnwULI.

89. David Cho and Brady Dennis, "Officials Knew of AIG Bonuses Months

Before Firestorm," *Washington Post*, May 13, 2009, http://www.washington-post.com/wp-dyn/content/article/2009/05/12/AR2009051203624.html.

90. *Reuters*, "AIG London Execs: Returning Bonuses Is Blackmail," March 26, 2009.

91.Jake DeSantis, "Dear A.I.G., I Quit!", *New York Times*, March 24, 2009, http://www.nytimes.com/2009/03/25/opinion/25desantis.html

92. Binyamin Applebaum, "Bailout Overseer Says Banks Misused TARP Funds," *Washington Post*, March 20, 2009, http://www.washingtonpost.com/wp-dyn/content/article/2009/07/19/AR2009071901770.html.

93. Project Censored, "Recession Causes States to Cut Welfare," http://www.projectcensored.org/top-stories/articles/21-recession-causes-states-to-cut-welfare/.

94. Marcy Kaptur, interview by Bill Moyers, *Bill Moyers' Journal*, PBS, October 9, 2009, http://www.pbs.org/moyers/journal/10092009/transcript4.html

3. THE CONSUMERIST AND TECHNOLOGICAL SCRIPTS

1. Walter Brueggemann, "Counterscript: Living with the elusive God."

2. Slavoj Zizek, "The Spectre Is Still Roaming Around!," Arkzin: Zagreb, 1998.

3. Walter Brueggemann, *The Prophetic Imagination*, 2nd ed. (Minneapolis, MN: Fortress Press, 2001), 3.

4. Walter Brueggemann, *The Prophetic Imagination*, 7.

5. Exodus 2:24.

6. Walter Brueggemann, *The Prophetic Imagination*, 13.

7. Walter Brueggemann, *The Prophetic Imagination*, 46.

8. Jurgen Habermas, "Religion in the Public Sphere," trans. Jeremy Gaines, *European Journal of Philosophy* 14:1 (2006).

9. Slavoj Zizek, "To each according to his greed," *Harper's Magazine*, October 2009, http://www.harpers.org/archive/2009/10/0082658

10. Walter Brueggemann, *The Prophetic Imagination*, 4.

11. Nicholas Adams, "Jürgen Moltmann" in *The Blackwell Companion to Political Theology*, ed. Peter Scott and William T. Cavanaugh, (Oxford: Wiley-Blackwell, 2003).

12. Walter Brueggemann, *The Prophetic Imagination*, 56-57.

13. Walter Brueggemann, *The Prophetic Imagination*, 64.

14. Walter Brueggemann, *The Prophetic Imagination*, 65.

15. Walter Brueggemann, *The Prophetic Imagination*, 66.

16. Walter Brueggemann, *The Prophetic Imagination*, 68.

17. *Associated Press*, "Foreclosures now affect 1 in 8 U.S. Homeowners,"

March 6, 2009, http://www.allbusiness.com/government/government-bodies-offices-legislative/11959368-1.html.

18. Bill McBride, "One Giant Wave, Still Building," Calculated Risk, August 6, 2009, http://www.calculatedriskblog.com/2009/08/foreclosures.html.

19. Mark R. Rank and Thomas A. Hirschl, "Estimating the Risk of Food Stamp Use and Impoverishment During Childhood," *Archives of Pediatrics and Adolescent Medicine*, 2009; 163.

20. Jesse, "Guest Post: Why the Austrian, Keynesian, Marxist, Monetarist, and Neo-Liberal Economists Are All Wrong," August 20, 2009, Naked Capitalism, http://www.nakedcapitalism.com/2009/08/why-austrian-keynesian-monetarist-and.html.

21. Duane Warden, "The Rich and Poor in James: Implications for Institutionalized Impartiality," *Journal of the Evangelical Theological Society*, 43, no. 2 (June 2000): 247–257.

22. Chris Hedges, "The Radical Christian Right Is Built on Suburban Despair," AlterNet, January 19, 2007, http://www.alternet.org/story/46908/.

23. Sarah Posner, *God's Profits: Faith, Fraud, and the Republican Crusade for Values Voters* (Sausalito, CA: Polipoint Press, 2008).

24. Walter Brueggemann, *The Prophetic Imagination*, 13.

25. Jane Lampman, "Fight against poverty unites Christian left and right," *Christian Science Monitor*, February 18, 2009, http://www.csmonitor.com/Money/2009/0218/p03s07-usec.html.

26. Walter Brueggemann, "Counterscript: living with the elusive God."

27. Stephen A. O'Connell, "Debt Forgiveness: Plainer Speaking, Please.," http://ww.swarthmore.edu/SocSci/soconne1/documents/forgive.pdf

28. Nick Baumann, "Your "Representatives" in Congress," *Mother Jones*, November 10, 2009, http://motherjones.com/mojo/2009/11/your-representatives-congress.

29. OpenSecrets.org, "Totals by Sector," http://www.opensecrets.org/bigpicture/sectors.php?cycle=2008

30. Walter Brueggemann, *The Prophetic Imagination*, 46.

31. Ezra Klein, "How Stupak's amendment could change the whole insurance market," *Washington Post*, November 13, 2009, http://voices.washingtonpost.com/ezra-klein/2009/11/is_stupaks_amendment_a_trojan.html.

32. Michael O'Brien, "Hoyer: Final health bill may include stronger abortion provisions," The Hill, October 30, 2009, http://thehill.com/blogs/blog-briefing-room/news/65621-hoyer-final-health-bill-may-include-stronger-abortion-provisions.

33. United States Conference of Catholic Bishops, "Bishops Urge Pas-

sage of Stupak-Ellsworth Anti-Abortion Amendment for Health Reform Bill," Press Release, November 7, 2009, http://www.usccb.org/comm/archives/2009/09-229.shtml.

34. Sarah Posner, "Bart Stupak's Demand: What It Would Mean," *Religion Dispatches*, October 30, 2009, http://www.religiondispatches.org/blog/1981/bart_stupak%E2%80%99s_demand%3A_what_it_would_mean/.

35. Robin Marty, "Will the Stupak Amendment Affect Insurance Coverage for Miscarriages? I Think So," RH Reality Check, November 9, 2009, http://www.rhrealitycheck.org/blog/2009/11/09/will-stupak-amendment-force-women-whove-miscarried-lose-insurance-coverage-i-think-so.

36. Frances Kissling, "Exploiting the healthcare debate to restrict abortion," *Salon*, September 14, 2009, http://www.salon.com/news/opinion/feature/2009/09/14/abortion/print.html.

37. Kapya Kaoma, *Globalizing the Culture Wars: U.S. Conservatives, African Churches, and Homophobia*, (Somerville, MA: Political Research Associates, 2009).

38. Brueggemann, *The Prophetic Imagination*, 28.

39. Jeffrey Kaplan, "The Gospel of Consumption," *Orion Magazine*, May/June 2008, http://www.orionmagazine.org/index.php/articles/article/2962.

40. Hubert Locke, "Our Faith and the Common Good," Progressive Christian Witness, January 24, 2006 , http://www.progressivechristianwitness.org/pcw.cfm?id=6&p=3.

41. CBS/Associated Press, "Man Dies After Wal-Mart Stampede," November 28, 2008, http://www.cbsnews.com/stories/2008/11/28/national/main4637170.shtml.

42. Eric Levine, "Fundamentalist Consumerism and an Insane Society," *Z Magazine,* February 2009, http://www.zcommunications.org/fundamentalist-consumerism-and-an-insane-society-by-bruce-e-levine.

43. Harvey Cox, "The Market as God: Living in the new dispensation," *Atlantic Monthly*, March 1999, http://www.theatlantic.com/past/issues/99mar/marketgod.htm.

44. Peter Laarman, "The Prophets of Neoliberalism," *Religion Dispatches*, March 16, 2008, http://www.religiondispatches.org/archive/human-rights/134/rdpulpit:_the_prophets_of_neoliberalism.

45. Peter Laarman, "I Owe, Therefore I Am: Why Struggling Against the Banks is a Holy Obligation," *Religion Dispatches*, April 6, 2009 http://www.religiondispatches.org/archive/economy/1297/i_owe%2C_therefore_i_am%3A_why_struggling_against_the_banks_is_a_holy_obligation.

46. Brueggemann, "Counterscript."

NOTES

47. Brueggemann, *The Prophetic Imagination*, 46.

48. Ibid.

49. E.J. Dionne, *Souled Out: Reclaiming Faith & Politics After the Religious Right*, (Princeton & Oxford: Princeton University Press:,2008), 89.

50. Ibid, 184.

51. Theresa Tamkins, "Medical bills prompt more than 60 percent of U.S. bankruptcies," CNN.com, June 5, 2009, http://www.cnn.com/2009/HEALTH/06/05/bankruptcy.medical.bills/.

52. William Greider, "Why Not Tax Wall Street?", *The Nation*, December 7, 2009, http://www.thenation.com/doc/20091207/greider.

53. Reinhold Niebuhr, *The Nature and Destiny of Man*, vol. II, (New York: Charles Scribner's Sons, 1943), 304.

54. John Arlidge, "I'm doing 'God's work'. Meet Mr Goldman Sachs," *The Sunday Times*, November 9, 2009, http://www.timesonline.co.uk/tol/news/world/us_and_americas/article6907681.ece.

55. Simon Clark and Caroline Binham, "Profit 'Is Not Satanic,' Barclays CEO Varley Says," *Bloomberg.com*, November 3, 2009, ttp://www.bloomberg.com/apps/news?pid=newsarchive&sid=aGR1F_bjSIZw.

56. *The Christian Century*, "Hard Times: Lessons of the economic downturn," July 28, 2009, http://www.christiancentury.org/article.lasso?id=7392.

57. Reinhold Niebuhr, *Moral Man And Immoral Society* (New York: Charles Scribner's Sons, 1932), 167.

58. Jacques Rancière, *Disagreement: Politics and Philosophy*, (Minneapolis: University of Minnesota Press, 1999): 11-12.

59. Reinhold Niebuhr, *Justice and Mercy*, (Louisville: Westminster John Knox, 1974).

60. Reinhold Niebuhr, *The Nature and Destiny of Man*, vol. II, (New York: Charles Scribner's Sons, 1943), 298.

61. Brueggemann, *The Prophetic Imagination*, 63.

62. Ibid, 64.

63. Brueggemann, *The Prophetic Imagination*, 65.

64. Ibid, 67.

65. Jeremiah Wright, "The Audacity of Hope," Preaching Today, http://www.preachingtoday.com/sermons/sermons/audacityofhope.html

66. Brueggemann, *The Prophetic Imagination,* 67.

67. Ibid, 74.

68. Ibid, 77.

69. Ibid, 78.

4. THE MILITARIST SCRIPT: TORTURE

230

1. Walter Brueggemann, "Counter-Script."

2. Alfred W. McCoy "The Hidden History of CIA Torture: America's Road to Abu Ghraib," TomDispatch.com, September 9, 2004.

3. Afua Hirsch, "A proud 700-year history of double standards on torture," *The Guardian*, August 4, 2009, http://www.guardian.co.uk/comment-isfree/2009/aug/04/torture-law-complicity-terror.

4. The Avalon Project, "English Bill of Rights 1689," http://avalon.law.yale.edu/17th_century/england.asp.

5. Eric Weiner "Waterboarding: A Tortured History," National Public Radio, November 3, 2007. See also Evan Wallach, "Waterboarding Used to Be a Crime," *Washington Post*, November 4, 2007, http://www.washington-post.com/wp-dyn/content/article/2007/11/02/AR2007110201170.html.

6. Ibid.

7. International Committee of the Red Cross, "The Geneva Conventions of 1949," http://icrc.org/Web/Eng/siteeng0.nsf/htmlall/genevaconventions.

8. Weiner, "Waterboarding."

9. Ibid.

10. Ibid.

11. US Army Field Manual 34-52, 1992; the War Crimes Act of 1996 makes it a crime for US military personnel to violate the provisions of the the Geneva Convention.

12. Glenn Greenwald, "Ronald Reagan: vengeful, score-settling, Hard Left ideologue," *Salon*, May 1, 2009, http://www.salon.com/news/opinion/glenn_greenwald/2009/05/01/shifts.

13. David Rose, "Tortured Reasoning," *Vanity Fair*, December 16, 2008, http://www.vanityfair.com/magazine/2008/12/torture200812?printable=true&currentPage=all.

14. Ibid.

15. Daphne Eviatar, "Declassified Docs Reveal Pentagon Ignored FBI's Warnings on Abusive Interrogations," *Washington Independent*, November 7, 2009, http://washingtonindependent.com/67016/declassified-docs-re-veal-pentagon-ignored-dojs-warnings-on-abusive-interrogations.

16. Sherwood Moran, "Suggestions For Japanese Interpreters Based On Work In The Field," July 17, 1943, http://mcittahistory.bravehost.com/aamitcsm.pdf.

17. Bobby Ghosh, "After Waterboarding: How to Make Terrorists Talk?", *Time*, June 8, 2009, http://www.time.com/time/magazine/article/0,9171,1901491,00.html.

18. Dick Cheney, interview with Tim Russert, *Meet the Press*, MSNBC.

com, September 16, 2001, http://www.msnbc.msn.com/id/3080244/

19. Richard Clarke, *Against All Enemies: Inside America's War on Terror* (New York: Basic Books, 2004), pp. 23-24.

20. Mark Danner, "US Torture: Voices from the Black Sites," *New York Review of Books*, Volume 56, Number 6, April 9, 2009, http://www.nybooks.com/articles/22530

21. Cofer Black, Testimony to National Commission on Terrorist Attacks Upon the United States, http://www.fas.org/irp/congress/2002_hr/092602black.html.

22. John Yoo, "The President's Constitutional Authority To Conduct Military Operations Against Terrorists And Nations Supporting Them," memo prepared for the White House Office of Legal Counsel, September 25, 2001...

23. George W. Bush, "Military Order: Detention, Treatment, and Trial of Certain Non-Citizens in the War Against Terrorism," November 2001, http://www.globalsecurity.org/military/library/news/2001/11/mil-011113-milorder.htm.

24. Carl Levin, "Statement of Senator Carl Levin on Senate Armed Services Committee Report of its Inquiry into the Treatment of Detainees in U.S. Custody," Senate Armed Services Committee Inquiry Into The Treatment Of Detainees In U.S. Custody, http://levin.senate.gov/newsroom/supporting/2008/Detainees.121108.pdf.

25. "Chris Mackey and Greg Miller discuss their book, 'The Interrogators,'" Fresh Air, *National Public Radio*, July 20, 2004 , quoted in Mark Danner, "The Red Cross Torture Report: What It Means," *New York Review of Books*, April 30, 2009, http://www.nybooks.com/articles/22614.

26. Lawrence Wilkerson, "Some Truths About Guantánamo Bay," The Washington Note, March 17, 2009, quoted in Danner, "The Red Cross Torture Report."

27. George W. Bush, "Humane Treatment of al Qaeda and Taliban Detainees," February 7, 2002, http://www.dod.mil/pubs/foi/detainees/dia_previous_releases/fourth_release/DIAfourth_release.pdf.

28. Danner, "The Red Cross Torture Report."

29. Carl Levin, "The origins of aggressive interrogation techniques," Senate Armed Services Committee Inquiry Into The Treatment Of Detainees In U.S. Custody, June 17 2008, http://levin.senate.gov/senate/statement.cfm?id=299242.

30. Mark Benjamin, "Bush's top general quashed torture dissent," *Salon*, June 30, 2008, http://www.salon.com/news/feature/2008/06/30/richard_myers.

31. John D. Rockefeller, "OLC Opinions On The Cia Detention And Interrogation Program," April 22, 2009.

32. Mark Danner, "US Torture: Voices from the Black Sites".

33. Peter Finn and Julie Tate, "CIA Mistaken on 'High-Value' Detainee, Document Shows," *Washington Post*, June 16, 2009, http://www.washingtonpost.com/wp-dyn/content/article/2009/06/15/AR2009061503045.html

34. John Bybee, "Interrogation of al Qaeda Operative," Memorandum prepared for John Rizzo, Acting General Counsel of the Central Intelligence Agency by the White House Office of Legal Counsel, August 1, 2002.

35. International Committee of the Red Cross, Report on the Treatment of Fourteen "High Value Detainees" in CIA Custody, February 2007.

36. McCoy, "The Hidden History of CIA Torture."

37. Senate Armed Services Committee, "Inquiry Into The Treatment Of Detainees In U.S. Custody," November 20, 2004; Dana Priest, "CIA Holds Terror Suspects in Secret Prisons," *Washington Post*, November 2, 2005, http://www.washingtonpost.com/wp-dyn/content/article/2005/11/01/AR2005110101644_pf.html.

38. Steven Bradbury, "Application of United States Obligations Under Article 6 of the Convention Against Torture to Certain Techniques that May Be Used in the Interrogation of High Value al Qaeda Detainees," Memorandum prepared for John Rizzo, Senior Deputy General Counsel Central Intelligence Agency by the White House Office of Legal Counsel, May 30, 2002.

39. Alberto Mora, "Statement For the Record: Office of General Counsel Involvement In Interrogation Issues," June 7, 2004.

40. John Yoo, "The President's Constitutional Authority To Conduct Military Operations Against Terrorists And Nations Supporting Them."

41. Daphne Eviatar, "Declassified Docs Reveal Pentagon Ignored FBI's Warnings on Abusive Interrogations."

42. Philip Zelikow, "Interrogations and Recordings: Relevant 9/11 Commission Requests and CIA Responses," December 13, 2007, http://www.fas.org/irp/news/2007/12/zelikow121307.pdf.

43. George W. Bush, "Statement by the President: United Nations International Day in Support of Victims of Torture," June 26, 2003.

44. Joby Warrick, "CIA Tactics Endorsed In Secret Memos," *Washington Post*, October 15, 2008, http://www.washingtonpost.com/wp-dyn/content/article/2008/10/14/AR2008101403331.html.

45. "Central Intelligence Agency Inspector General Special Review

Counterterrorism Detention And Interrogation Activities (September 2001 - October 2003)," May 7, 2004.

46. Mark Danner, "Torture and Truth," *New York Review of Books*, June 10, 2004, http://www.nybooks.com/articles/17150.

47. Seymour M. Hersh, "Torture at Abu Ghraib," *The New Yorker*, April 30, 2004, http://ww.newyorker.com/printables/fact/040510fa_fact.

48. Antonio Taguba, "Article 15-6 Investigation Of The 800th Military Police Brigade," n.d.

49. Scott Wilson and Sewell Chan, "As Insurgency Grew, So Did Prison Abuse," *Washington Post*, May 10, 2004, http://www.washingtonpost.com/ac2/wp-dyn/A13065-2004May9?language=printer.

50. Taguba Report.

51. Jan Crawford Greenburg, Howard L. Rosenberg and Ariane de Vogue, "Sources: Top Bush Advisors Approved 'Enhanced Interrogation'" ABC News, April 9, 2008, http://abcnews.go.com/TheLaw/LawPolitics/story?id=4583256&page=1.

52. Dennis Blair, "[Congressional] Member Briefings on Enhanced Interrogation Techniques (EITs)," document released May 6, 2009, https://docs.google.com/viewer?url=http://ftp.fas.org/irp/congress/2009_cr/eit-briefings.pdf.

53. Josh White and R. Jeffrey Smith, "White House Aims to Block Legislation on Detainees," *Washington Post*, July 23, 2005, http://www.washingtonpost.com/wp-dyn/content/article/2005/07/22/AR2005072201727.html.

54. George W. Bush, "President's Statement on Signing of H.R. 2863, the 'Department of Defense, Emergency Supplemental Appropriations to Address Hurricanes in the Gulf of Mexico, and Pandemic Influenza Act, 2006,'" December 30, 2005.

55. Glenn Greenwald, "Democratic complicity in Bush's torture regimen," *Salon*, December 9, 2007, http://www.salon.com/news/opinion/glenn_greenwald/2007/12/09/democrats.

56. Scott Horton, "The Guantánamo 'Suicides': A Camp Delta sergeant blows the whistle," *Harper's Magazine*, January 2010, http://www.harpers.org/archive/2010/01/hbc-90006368.

57. Glenn Greenwald, "Obama's efforts to block a judicial ruling on Bush's illegal eavesdropping," *Salon*, February 28, 2009, http://www.salon.com/opinion/greenwald/2009/02/28/al_haramain/.

58. Glenn Greenwald, "Obama's latest effort to conceal evidence of Bush era crimes," *Salon*, May 13, 2009, http://www.salon.com/news/opinion/glenn_greenwald/2009/05/13/photos.

59. Glenn Greenwald, "Obama contemplates Executive Order for detention without charges," *Salon*, June 27, 2009, http://www.salon.com/news/opinion/glenn_greenwald/2009/06/27/preventive_detention.

60. Alissa J. Rubin, "Afghans Detail Detention in 'Black Jail' at U.S. Base," *New York Times*, November 28, 2009, http://www.nytimes.com/2009/11/29/world/asia/29bagram.html

61. Scott Horton, "The Guantánamo 'Suicides'".

62. Foon Rhee, "Obama opens door on torture prosecutions," *Boston Globe*, April 21, 2009, http://www.boston.com/news/politics/politicalintelligence/2009/04/obama_opens_doo.html.

63. *Associated Press*, "In reversal, Obama seeks to block abuse photos," May 13, 2009, http://www.msnbc.msn.com/id/30725189/.

64. Human Rights First, "Command's Responsibility: Detainee Deaths in U.S. Custody in Iraq and Afghanistan," February 2006, http://www.humanrightsfirst.org/us_law/etn/dic/exec-sum.aspx.

65. George W. Bush, "Remarks by the President on Iraq, Cincinnati Museum Center - Cincinnati Union Terminal, Cincinnati, Ohio," October 7, 2002.

66. CNN, "Transcript of Powell's U.N. Presentation," February 6, 2003, http://www.cnn.com/2003/US/02/05/sprj.irq.powell.transcript/; Condoleezza Rice, interviewed by Wolf Blitzer, CNN, September 8, 2002, http://www.cnn.com/TRANSCRIPTS/0209/08/le.00.html.

67. Julian E. Barnes and Greg Miller, "Detainee says he lied to CIA in harsh interrogations," *Los Angeles Times*, June 16, 2009, http://rticles.latimes.com/2009/jun/16/nation/na-cia-detainee16

68. Dan Froomkin, "Krauthammer's Asterisks," *Washington Post*, June 26, 2009, http://voices.washingtonpost.com/white-house-watch/torture/krauthammers-asterisks.html.; emptywheel (Marcy Harris), "Khalid Sheikh Mohammed Was Waterboarded 183 Times in One Month," FireDogLake, April 18, 2009, http://emptywheel.firedoglake.com/2009/04/18/khalid-sheikh-mohammed-was-waterboarded-183-times-in-one-month/.

69. Lawrence Wilkerson, "Some Truths About Guantánamo Bay".

70. Glenn Greenwald, "The degrading effects of terrorism fears," *Salon*, January 2, 2010, http://www.salon.com/news/opinion/glenn_greenwald/2010/01/02/fear.

71. Glenn Greenwald, "Cause and effect in the 'Terror War,'" *Salon*, December 29, 2009, http://www.salon.com/news/opinion/glenn_greenwald/2009/12/29/terrorism.

72. David Brooks, "The God That Fails," *New York Times*, December 31, 2009, http://www.nytimes.com/2010/01/01/opinion/01brooks.html.

73. Gary Younge, "The war on terror has been about scaring people, not protecting them," *Guardian U.K.*, January 3, 2010, http://www.guardian.co.uk/global/2010/jan/03/yemen-anti-terrorism-rendition-security.

74. Alfred W. McCoy "The Hidden History of CIA Torture: America's Road to Abu Ghraib," "Confronting the CIA's Mind Maze: America's Political Paralysis Over Torture", Tom Dispatch, http://www.tomdispatch.com/post/1795/%20alfred_mccoy_on_the_cia_s_road_to_abu_ghraib.

75. Mark Danner, "The Red Cross Torture Report: What It Means", *New York Review of Books*, Volume 56, Number 7, April 30, 2009, http://www.nybooks.com/articles/22614.

76. McCoy, "The Hidden History".

77. Scott Horton, "Six Questions for Darius Rejali, Author of 'Torture and Democracy,'" *Harper's Magazine*, December 2009, http://www.harpers.org/archive/2008/02/hbc-90002387.

78. meteor blades (Tim Lee), "Moving Forward REQUIRES Looking Back," Daily Kos, May 21, 2009, http://www.dailykos.com/story/2009/5/21/734083/-Moving-Forward-REQUIRES-Looking-Back.

79. "Dollar Glut Finances US Military Expansion," in Top 25 Censored Stories For 2010 at ProjectCensored.org, http://www.projectcensored.org/top-stories/articles/24-dollar-glut-finances-us-military-expansion/.

80. Glenn Greenwald, "The bipartisan consensus on U.S. military spending," *Salon*, January 2, 2008, http://www.salon.com/news/opinion/glenn_greenwald/2008/01/02/military_spending.

81. Glenn Greenwald, "The sanctity of military spending," *Salon*, January 26, 2010, http://www.salon.com/news/opinion/glenn_greenwald/2010/01/26/defense/index.html.

82. Theodore M. Vestal, *Ethiopia: A post-Cold War African State* (Westport, CT: Praeger Publishers, 1999), p.17.

83. Robert Altemyer, The Authoritarians, http://home.cc.umanitoba.ca/~altemey/.

84. Christopher L. Blakesley and Thomas B. McAffee, "The Bush Theory of the War Power: Authoritarianism, Torture and the So-Called "War on Terror"- A Critique, n.d., http://works.bepress.com/cgi/viewcontent.cgi?article=1000&context=christopher_blakesley.

85. Darius Rejali, *Torture and Democracy*, (Princeton, New Jersey: Princeton Press, 2007), pp. 4-ff.

86. George W. Bush, State of the Union Address, January 29, 2002.

87. Michael M. Phillips "Cheney Says He Was Proponent for Military Action Against Iran," *Wall Street Journal*, August 30, 2009, http://online.wsj.com/article/SB125164376287270241.html

88. James Richardson, "I think Joe Scarborough just gave the game away,"Daily Kos, May 25, 2009, http://www.dailykos.com/story/2009/5/25/735352/-I-think-Joe-Scarborough-just-gave-the-game-away.

89. Glenn Greenwald, "Craving terrorist melodrama," *Salon*, December 30, 2009, www.salon.com/opinion/greenwald/2009/12/30/hysteria.

90. Pew Forum on Religion & Public Life, "The Religious Dimensions of the Torture Debate," April 30, 2009, http://pewresearch.org/pubs/1210/torture-opinion-religious-differences.

91.Tom Schaller, "Authoritarianism in American Politics," FiveThirtyEight.com,December 12,2009,http://www.fivethirtyeight.com/2009/10/authoritarianism-in-american-politics.html.

92.James Wellman, "Cheerleading for war?"The Immanent Frame, April 15, 2009, http://blogs.ssrc.org/tif/2009/04/15/cheerleading-for-war/.

93. Jonathan Weiler and Marc J. Hetherington, "Authoritarianism and the American Political Divide,"The Democratic Strategist, September 21, 2006, http://www.thedemocraticstrategist.org/ac/2006/09/authoritarianism_and_the_ameri.php.

94. William T. Cavanaugh, "Threat of Torture Plays with More Minds than You Might Have Imagined," Vital Theology, n.d., https://docs.google.com/viewer?url=http://www.vitaltheology.com/VTV3I6page3.pdf.

95. Babak Dehghanpisheh, John Barry and Roy Gutman, "The Death Convoy Of Afghanistan," *Newsweek*, August 26, 2002, http://www.newsweek.com/id/65473.

96. Dick Cheney, *Meet the Press*, MSNBC.com, September 16, 2001.

97. Juan Gonzalez, "Exclusive: John Walker Lindh's Parents Discuss Their Son's Story, from Joining the US-Backed Taliban Army to Surviving a Northern Alliance Massacre, to His Abuse at the Hands of US Forces," *Democracy Now!*, July 31, 2009, http://www.democracynow.org/2009/7/31/exclusive_john_walker_lindhs_parents_discuss.

98. Michael Teitelman, "Obama, Torture and John Walker Lindh," *Counterpunch*, May 22-24, 2009, http://www.counterpunch.org/teitelman05222009.html.

99. Spencer Ackerman, "Rumsfeld's Lawyer in 2001: "Take the Gloves Off" on Lindh," TPM Muckraker, June 25, 2007, http://tpmmuckraker.talkingpointsmemo.com/archives/003522.php.

100. Nina Totenberg, "U.S. Faces Major Hurdles in Prosecuting Padilla," *National Public Radio*,January 3, 2007, http://www.npr.org/templates/transcript/transcript.php?storyId=6682846.

101. Digby (Heather Parton), "Psikhushka," Hullabaloo,January 3, 2007,

http://digbysblog.blogspot.com/2009/05/psikhushka-by-digby-in-case-anyones.html.

102. Cavanaugh, "Threat of Torture".

103. John Howard Yoder, "Are The Tyrants Really in Charge? Realism and Radical Change," unpublished, 1993, http://theology.nd.edu/people/research/yoder-john/documents/ARETHETYRANTSREALLY-INCHARGE.pdf.

104. Evangelicals for Human Rights, "Evangelical Declaration Against Torture," released in March 2007 and later endorsed by the National Association of Evangelicals, http://www.evangelicalsforhumanrights.org/index.php?option=com_content&task=view&id=14&Itemid=54.

105. Walter Brueggemann, "Full of Truth and Hope," paper presented at the Wisconsin Council of Churches Forum on Ethics and Public Policy, September 25, 2007, http://www.wichurches.org/Brueggemann2007.pdf.

106. AP-GfK Poll conducted by GfK Roper Public Affairs & Media. May 28-June 1, 2009, http://bs4.com/national/aclu.abu.ghraib.2.1029480.html.

107. Pew Forum on Religion & Public Life, "The Religious Dimensions of the Torture Debate."

108. Robert Parry, "Dick Cheney Admits to Torture Conspiracy," AlterNet/Consortium News, February 15, 2010, http://www.alternet.org/story/145671/dick_cheney_admits_to_torture_conspiracy.

109. John Howard Yoder, "The 'Power' of 'Non-Violence'" unpublished, 1994, http://theology.nd.edu/people/research/yoder-john/documents/THE1.pdf.

110. William T. Cavanaugh, "Killing For the Telephone Company: Why the Nation-State is not the Keeper of the Common Good," *Modern Theology 20:2*, April 2004, http://www.jesusradicals.com/library/cavanaugh/telephone.pdf.

111. Yoder, "The 'Power' of 'Non-Violence'".

112. Timothy Gorringe, "Atonement," in *The Blackwell Companion to Political Theology*, Peter Scott and William T. Cavanaugh, editors, (London: Wiley-Blackwell, 2003), pp. 363-376;

113. Esther D. Reed, "Redemption," in *The Blackwell Companion to Modern Theology*, Gareth Jones, editor, Wiley-Blackwell (2004), p. 231.

114. Jim Wallis, "Cut the Deficit–Cut Military Spending," God's Politics Blog, February 4, 2010, http://blog.sojo.net/2010/02/04/cut-the-deficit-cut-military-spending/.

115. Glenn Greenwald, "Helen Thomas deviates from the terrorism script," *Salon*, January 9, 2010, http://www.salon.com/news/opinion/glenn_

greenwald/2010/01/09/thomas.

116. Gorringe, "Atonement," p. 367.

117. Douglas Harink, "Doing Justice to Justification," *The Christian Century*, June 14, 2005, http://www.religion-online.org/showarticle. asp?title=3206.

118. John William Drane, *Introducing the New Testament* (Minneapolis: Fortress Press, 2000), p. 83.

119. Gorringe, "Atonement," p.370.

120. John Howard Yoder, "The Unique Role of the Historic Peace Churches," Brethren Life and Thought, 14, (Summer, 1969), 136, quoted in Stanley Hauerwas, "Democratic Time: Lessons Learned from Yoder and Wolin," http://www.crosscurrents.org/hauerwas200506.htm.

121. John Howard Yoder, *The Priestly Kingdom: Social Ethics as Gospel* (University of Notre Dame Press, 1984), p. 158, quoted in Hauerwas, "Democratic Time".

122. Gorringe, "Atonement," p.371.

123. Ibid, pp. 371-372.

124. Jan Milic Lochman, *Reconciliation and Liberation* (Minneapolis: Fortress Press, 1980), p. 107.

125. Gavin Lee, "Guantanamo guard reunited with ex-inmates," BBC, January 12, 2010, http://news.bbc.co.uk/2/hi/8452937.stm.

126. Gorringe, "Atonement", p.373.

127. Rekha Basu, "From an unlikely source, a plea for forgiveness," *South Florida Sun-Sentinel*, September 18, 2001, http://www.racematters.org/terryandersonss.htm.

128. James Ridgeway, "GOP Target: Terry Anderson," *Village Voice*, Ocotober 19, 2004, http://www.villagevoice.com/2004-10-19/news/goptarget-terry-anderson/.

129. Walter Wink, *When the powers fall: reconciliation in the healing of nations* (Minneapolis: Fortress Press, 1998), pp. 39-40.

130. Gorringe, "Atonement", p.373.

131. Johann Baptist Metz, "'Politische Theologie' in der Diskussion," quoted in James Matthew Ashley, *Interruptions: Mysticism, Politics, and Theology in the Work of Johann Baptist Metz* (South Bend, IN: University of Notre Dame Press, 1998), p. 117.

132. William Cavanaugh, "Telling the Truth about Ourselves: Torture and Eucharist in the U.S. Popular Imagination," *The Other Journal*, May 4, 2009, http://www.theotherjournal.com/article.php?id=764.

133. Jonathan Weiler and Marc J. Hetherington, "Authoritarianism and the American Political Divide."

POSTSCRIPT

1. John F. Haught, The Revelation of God in History http://www.religion-online.org/showbook.asp?title=1946

2. Brueggemann, "Counterscript."